The Writing or the Sex?

Pergamon Titles of Related Interest

Spender MEN'S STUDIES MODIFIED: The Impact of Feminism on the Academic Disciplines
Newman MEN'S IDEAS/WOMEN'S REALITIES: Popular Science, 1870-1915
Christian BLACK FEMINIST CRITICISM: Perspectives on Black Women Writers

Related Journals
(Free sample copies available upon request)

REPRODUCTIVE AND GENETIC ENGINEERING: Journal of International Feminist Analysis
WOMEN'S STUDIES INTERNATIONAL FORUM

The ATHENE Series

General Editors
Gloria Bowles
Renate Klein
Janice Raymond

Consulting Editor
Dale Spender

The Athene Series assumes that all those who are concerned with formulating explanations of the way the world works need to know and appreciate the significance of basic feminist principles.

The growth of feminist research has challenged almost all aspects of social organization in our culture. The Athene Series focuses on the construction of knowledge and the exclusion of women from the process—both as theorists and subjects of study—and offers innovative studies that challenge established theories and research.

On Athene—When Metis, goddess of wisdom who presided over all knowledge was pregnant with Athene, she was swallowed up by Zeus who then gave birth to Athene from his head. The original Athene is thus the parthenogenetic daughter of a strong mother and as the feminist myth goes, at the "third birth" of Athene she stops being Zeus' obedient mouthpiece and returns to her real source: the science and wisdom of womankind.

The Writing or the Sex?

or

why you don't have to read women's writing to know it's no good

by
Dale Spender

PERGAMON PRESS
New York Oxford Beijing Frankfurt
São Paulo Sydney

Pergamon Press Offices:

U.S.A.	Pergamon Press, Inc., Maxwell House, Fairview Park, Elmsford, New York 10523, U.S.A.
U.K.	Pergamon Press plc, Headington Hill Hall, Oxford OX3 0BW, England
PEOPLE'S REPUBLIC OF CHINA	Pergamon Press, Qianmen Hotel, Beijing, People's Republic of China
FEDERAL REPUBLIC OF GERMANY	Pergamon Press GmbH, Hammerweg 6, D-6242 Kronberg, Federal Republic of Germany
BRAZIL	Pergamon Editora Ltda, Rua Eça de Queiros, 346, CEP 04011, São Paulo, Brazil
AUSTRALIA	Pergamon Press Australia Pty Ltd., P.O. Box 544, Potts Point, NSW 2011, Australia
JAPAN	Pergamon Press, 8th Floor, Matsuoka Central Building, 1-7-1 Nishishinjuku, Shinjuku-ku, Tokyo 160, Japan
CANADA	Pergamon Press Canada Ltd., Suite 271, 253 College Street, Toronto, Ontario M5T 1R5, Canada

Copyright © 1989 Dale Spender

First edition 1989

Library of Congress Cataloging in Publication Data

Spender, Dale.
   The writing or the sex? : or why you don't have to read women's writing to know it's no good / by Dale Spender. -- 1st ed.
      p.   cm. -- (The Athene series)
   Bibliography: p.
   Includes index.
   ISBN 0-08-033180-7 :   -- ISBN 0-08-033179-3 (pbk.) :
   1. Literature--Women writers--History and criticism. 2. Feminism and literature. 3. Sexism and literature. 4. Women and literature.
I. Title. II. Series.
PN471.S64   1989
809'.89287--dc19   88-26771
                                                                          CIP

Printed in the United States of America

∞™ The paper used in this publication meets the minimum requirements of American National Standard for Information Sciences -- Permanence of Paper for Printed Library Materials, ANSI Z39.48-1984

For my sister, Lynne Spender, without whom there would have been no reason for writing

As the following history is the product of a female pen, I tremble for the terrible hazard it must run in venturing into the world, as it may very possibly suffer, in many opinions without perusing it; I therefore humbly move for its having the common chance of a criminal at least to be properly examined before it is condemned.

From
A NARRATIVE OF THE LIFE
OF MRS CHARLOTTE CHARKE
1755

Contents

Acknowledgements

My thanks first of all to Renate Klein and Stephanie Boxall for waiting so patiently for this manuscript; it was one of the tasks I was working on when I gave up smoking, and it has taken me some time to "recover" and to complete it. But it does indicate that there is life after quitting, particularly if you have the support of Renate Klein.

I must also thank my sister, Lynne Spender, who has been such a constant source of support, who not only takes on some of the responsibility for my emotional and physical well being, but who also provides me with that precious commodity—*instant feedback* on my work. I am also indebted to her for her diligent documentation of the review space accorded women's books in Australia.

Margaret Littlewood, Richelle Van Snellenberg, Mandy Spry, and the British "Women in Publishing" Collective provided invaluable assistance with surveys of the review rate of women's books; I am grateful too for the commentary and statistics supplied by Marilyn French which have allowed for the development of an international profile on this particular form of prejudice.

Frances McHarg and St Lucia Secretarial Services have carefully transformed some of my purple prose (I write with a purple pen and ink) into "clean copy" in record time, and have proved to my satisfaction that "secretaries" are infinitely superior to computers.

Candida Lacey, Susan Martin, Debra Adelaide, Catherine Wearing, and Kirsten Lees have helped to check references and locate sources, and have given generously of their good will and expertise. And I am very grateful to Marion Glastonbury and Hilary Simpson for the pioneering work they have published on the working conditions of women writers. For his comments and contributions on Thomas Hardy—about whom I knew little and lacked inclination to know more—I am grateful to Dale Kramer.

Cheris Kramarae has been a wonderful correspondent and source of encouragement over the years, and I thank her—and Brinlee and Jana and their vacated bedroom—for the many conversations we have had on women and literature.

The major forum in which some of these ideas have been discussed is SKMSKI, an association of feminist literary scholars. For their scholarship, sisterliness, and scintillating discussions on women's literary traditions (and their quotes on the limitations and logic of literary men) I would like to thank Cathy Davidson, Annette Kolodny, Susan Koppelman, Emily Toth, Joanna Russ—and Elaine Showalter.

Finally, I would like to acknowledge my debt to all the many women writers and critics whose words of wisdom form the substance of this book; and I would like to thank Ted Brown who has provided me with £500 a year and "A Room of My Own" in order that I could complete it.

Dale Spender
Brisbane
May 1988

Introduction

The basic theme of this book is very simple. It is that men have been in charge of according value to literature, and that they have found the contributions of their own sex immeasurably superior. The basic assertion of this book is that it is time for a change.

The criteria that men have used, and the rationales that they have engaged in to justify their choice of their own work, are the concerns of the first part of this volume—On the Judgement of Literary Men. One consequence of this male judgement has been that little or no representation has been given to women in the literary canon, and it is widely assumed and wantonly asserted that the reason for the absence of women is that women have not written in the past—or that what they have written is not very good. The underlying implication, throughout the world of letters, is that the writing of women has been evaluated and found wanting—which is why it has so little prominence in the literary heritage.

But such an assumption can be readily discounted. The men of letters have *not* read the writings of women and found them unworthy of inclusion; quite the reverse. On the grounds that it is the work of women, literary men have disqualified women's writing from even being considered as worthy of inclusion in the canon. For women it has been much more than a case of an *unfair* hearing, it has often been a case of no hearing at all.

Hence the initial full title of this volume: The Writing or The Sex? Judgement of Literary Men—or why you don't have to read women's writing to know it's no good. (Not even computers could cope with a title of this length; hence the abridgement.)

Every facet of the literary process, from start to finish, is examined on the basis that it is not the writing, but the sex which is responsible for the poor ratings given to women's work in the literary world of men. The extent to which women are debarred from entering mixed-sex conversations, and the extent to which men have set up the discipline of "lit-crit"—so that simply by following all its rules preferential treatment is given to men—form the sub-stance of the first two chapters. They give some idea of the nature of the obstacles that women writers are up against, in their struggle for a fair hearing within society, and within literary circles. They also expose the blatant self-interest of much male "lit-crit" and the false arguments that have been used to sustain the prominence and primacy of men.

While such crass considerations as publishing and reviewing may have been kept out of the more purified literary environment, women writers and critics cannot leave these areas out of their sphere of interest. If a woman writer does not get published, or reviewed, then in many respects she does not exist in the literary community. The fact that there are "gatekeepers" in both these areas, who can use sex/gender to deny women a place in the literary heritage, means that publishing and reviewing are processes of vital importance to women writers; they warrant a central place in women's lit-erary criticism.

Education is the focus of the last chapter in Part One; there is a basic contradiction in our society which allows females to be the better literary students and educational writers—but to have minimal presence in the pro-fessional world of letters. In the words of Paul Theroux (1987) " . . . it has always been easier for women to write and for men to be published." The question is whether this is the case, and if so, why is it? And again, the judgement of literary men is seen as problematic.

Throughout Part One runs an underlying theme. It is that again and again it can be established that women enjoy so few resources in a male-dominated society; women get so little space in conversations with men, such minimal representation in the canon and the curriculum, such a small percentage of publications and such a sparse allocation of review space. Yet again and again it has been asserted that women are getting more than their share.

This problem of perception is regularly addressed, along with the crucial issue that it raises; when women's presence is less than 30% and still gives men cause for complaint, how much space are women entitled to? What is women's share?

But if women must learn to read literature through men's eyes, this is not the only view. Part Two of this volume starts to sketch the outlines of literary criticism, from women's point of view. And women judge the men who have made themselves "superior" and who have done so at women's expense.

"Women's Work and Women's Criticism" looks at the conditions under which women's writing has been produced and illustrates how markedly different they are from those which have pertained for men. And "Polish, Plagiarism, and Plain Theft" contains an extended discussion on the way men have robbed women of their labour, literary labour included. The book concludes with the case histories of Colette, Sonya Tolstoy, and Zelda Fitzgerald (and more)—and points out that they are not "isolated examples" but part of the pattern of literary production and the relationship between the sexes. The evidence is presented for a form of women's literary criticism, which takes account of the exploitative practices of men. It seems little short of folly to argue for a free, open, and blameless literary community when there are so many profiteers standing by the door.

And because it is time that we put in print some of the gems of literary logic which so many women writers and critics are obliged to hear, an appendix has been attached. Perhaps the day will come when it will be obvious to all that the statements contained therein are foolish as well as fallacious, and they will cease to be made. Though I think it is unlikely that it will happen in my time.

In the interim, have a good read.

I

ON THE JUDGEMENT OF LITERARY MEN

1

Language Studies: From the Spoken to the Written Word

In some ways this book began almost twenty years ago when I first started asking questions about how, when, and why women spoke differently from men—and with what effect? As I was informed then (by authorities in various departments, in various universities in Australia) that such questions were "not a topic" and therefore could not be the substance of research, it is gratifying now to see a well established and ever increasing body of knowledge which encodes information and insights under the rubric of *Language and Sex*, or, more recently, as *Language and Gender*.

Because of the understandings provided by research and discussion in this area, there is now a much greater and more sophisticated awareness of the "conversation codes" that set up the patterns of talk between the sexes. There is also the recognition that beliefs about these patterns of mixed sex talk are often very far removed—and sometimes even diametrically opposed to—the empirical reality.

Despite the protests of women over the centuries—Elizabeth Cady Stanton among them[1]—twenty years ago it was still widely and unwaveringly accepted that women were *the talkative sex*. Women were the empty vessels that made the most sound, according to such eminent linguists as Otto Jesperson: Without one shred of supportive evidence, he insisted that women were linguistically incompetent and went so far as to argue that women had a debilitating effect on the language (1922: p. 246). It was partly because male linguists presented such a long list of women's language sins (sins that women were supposed to have committed) that I became so interested in

---

[1]See Elizabeth Cady Stanton et al. 1881, Vol. 1, p. 110 for the steps she took at women's conventions to ensure that the few men present did not dominate the conversation.

documenting some of the dynamics of women's talk: Well can I remember some of my own initial and tentative ventures into the tape-recording arena.

I elected then to study the interactions between women and men and my method was to make tapes of their conversations in a variety of "natural" and "controlled" contexts. My goal was simple: To analyse the taped interactions and to establish any differences between the sexes in patterns of speech. But after weeks—indeed months—of making tapes and listening to them with the aim of identifying the characteristics of women's speech and the differences in the speech of men, I began to suspect that as a linguistic researcher, I was a distinct failure. Although I had hours of tapes of conversations between women and men it did not seem to me that I had enough data from women to draw any conclusions. At that stage I thought there was a limit to the informa-tion that could be gleaned from women's encouraging expressions—such as "Really," "Goodness me," "And then?" etc. Later I came to regard these as supportive/eliciting comments which kept (men's) conversations going: But at the time I saw them as non-data and I almost despaired of ever being able to record sufficient sustained speech to identify any possible features specific to women.

Of course it took some time for me to appreciate that the salient character-istic of women's talk in conversation with men was *silence*; this was an understanding I did not reach unaided. As an unquestioning believer in the received wisdom that women were exceedingly garrulous, I just kept on trying to make more tapes of more woman-talk, before Cheris Kramarae suggested that perhaps the problem was not my research procedures, but the speech conventions of a male-dominated society.

So I stopped dwelling on my own ostensible failure to obtain data and rephrased my questions about the language of women and men. Not just about why women talked so little in the presence of men, but why in the face of such overwhelming evidence to the contrary, we could continue to believe that women were the talkative sex?

Again it was Cheris Kramarae who found the key to the contradiction of women's silence—and loquaciousness. She suggested that "Perhaps a talka-tive woman is one who does talk as much as a man" (Cheris Kramer, 1975: p. 47).

From this shift in perspective came a new set of insights—and explana-tions.

Within language studies it has now been established that over the centu-ries women have been enjoined by men to be silent. Sophocles might not have started it, but when he suggested that "silence gives the proper grace to women," he made a contribution to the image of a good woman as a silent woman in the western tradition. And once it is realised that silence is an attitude that men desire in women, there is no longer any apparent contradic-tion between the infrequency of women's utterances and the insistence that they talk too much. Quite simply, if a woman is expected to be quiet then any woman who opens her mouth can be accused of being talkative.

But if for me—all those years ago—this insight into women's language eliminated some of the inconsistencies in my research, it also introduced a whole new range of problems. (And one new inconsistency emerged: that of trying to *articulate* women's *silence*, a problem which plagues all who work in this area.) One of the consequences of my discovery that women talked so little, when I had assumed they talked so much, was that I became a committed non-believer. Never since have I trusted linguistic authorities or the supposed evidence of my senses. Assured and reassured by countless women and men that they have a fair share of the conversation, I have remained completely unconvinced and have gone on to make my own tapes, develop my own records, and to count for myself the space allocated to women. Not terribly rigorous as research activity goes, but richly rewarding and revealing. The discrepancy between people's perceptions (my own included) and empirical reality has become a cornerstone in much of my research.

And I never cease to be amazed at the extent to which our reality is predicated on the premises with which we begin; or the extent to which measurement is in the eye of the beholder—or the ear of the listener.

So when a few years ago I was challenged by some assertive women at a meeting where I suggested that women did not enjoy the same rights or opportunities to talk as did men, I again got out the tape recorder to check— not on women in general, but on particular women who took pride in their talking achievements with men.

Within a university context I made twenty tapes of academic feminists in conversation with an assortment of academic men. I set up the concealed tape recorder, and only after the conversation concluded did I introduce myself, indicate the existence of the tape recorder, and seek permission to simply count the number of minutes taken by each speaker. Four men considered their conversations private so I erased the tapes and this left me with sixteen samples (of varying length). In each case, before counting the minutes taken by each sex, I asked just one question: *Do you think you had a fair share of the conversation?* All the women said yes, one declaring that she had had more than her share; twelve men said yes; and four said no.

When I analyzed these tapes I found that fourteen feminists who believed that they had had a *fair* share of the conversation, spoke between 8% and 38% of the time. In this group were two of the men who were of the opinion that they had *not* had a fair share and they spoke for 75% and 67% of the time respectively. Two of the women did slightly better, with one achieving 40% of the conversation time and the other 42%. Both of the men in these interactions had stated that they had not enjoyed a fair share. Given that 60% and 58% do not feel like a fair share to men, the question of course arises as to what they think they are entitled to. And what do women think is their fair share of the conversation cake? The woman who thought that she had received more than her fair share spoke for 35% of the time.

While some of the women involved were incredulous when confronted with these results (and wherever possible I took the precaution of checking the tape in the presence of the speakers) I was not at all surprised by these statistics. I have always used my own life as a source for research and it seems to me that in general a woman is allowed up to about one third of the conversation time in interactions with male peers. Beyond this point, *both women and men* are likely to perceive the contribution of the woman as domineering.

In my own case I have found it difficult—and impossible—to discover what happens if women aim, not for what feels like a *fair* share, but for *half* the conversation time. Difficult because a woman has to break every rule in the polite conversation book if she tries to talk for half the time: It *feels* unfair, rude, and objectionably overbearing. For me it has also been impossible to talk for 50% of the time because no man has stayed "conversing" with me for the mandatory three minutes—the time I set for the minimal unit of interaction. The highest score I have ever attained (in conversation with a male colleague) was 44% and this was accompanied by angry assertions on his part that I was "impossible," "unreasonable," and that I "didn't listen to a word that was being said." At the time—before the tape had been analysed—I felt he was probably right.

Of course there are some contexts in which women are the authority figures and where it is possible for them to talk for more than 50% of the time without necessarily feeling any guilt.[2] I have many tapes of myself talking to male students and in these circumstances my language behaviour is similar to that of many men talking to women. I am the authority, I set the terms, I do most of the talking, interrupting, and legislating of experience.

No doubt a comparable pattern would also emerge were tapes to be made of Mrs. Thatcher addressing her all-male cabinet. And what this implies is that it is not the *sex*, but power and authority which determines the right to talk: It is interesting that so many men still possess such power and authority *vis à vis* women.

It is not just a simple *reversal*, however, when women have the power to talk, and men find it in their own interest to listen. For unlike women, men do not use the small amount of talking time they have available to encourage the talk of an authoritative woman. Male behaviour in this context is in line with other patterns of power, for students do not ordinarily encourage the authority figure—the teacher—to speak, and patients do not generally make

---

[2] I have no tapes of white women talking to black men and no means of hypothesising about the nexus of gender and ethnicity.

supportive comments to doctors, designed to "draw them out." It seems that the phenomenon of the eliciting utterance—"Did you really?", "Do go on", "And then?", "How interesting" etc.—is confined to women talking to men and is noted primarily in its absence: Women who do not use such devices are invariably seen as rude or revolting as linguist Pamela Fishman (1977) has suggested.

Because there is such a vast difference between what people believe to be happening in conversations, and what the tape recorder reveals, it has taken some time to discredit—and discard—many of these language myths. That so many open-minded and perspicacious women can continue to think that they are enjoying a fair share of the conversation when they get to talk for about one third of the time is an indication of the power of unwritten social codes to determine perception. That so many astute and aware women can continue to think that they do not modify their behaviour with the entry of a man to their conversation is evidence of the extent to which human beings can be oblivious to some of their own actions and their implications.

But far from being discouraged by this "discrepancy," I find it quite an exciting challenge. One of the difficulties—and the delights—of undertaking research in this area is in identifying the various "codes" that play such a crucial role in daily life but that can rarely be articulated and are often fervently denied.

So teachers will insist that they spend as much time with the girls as the boys, parents will assert that they treat their daughters and their sons precisely the same, and literary critics will argue that sex and gender have absolutely nothing to do with their literary evaluations. Yet all these individuals who are so convinced that they do *not* discriminate can readily be shown to be operating a sexual double standard. No sophisticated research project is required to demonstrate that teachers (feminists included!) spend more time with boys than with girls (even—or especially—if boys are the minority). Parents can be shown to operate totally different codes of behaviour in relation to their daughters and their sons, and literary critics can certainly be shown to utilise a sexual double standard, despite their protests to the contrary.

That there can be such a *gap* between belief and behaviour is not (necessarily) because people are trying to conceal sexist (or racist) actions: On the contrary they can genuinely feel that there is nothing problematic about their behaviour and that they are performing in a perfectly honourable manner— even as they engage in the most blatantly discriminatory practices. Because they don't *feel* as though they are doing the wrong thing, because they don't feel as though they are operating a double standard, they can classify their conduct as reasonable—even right. And while ever discrimination is presented as something dreadful people do, as distinct from the *routine* practice of *all* members of the society, we can expect this discrepancy between belief and behaviour to continue.

The fundamental importance of gender as a factor in daily life is not often appreciated. While everyone who has ever tried will know how difficult—impossible?—it is to talk to a baby of unknown sex, the implications of this situation are rarely spelled out. For in order to know what to say and how to say it—what stance to assume, what tone to adopt, what information to impart—it is necessary to know the sex of the conversation partner, even when it is a baby! The embarrassment can be acute if one gets "caught out" making conversation on the basis of the wrong sex: The speaker who finds that the supposed girl is really a boy is distressed, and not just because it is a case of mistaken identity but because the wrong thing may have been said, in the wrong form. Everything from body posture to vocabulary and volume can be governed by considerations of gender which is why it can be disorienting and confusing when the sex of the conversation partner is not known: The speaker simply does not know how to relate to the audience, or where to begin.

From birth the two sexes are treated very differently: They are addressed in different ways, provided with different information and expectations, and evaluated according to very different criteria. And so different are these sexual standards that even when females and males do the *same* thing, completely different constructions can be placed upon their actions. As Muriel Schulz (1975) has pointed out, spinsters and bachelors may both be unmarried adults but references made to the two categories cannot involve a comparison of like with like: There is a substantial difference between an old woman—and an old man. Even between a woman—and a man.

The double standard permeates just about every facet of language behaviour so that it is extremely difficult trying to work out what knowledge is to be "trusted." When women can be held to talk too much when they talk less than a man, while men can still be regarded as the strong silent type, even when they do most of the talking, the way through the language and gender mine field is not always clear. When a woman who gives her opinion can be categorised as rude, pushy, aggressive and bitchy, while a man who gives his opinion can be rated as masterful, forceful, authoritative—and revealing leadership qualities—the need for guidelines about reliable evidence becomes obvious.

Nowhere is this more clearly demonstrable than in the case of transcript evaluations (where the sex of the speaker cannot be identified from the voice). Again and again I have asked people to rate transcripts and the very same speech can be rated as positive or negative, depending on the presumed sex of the speaker. When I have indicated, for example, that a lengthy expression of opinion is the pronouncement of a man, it has invariably been rated as impressive, thoughtful, informative, and useful: the same speech, when attributed to a woman has been dismissed as rambling, irrational, tedious, and (once)—"a waste of words."

Such a sexually discriminating response should not be all that surprising: As Cheris Kramarae found as early as 1977, English speakers *of both sexes*, believe that men's speech is forceful, efficient, blunt, authoritative, serious, sparing, and masterful, while that of women is considered weak, trivial, ineffectual, hesitant, hyperpolite, euphemistic—and is often marked by gossip and gibberish. And when women and men believe that this is the way that women and men talk, they are predisposed to find such characteristics when asked to assess the spoken—or the written word—of women and men.

One of the classic studies of the extent to which measurement exists in the mind of the beholder was conducted in 1974 by Philip Goldberg. Using professional literature from six fields (encompassing both traditionally masculine and feminine areas), he compiled two sets of booklets in which "the same article bore a male name in one set of booklets, a female name in the other" (p. 39). He then asked women students to rate the contributions of the writers.

Of course they rated the male author John T. McKay as superior to Joan T. McKay across the various areas. "Of all nine questions," comments Philip Goldberg, "regardless of the author's occupational field, the girls [sic] consistently found an article more valuable—and its author more competent—when the article bore a male name. Though the articles themselves were exactly the same, the girls felt that those written by the John T. McKays were definitely more impressive and reflected more glory on their authors than did the mediocre offerings of the Joan T. McKays" (pp. 40–41).

Interestingly, Philip Goldberg confined his study to women. He seems to think that the important point of his exercise was to demonstrate that women are biased against women: "Women," he says, "seem to think men are better at everything." But, of course, it isn't only women who believe this; the whole society, men included, believe it too. This is what the sexual double standard is all about. This is why it can be stated with a degree of certainty that it is not the talking or the writing, but the sex, which can determine the worth of a particular contribution.

That men can base their judgements on women's sex, as distinct from women's performance, is a thesis that has been more recently and fully substantiated by Bernice Lott: "Findings generally support the hypothesis," she says "that the typical responses (of men, primarily) to a competent woman include prejudice, stereotyped beliefs, and overt or subtle discrimination" (1985: p. 43): and she goes on to summarise the research results in this area:

> Goldberg (1968) using only women participants found that the same article was judged to be more valuable, and the author more competent, if authored by a man than a woman. Since then, college students of both genders have

been shown to: select women for a managerial position less than men (Cann, Siegfried and Pearce, 1981; Rosen and Jerdee, 1974) and reject women even more sharply if the position is highly demanding (Rosen and Jerdee, 1974); rate men instructors (not their own) in a generally more favourable way than women (Denmark, 1979); evaluate men instructors as more intelligent and motivating than equally presented women teachers (Bernard, Reefauver, Elsworth and Naylor, 1981); rate men instructors as more powerful and effective (Kaschak, 1981) and prefer to take a course from a man (Lombardo and Tocci, 1979); rate a female applicant for an insurance agent's job as less suitable for the job than a similarly high-scoring man (Heneman, 1977); hire a man over a woman judged equally suitable for a department store job and try harder to persuade a man than a woman to stay with the firm (Gutek and Stevens, 1979); be more willing to recommend hiring a man than a woman for a sales management traineeship and at a higher salary (Dipboye, Arvey and Terpstra, 1977); and give more favorable evaluations to male than female applicants for a newswriting job on such attributes as professional competence, predicted job success, value of a word sample, dedication to journalism, and writing style (Etaugh and Kasley, 1981). In some of the above studies bias against women was greater on the part of men than of women respondents (Bernice Lott, 1985: p. 47).

And there is every reason to believe that the same value judgements operate in the world of letters. Such findings have enormous implications for literary studies, and for the assessments and judgements which are at the core of the entire literary profession and its practices.

That literary critics have not looked to some fields of social science to provide insights on their own evaluative practices says more about their intellectual insulation than—in this instance—the absence of reliable information. For there is a great deal of evidence available from a wide variety of sources which suggests that no member of society can be value-free in relation to gender. Numerous studies in a range of disciplines suggest that like the women in Philip Goldberg's sample, teachers, examiners, editors—and referees of academic journals, not to mention literary critics—predictably provide different evaluations on the basis of perceived sex. Even within the field of literary criticism itself there is sufficient data available for the critics to be informed that works are rated differently according to sex.

Real-life situations as distinct from experiments, the cases of Charlotte Brontë, Emily Brontë, and Elizabeth Gaskell nonetheless provide convincing documentation on the way the sex of the writer influences the assessment of even the most eminent and respected scholars and critics. The double standard in literary evaluation was blatantly exposed when on the publication of *Jane Eyre* by Currer Bell it was decreed that such a novel was a remarkable achievement if written by a man. But the same work was considered a disgrace if written by a woman (see Margot Peters, 1977: p. 205).

And Emily Brontë fared little better: Carol Ohmann (1986) has traced the response to the first edition of *Wuthering Heights* when Ellis Bell was as-

sumed to be male, and contrasted it with the reaction to the second edition
when it was known that Emily Brontë was the author:

> There are not so many reviews of the second edition of *Wuthering Heights*. But
> there are enough, I think, to show that once the work of Ellis Bell was identified
> as the work of a woman, critical responses to it changed. Where the novel had
> been called again and again "original" in 1847 and 1848, the review in the
> *Athenaeum* in 1850 began by firmly placing it in a familiar class, and that class
> was not in the central line of literature. The review in the *Athenaeum* began by
> categorising *Wuthering Heights* as a work of "female genius and authorship".
> The reviewer was really not surprised to learn that *Jane Eyre* and its "sister-
> novels" were all written by women . . . "
>   It is on Emily Brontë's *life* that the review spends most of its 2,000 words.
> References to *Wuthering Heights* are late and few and then it is grouped not
> only with *Jane Eyre* but also with *Agnes Grey*. All three are "characteristic
> tales"—characteristic of the Bell, that is to say the Brontë sisters, and, more
> generally, of tales women write. A single sentence is given to *Wuthering
> Heights* alone: "To those whose experience of men and manners is neither
> extensive nor various, the construction of a self-consistent monster is easier
> than the delineation of an imperfect or inconsistent reality . . . " The review
> ends there, repeating still another time its classification of the novel. *Wuthering
> Heights* . . . is a "more than unusually interesting contribution to the history of
> female authorship in England." (Carol Ohmann, 1986: p. 72)

In emphasising that the work is the product of a woman's pen, and in
lumping together "the sisters" in an undifferentiated mass, the reviewer in
the *Athenaeum* engages in the classic "put down": to suggest that the
experience of the woman writer is inevitably limited by her sex and that for
her the less demanding course of action is preferable, is to make the typical
value judgement about women which has persisted for centuries (see for
example Dale Spender, 1982(a), *Women of Ideas—And What Men Have
Done to Them*).

I wouldn't want to give this particular *Athenaeum* reviewer too much
attention—after all, it's a pretty silly assessment which is being made. However, I would want to point out that the reviewer is but one of scores of critics
who have indulged in making comparably silly assertions and yet have been
taken seriously.

And the question which arises in these circumstances is—why do critics
not monitor their own practices? Why is there no established forum for
debate on the way in which gender—or ethnicity—influences the judgement
of literary professionals? Why no courses in the academy on the reasons that
Mary Ann Evans chose the pen name of a man, or on the dramatic shift in the
response to Elizabeth Gaskell's novel of social protest when it was known the
author was female? (Dale Spender, 1985: p. 207). Why no courses on the
views, values, and vagaries of the men who have decreed society's literary
standards? I am sure there would be no shortage of students for courses on

the prejudices of the profession—on the habits of editors, publishers, reviewers, literary judges, and academics.

The means by which the written word gets accepted for publication, and
for promotion, review, validation, and inclusion in the literary curriculum to
become part of the cultural heritage, would have to be one of the most underresearched and least-taught areas of intellectual endeavour. And this cannot
be because the process is unimportant: The production of the printed word in
our society—and the role that *gatekeepers*[3] play in it—is centrally significant
and should be open to investigation. But currently, it seems that a policy of
"no questions asked" is being employed in the world of letters. This in itself
is cause for concern.

Of course one reason that there is not more research undertaken in this
critical area (and one reason the research that has been done is not always
widely known) is that the findings can have educational and social as well as
literary implications. Measurement of the judgement of assessors can make a
mockery of much of our sacred marking system on which a meritocracy
depends: Were society to lose faith in the efficacy of marking—in exams and
entrance qualifications, in appointments and degrees— chaos could quickly
ensue.

For what has emerged, particularly in the educational realm, is that it is
not just that the *same* contribution can be accorded a different mark or status
on the basis of perceived sex, but that the same status and mark can be
granted different weightings on the basis of sex.

It borders on the astonishing, but it can be shown that in the study of
English, for example, when girls and boys get the same mark, teachers (and
students) can invest it with systematically different meanings. Girls can have
their performance denigrated on the grounds that it was only conformity and
conventional correctness which was responsible for their "good" marks,
while the boys—*who have been given the same grade*—are assumed to have
attained their marks by virtue of their genuine *intellectual* ability.[4]

Instances have been documented where girls have been awarded higher
marks than boys, but the teachers—like the women students in Philip Goldberg's study—will continue to insist that the boys are brighter and that the
girls lack creativity. Like those of us who maintain the mindset that women
are talkative, despite the dramatic evidence to the contrary, teachers can be
committed to the premise that boys are brighter and proceed to substantiate
their belief regardless of the data they are confronted with.

The existence of such entrenched bias in educational contexts has serious
ramifications, not the least of which is that girls are being robbed of their

---

[3] For further discussion on "Gatekeeping" see Dale Spender and Lynne Spender, 1983, and Dale
Spender, 1981.
[4] For further discussion see Chapter Five.

intellectuality and creativity as Katherine Clarricoates (1978) has so uncompromisingly pointed out. And there are of course no grounds for assuming that this theft of women's creativity is being confined to the classroom.[5] Comparable practices are to be found across social, political, and business institutions. And their presence can be readily documented in the literary studies curriculum: The "marks" and status given to Emily Brontë and Elizabeth Gaskell once their sex was known are essentially the same as the marks and status given to the girls Katherine Clarricoates observed in school.

One finding that emerges from linguistic and educational research on the importance of gender in perceptions is that all members of society learn the rules for the construction of reality—in this case that "men are better." While there are varying degrees of commitment to this principle (my own exacted unwillingly), no one can be completely free from such distortions and some who insist on their purity (as some critics are prone to do), simply proclaim their ignorance.

Not even knowledge about the sexual double standard and its operation guarantees immunity. Whenever I include my own responses in my own research, in spite of the compensatory adjustments that I make, I too continue to rate John McKay as (marginally) superior to Joan McKay. I too need to know the sex of my conversation partner before I know what to say and how to say it. I can still think that I have had more than my fair share of the conversation when I have spoken for approximately one third of the time, and my tape recorder continues to inform me that I modify my language behaviour when a man enters the conversation. I defer to men, I develop their conversation topics at the expense of my own, and sometimes knowingly, but sometimes not, I behave (according to my own criteria) as a bit of a wimp!

In a classroom I can still give disproportionate attention to males and be far more concerned about not hurting men's feelings. To my eternal shame I continue to be ultra-sensitive to the male response when I deliver "fierce feminist" lectures to a mixed audience. And to this day I expect more from women than I do from men across a whole range of areas. To declare otherwise would be to defy the evidence of my tape recorder and my written responses. While it might feel as though this time I really am taking a *half* share in the conversation, that I really am treating my students equally, that I really am operating a single rather than a double sexual standard, empirical evidence belies my beliefs. There seems to be no way of avoiding this dilemma: To be a member of this society is to use its "rules" even when they encode offensive forms of sexual discrimination.

Which is why I laugh (or cry!) when members of the literary profession

---

[5]This phenomenon is discussed at greater length in Chapter Seven "Polish, Plagiarism and Plain Theft", page 140.

persist with their claims that their judgement is never clouded by issues of gender. Terrible that so many of them should be so arrogant, but worse that they should be so assiduously ignorant and disregard the implications of so much relevant research. If it were not so awful it could be extremely amusing to detect the eminent literary academics and critics running for the cover of "certainties" rather than confronting and examining the biases and limitations of their own processes of assessment. But instead of coming to terms with the *subjective* nature of their activities (which has connotations of "soft data" and the feminine), many male academics have scrambled to stake their claim to "hard data" and are—in the opinion of Elaine Showalter (1986)— trying to establish a second and more scientifically prestigious form of literary criticism:

> The new sciences of the text based on linguistics, computers, genetic structuralism, deconstructionism, neoformalism and deformalism, affective stylistics and psychoaesthetics, have offered literary critics the opportunity to demonstrate that the work they do is as manly and aggressive as nuclear physics—not intuitive, expressive and feminine, but strenuous, rigorous, impersonal and virile. (Elaine Showalter, 1986: p. 140)

This is not to suggest that such activities should be outlawed. However it is to suggest—as Elaine Showalter does—that these activities are a long way from reading books. And if the object of the exercise is to read books—to enjoy them and reflect upon them, to discuss their meanings and speculate on the worlds they create—then many of these new "sciences of the text" have little or nothing to offer. As simplified symbolic systems which allow for finite meanings—for certainties and proof—they need not be concerned with the richness, complexity, and infinite variations of the written word. The new sciences can steer clear of the challenges provided by the more open-ended questions of interpretation and appreciation.

But where the object of the exercise *is* to read books and to discuss the intellectual, philosophical, and pleasurable responses that they afford, then an appropriate frame of reference is called for, one which can take acount of meaning, of language and its oppressive and liberating uses. And this is where research on the spoken word can be relevant and helpful.

At one level, of course, it is absurd that the studies of the spoken and written language should ever have been split and that they should have for so long been separated, but when some of the findings that have emerged in the context of language and gender studies are listed and linked with some of the issues in "lit-crit," the parallels between the two can be observed readily.

For example, when men today dominate the conversation and determine the agenda, they are behaving in much the same manner as the literary men who, over the centuries, have insisted that their words warrant more space in the canon and that their concerns are the significant and universal ones. And just as men have protected and perpetuated their primacy with the assertion that women talk too much, so have the men of letters protested when they have perceived women trespassing in what they have decreed is male literary territory. Although when it comes to publication rates, review space, and curriculum representation—and the status stakes—women have nothing like a half share in resources and recognition,[6] there are literary men who can continue to carp that women are getting more than their share. Just as women talkers are confined to about one third of the conversation space, so too are women writers allocated only a small percentage of space in the literary curriculum. While there may be those who insist that there are too many women studied these days, that they are swamping the men writers—and *lowering the standards*—women don't ever seem to exceed 10% of the writers represented in mainstream literature courses. They were never more than 7% when Elaine Showalter (1974) conducted her study in 1970, they were 7% when Jean Mullen conducted hers in 1972, and between 5% and 8% when Joanna Russ (1984) conducted hers in 1977. And there is evidence which suggests there is a "backlash" against women writers and that things are getting better rather than worse. There are universities in Australia and England, for example, where there are courses on nineteenth century poets and twentieth century writers where not one woman is included on the reading list!

To assume that "progress" has been made since the startling studies of the seventies made the inequities of women's literary representation quite clear, is to be gravely misled. It isn't necessarily any easier now for women to attain a *half* share in any linguistic framework. Women who want to contribute equally with men in conversation have to be committed and courageous. A veritable battery of insults is available to intimidate them, to undermine their confidence, and ensure their withdrawal. "Domineering," "aggressive," "rude," "bitchy," and "disagreeable" are but some of the terms designed to end women's spoken participation, and they have their parallels in the counsel and criticism—commented on in greater length later— that men have directed towards literary women.

When today men repeatedly interrupt women in conversation—and silence them—they are replicating a pattern that for hundreds of years has characterised the response to women's written words. Both Tillie Olsen (1980) and Adrienne Rich (1980) have stated unequivocally that the history of women and their literature is the history of interruption—and silence:

> The entire history for women's struggle for self determination has been muffled in silence over and over. One serious cultural obstacle encountered by any feminist writer is that each feminist work has tended to be received as if it emerged from nowhere; as if each of us had lived, thought and worked without

---

[6]See *Women in Publishing*, 1987 for more definitive statistics.

any historical past or contextual present. This is one of the ways in which
women's work and thinking has been made to seem sporadic, errant, orphaned
of any tradition of its own. (Adrienne Rich, 1980: p. 11)

The conditions under which women write are not dissimilar to the conditions under which women talk: They can attend to their own needs only *after*
they have met some of the physical and psychological needs of men. Tillie
Olsen (1980) has movingly attested to the way in which women are required
to do the "shitwork" in the home, and the extent to which marriage and
motherhood curtail women's opportunities to write. Pamela Fishman (1977)
in her classic study of mixed sex talk has shown how women are required to
do the "shitwork" in conversation—to do all the routine and invisible chores
which keep conversations going and which, of course, put women in the
position of developing men's talk and topics at the expense of their own. All
those helpful touches—the clean shirts and the supportive comments—the
"emotional management" as women put their energy into making men feel
comfortable.

This is a phenomenon that many women have written about—Virginia
Woolf among them. Because it has been widely recognised within women's
literary history that women's words are being judged by men (and that it
doesn't pay to antagonise them) extensive constraints have been placed upon
women's work which have no counterparts among men:

> No male writer has written primarily or even largely for women, or with the
> sense of women's criticism as a consideration when he chooses his materials,
> his themes, his language. But to a lesser or greater extent every woman writer
> has written for men, even when, like Virginia Woolf, she was supposed to be
> addressing women. (Adrienne Rich, 1980: pp. 37–38)

Virginia Woolf was herself aware of this "influence" in her writing: She
gave it substance in her references to the "Angel in the House," the figure
"who used to come between me and my paper when I was writing" and who
used to "seduce" her by whispering—

> Be sympathetic, be tender; flatter; deceive, use all the arts and wiles of our sex.
> Never let anyone guess that you have a mind of your own. Above all, be pure!
> (Virginia Woolf, 1972: p. 285)

It has been widely accepted among women that certain forms must be
followed if they are to get a hearing from men. With the spoken word and the
written word women have tried to be polite, pure—and *supportive*—on the
premise that they would be heard and heeded. But unfortunately the double
standard can also give rise to the double bind with the result that women
who practise politeness may get just as negative a reception as women who
are "rude and disagreeable." Peter Trudgill (1975) is just one of the linguists
who has suggested that it is because women speak more politely than men
that their voice lacks authority.

So women are damned if they do and damned if they don't: Damned if they are assertive (and talk like men), and damned if they are supportive—"hesitant"—and polite, and talk like women!

The similarities with the written word are obvious: Women are damned for writing like women ("domestic dramas and tragedies at tea parties"), and they are damned for writing like men—when, of course, it is known that women are the authors.

When I was doing my own research on language and sex, I was often perplexed by the way in which women's talk was categorised as "gossip"[7] (and dismissed) frequently without a hearing. To satisfy my own curiosity, I did a content analysis of women's talk and compared it with men's talk on a number of occasions. When I realised that women could be talking philosophically about the rearing of the next generation while men were revealing a partisan preference for particular football teams—*and that the women's talk was dismissed as gossip while the men's was held to be more important and interesting*—I concluded that the values being ascribed were based on the sex and not the talk. The only sensible statement that I could make on the basis of my comparison was that when men "gossip" it is called something different.

The same thesis applies to the written word as well and has a distinct counterpart in the novel. Again, I have often been perplexed by the way women writers are undifferentiated and seen to write, en masse, the lowly form of romantic fiction. From Jane Austen to Barbara Cartland—and despite all the dramatic diversity in between—there is the implication that *all* women's writing is romance, in much the same way as all women's talk is gossip.

And a content analysis of the writing cannot possibly support such a classification scheme. Look at the domestic melodramas of Thomas Hardy, at the romances of D. H. Lawrence. Clearly when men write romance it's called something different. It is the *sex* and not the *writing* that is responsible for such judgement.

Not surprisingly a long list could be compiled of the similarities in the treatment of women's spoken and written language in a male-dominated society. The overview contained here is not intended to be exhaustive but it is meant to make some of the connections and to state the case for looking at sex and gender as a central factor in literary judgement. However, no summary, no matter how brief, could be adequate if it did not include mention of the appropriation of women's words by men.

Few women could be unaware of the way in which their words can be

---

[7]A *Feminist Dictionary* (Cheris Kramarae and Paula Treichler, 1985) defines "gossip"—"a woman's female friend invited to be present at a birth . . . " (p. 179)

"ignored" only to be taken up by men, minutes, sometimes even seconds, later, and accorded approval. So common is this practice that it has become "a joke" among multitudes of women. Numerous versions abound of "That's a good suggestion Miss Jones, we'll wait for a man to make it," and it points to the phenomenon whereby men readily avail themselves of the resources of women—without acknowledgement.

Pamela Fishman (1977) has declared that women are supposed to be good at the art of conversation—and that for women, the art of conversation is getting men to talk. At the crux of her somewhat facetious explanation for sexual inequalities in interaction is the far-reaching premise that women's linguistic resources are supposed to be put at the service of men. That women have no linguistic rights of their own, no linguistic autonomy; that their contribution is justified only in so far as it affords ideas, opportunities, encouragement, support for the linguistic achievements of men is one insight that her study provides.

And the same premise can be transferred to the written word where women's efforts have frequently—one might go so far as to say ordinarily—been used by men to enhance their own records of performance.

Not that this habit has been confined to language: There are now numerous studies in the history of music and art that provide a very simple explanation for the presumed absence of women in these fields. According to Joanna Russ (1984), with whom I completely concur, one of the reasons that there have been few "great" women musicians and artists is that their work has been attributed to or appropriated by men (pp. 50–51). Cynthia Fuchs Epstein has described the literary arrangements:

> I have begun to collect gracious acknowledgements to wives which indicate the intellectual contribution of the wife to a piece of work, but which do not give professional credit to her. An early example is the acknowledgement of Gabriel Kolko . . . in *Wealth and Power in America* (Praeger, paperback edition, 1967) which states: 'To my wife, Joyce, I owe a debt that mere words cannot express. This book is in every sense a joint enterprise and the first in a series of critical studies on which we're presently engaged' (p. xi) . . . the wife did not appear as co-author or junior author. (Cynthia Fuchs Epstein, 1976: pp. 193–194)

This is just another variation on the theme of "That's a good idea Miss Jones, we'll wait until it's put forward by a man"; it is the means whereby the work of many women is taken over by men. And it is a practice about which few great male writers have felt much guilt. The assumption that women's resources are available to men and that women's creativity is but the raw material waiting to be wrought into artistic shape by gifted men is one which is prevalent in literary circles—and one which demands serious and systematic attention. It is not too much to assert that there have been eminent literary men who have not only *stolen* women's words but who have seen nothing problematic about the practice because they have believed they were only taking what they were entitled to! This form of language acquisition is the focus of the final chapter of this volume—"Polish, Plagiarism, and Plain Theft."

But much of the discussion in this chapter has been based on the premise that men have *first* read the words of women before they have found them wanting. This too is the premise of much feminist literary criticism which challenges the exclusion of women from the canon. While this is part of the picture, it is not the whole picture. Just as Cheris Kramarae (1977) found there are stereotypes of women's and men's language which mean people don't actually have to listen to women and men speaking to know that the women are "pathetic" and the men are "masterful," so too (as Philip Goldberg, 1974, pointed out) are stereotypical judgements being made about the written word of women. It is my contention that the population in general and male literary critics in particular entertain a negative image of women and their words, to the extent that it is widely believed that you don't have to read women's writing to know it's no good!

Kate Wilhelm (1975) has summed up what many women know—"My first husband never read a word I wrote. . . . He knew it was all trivial." (p. 22)

To challenge literary men on the grounds that they do not give women a fair hearing is one thing, to charge them with giving women no hearing at all is quite another. Yet when the words of women do not even qualify for a reading and an evaluation then the evidence that it is the sex and not the writing which is being judged is incontrovertible. It is because women have been dismissed as *women*, and then as writers, that it has become necessary to call to account the judgement of literary men.

2

Literary Criticism: Making It for Men

Literary criticism is an activity and a body of knowledge that is dominated by men; it was men who made up the rules, who constructed the theory and practice of "lit-crit," who decreed what was good, bad, and indifferent long before they allowed women educational and occupational rights. It is partly because men were allowed to take up their powerful positions before women started knocking at the door that they have been able to preserve and protect their primacy. And this is part of the problem. For, while there are many debates about standards, about content, form, and style, at the centre of tension between women and men in the world of letters is the issue of power—as Maggie Humm has suggested (1986). Men have it, and they are using it to try and keep women out. And the louder women knock, and the more claims they make for entry, the more many men are determined to defend what they have come to regard as their property. The tactics they have used to discourage women and to prevent them from trespassing range from the trite to the terrible, but unfortunately more than a few of them have proved to be very effective.

Of course the male desire to dissuade women from taking up their pens is not new. Since Aphra Behn (1640–1689) made her appearance on the Restoration Drama scene and, along with other women playwrights, made it perfectly plain that it was possible for women to be at least as popular and profitable as men, male members of the literary profession have been trying to eliminate any competition from women. When in 1728 Alexander Pope wrote The Dunciad and engaged in a vituperative attack on women writers, it was partly because he found it so galling that they should do so well as dramatists and novelists, and could command such attention. It is no coincidence that he unleashed his most vicious assault on the popular and prolific writer, Eliza Haywood (1693–1756) who—as Walter and Clare Jerrold (1929) have indicated—did not publish under her own name for some time after his vilification.

The insistence that women should not write has often been transformed (in the minds of many men) into the edict that women could not write. So along with their public denunciations and deprecations of women's creative efforts have been their private and cruel condemnations and counsel, intended to divert women from the world of letters.

Uneasy about the contradictions between being a woman and a writer, Charlotte Brontë turned to one of the most eminent literary men of her time for advice on the matter. When in deliberately didactic style Robert Southey delivered some of the most callous and calculatedly self-interested admonishments ever directed to an aspiring writer in literary history, he set an example which to this day still has its followers:

> The day dreams in which you habitually indulge are likely to induce a distempered state of mind; and, in proportion as all the ordinary uses of the world seem to you flat and unprofitable, you will be unfitted for them without becoming fitted for anything else. Literature cannot be the business of a woman's life and it ought not to be. The more she is engaged in proper duties, the less leisure she will have for it, even as an accomplishment and a recreation. (Robert Southey, quoted in Margot Peters, 1977: p. 54)

It must have taken the determination of desperation for Charlotte Brontë to have recovered her sense of self and to have persevered with her writing after such a harsh and intimidatory "corrective." Yet, while her case is awful, she is by no means the only woman to have been subjected to such harassment. A common entry in the annals of literary women is the documentation of the discouragement, the deflection, and the despondency they have experienced when they have set their sights on being writers. Tillie Olsen (1980) is but one of the latest in the long line of women authors who have appreciated the extent to which women's constancy and confidence is sapped by the systematic devaluation of their sex, and their work:

> . . . The will, the measureless store of belief in oneself to be able to come to, cleave to, find the form for one's own life comprehensions. Difficult for any male not born into a class that breeds such confidence. Almost impossible for a girl, a woman. (Tillie Olsen, 1980: p. 27)

In these days of what some would call post-feminism, there is sometimes an assumption that blatant intimidatory tactics designed to keep women out of the literary arena are a thing of the past. There is the acceptance that the women's movement has been responsible for certain gains and that as a result men are now more inclined to open the educational and occupational doors for women, and to accept them as equals. Perhaps this is the case in some areas; perhaps progress has been made, particularly in the non-traditional fields that women have entered. But that no such improvements have been forthcoming in the context of lit-crit (as distinct from publishing) is patently demonstrable. There are male critics, academics, and authors who continue in the same vein as the disturbed Alexander Pope and the disdainful Robert Southey. And there are those who are even worse.

The history of women's writing is the history of discouragement which continues to this day and this is—as Erica Jong points out—the fundamental consideration in any study of the woman writer:

> For women writers the systematic discouragement even to *attempt* to become writers has been so constant and pervasive a force that we cannot consider their literary productions without somehow assessing the effects of that barrage of discouragement. Often discouraged in the home, often at school, often by family and spouses, the rare woman writer who does not lose her determination along the way is already a survivor. That one should next have to face the systematic discouragement of a male-oriented literary establishment is absurd and sad but nonetheless a real fact of life for many women writers. The truth is that many of us are doomed to do our best work in an atmosphere of condescension and loneliness . . . we cannot truly understand the situation of the woman writer unless we are honest about this systematic discouragement and unless we try and see clearly the form it takes, and the strategies of survival it imposes on the individual artist. (Erica Jong, 1980: pp. 169–170)

Since women have shown themselves to be serious competition as writers, there have been men who have been prepared to say almost anything—to use almost any ploy—to get women to put away their pens. They have sneered, jeered, and threatened, often delivering disgraceful diatribes against individual women, invariably disqualifying the female sex in their effort to discredit women's writing. If it were not such an abhorrent task it would surely be salutary to compile a record of the resistant, ruthless, and irrational remarks made by men about women and their writing. Such an inventory is a painful prospect to contemplate: In even envisaging such a collection of comments I am mindful of Germaine Greer's (1970) incredulous statement that women have no idea how much men hate them (p. 249). Clearly, when men's "criticisms" of women and their writing are gathered together, it simply isn't possible to maintain the myth that males have been impartial judges of women's literary efforts. On the contrary, it could be said that the salient characteristic of men's response is misogyny.

On the occasions when women have assembled and assessed some of the judgements of literary men, the evidence against the men has been damning. Apart from Germaine Greer (1970), Kate Millett (1972), and Joanna Russ (1984), there have been Sandra Gilbert and Susan Gubar (1979) who, in *The Madwoman in the Attic*, have put together quite a list of men who have claimed that the pen is a metaphorical penis—which is why women cannot qualify as writers. Elaine Showalter (1986) has exposed the pride and the prejudice in the pronouncements of such critics as Robert Partlow and Robert Boyers (p. 126) who have contended that feminist literary criticism is a form of deviancy and that there can be no dialogue between the sexes until women talk in terms that are intelligible to men. As Elaine Showalter declares, their "terminology is best understood as a form of intimidation, intended to force women into using a discourse more acceptable to the academy" (pp. 126–127). It has counterparts too with the spoken word where men are intent on defining the topic, deciding the agenda, and determining when women are "out of order." The most common utterance that men make to women (on the tapes I possess) as they try to take over the topics and frame them from their own perspective is: "What you mean is . . . " The parallels in relation to feminist literary criticism are striking when men declare that women's theories and explanations are not up to standard until they are couched in the terms of men.

Just as abusive terms in the spoken language can be used against women, to scare them off and keep them quiet, so are some of the insults directed against women within literary criticism designed to discourage them from participation. After reading the recital of invective that comprises some of the literary men's "criticisms" of women's writing—including that of feminist literary criticism—no one could continue to believe that, in the world of letters, men have seen the error of their sexist ways and resolved recently to give women a fair hearing.

If more evidence were needed to reveal the depths to which contemporary man can descend to deflect women from writing, the younger generation of women—who have not given way under this pressure—can readily provide it. Erica Jong and Mary Gordon, for example, recall some of the threats that they experienced and, because they are of the opinion that such harassment is the rule rather than the exception, their testimony helps to support the case that the intimidation of writing women is routine.

Erica Jong speaks now from the position of one who did not heed the voice of authority:

> One of the most notable (and faintly horrifying) memories from my college years is the time a Distinguished Critic came to my creative writing class and delivered himself of the following thundering judgement:
>
> "Women can't be writers. They don't know blood and guts, and puking in the streets, and fucking whores, and swaggering through Pigalle at 5:00 a.m. . . . "
>
> But the most amazing thing was the *response*—or lack of it. It was 1961 or '62 and we all sat there—aspiring women writers that we were—and listened to this Maileresque claptrap without a word of protest. Our hands folded on our laps, our eyes modestly downcast, our hearts cast even lower than our eyes, we listened meekly—while the male voice of authority told us what women could or couldn't write. (Erica Jong, 1980: pp. 170–171)

How many other members of the class did listen—and decide to abandon any hopes they might have of being a writer?

It is awful to have to confront some of these crude intimidatory tactics: It is even worse to contemplate the fact that they can work, as Mary Gordon acknowledges:

> Once I was told a story by a famous writer. "I will tell you what women writers are like," he said. The year was 1971. The women's movement had made a lot of women write. "Women writers are like a female bear who goes into a cave to hibernate. The male bear shoves a pine cone up her ass, because he knows if she shits all winter, she'll stink up the cave. In the spring, the pressure of all that built up shit makes her expel the pine cone, and she shits a winter's worth all over the cave." That's what women writers are like said the famous writer.
>
> He told the story with such geniality; he looked as if he were giving me a wonderful gift. I felt I ought to smile; everyone knows there's no bore like a feminist with no sense of humor. I did not write for two months after that. It was the only time in my life I ever suffered from writer's block . . . (Mary Gordon, 1980: pp. 27–28)

The "Distinguished Critic" and the "Famous Writer": These are their words of wisdom, their assessments of women's potential and place, and these are the statements that are advanced as *fair judgement*. They are by no means isolated cases. (Maya Angelou, 1985, says it was precisely because she was told that a literary autobiography was the most difficult thing to write that she was propelled into doing it: see page 7)

There's more than one form of intimidation, however. While some men may have tried to protect their territory by actively frightening women away, there are others who have been a little more subtle and indirect: They have ingenuously sought to suggest that the doors to literary achievement are wide open and that the only obstacles to entry reside in the women themselves. If women are not proportionately represented in the literary world—they argue—it's women's fault; you can't accuse men of doing anything to keep them out.

Certain subscribers to this school of thought have been named by Sandra Gilbert and Susan Gubar (1979) who have suggested that by insisting that creativity is a male prerogative these men have been able to distance themselves from the direct pressure applied to women while at the same time they have defined women as non-starters in the literary events. Gerard Manley Hopkins, for example, did not go around addressing aspiring young women writers, or inform them that there was no point in trying to produce great work because they were women. But as a highly esteemed poet and an honourable man of the cloth who spoke with authority on the nature of creativity, he would have planted doubts in the minds of countless women when he declared that "The artist's most essential quality is masterly execution which is a kind of male gift and especially marks off men from women" (see Sandra Gilbert and Susan Gubar, 1979: p. 3).

If women can begin to believe that because they are women they simply have not got what it takes there may be no need to drive them from the literary door: They may decide for themselves that it's not worth knocking and stay away. And for this you could not possibly blame the men!

In asking whether the pen is a metaphorical penis—and for whom?— Sandrà Gilbert and Susan Gubar have exposed a powerful strategy designed to disqualify women writers—without reference to their work, of course. When Anthony Burgess announces that "Jane Austen's novels fail because her writing lacks a male thrust" his case does not rest upon supporting examples. It is sufficient for him to say that she lacks maleness for her writing to automatically become suspect. When William Gass expresses regret that "Literary women lack that blood congested genital drive which energises great style" *he* expects to be taken seriously though the mind boggles at the thought of the evidence he would need to support such an assertion. But these men are not really making literary assessments at all: They are simply stating the certainty of their sex (and the deficient nature of women) and providing variations on Norman Mailer's basic assertion that what a writer needs is balls. For some mysterious reason there's no point in putting pen to paper without them.

On a more substantive note, the belief that only men can reach the lofty heights as artists and writers not only helps to explain and justify women's relative absence from legitimated creative endeavours; it also introduces an element of determinism and—for women—defeat and despair. They are deflected from their talking/writing before they begin. For if it is the case that no matter how hard they try they will never be great—never the masterful speakers or the fathers of the texts—then the clear conclusion to draw is that they may as well accept the advice offered to Charlotte Brontë more than a century ago, and abandon their literary aspirations and assume the duties of home.

If these are the dimensions of "discouragement" as they are directed against white women, how much greater is the denial of opportunity for black women who must break the double silence of race and sex; how much greater the pressure to stay in their proper place and perform their servicing (as distinct from creative) tasks. And, as Audre Lorde has commented, it is not just the white community that constrains black expression; the concept of what it is appropriate for a black woman (lesbian) to write, permeates the black community too:

> Black writers, of whatever quality, who step outside the pale of what black writers are supposed to write about, of who black writers are supposed to be, are condemned to silences in black literary circles that are as total and destructive as any imposed by racism. This is particularly true for black women writers who have refused to be delineated by male-establishment models of femininity, and who have dealt with their sexuality as an accepted part of their identity . . .
> (Audre Lorde, 1985: p. 101)

Charlotte Brontë persevered despite the odds; so too did Zora Neale Hurston in the face of greater odds. And Maya Angelou, Toni Cade Bambara, Audre Lorde, Toni Morrison, Ntozake Shange, and Alice Walker (see Claudia Tate, 1985).

As if threats and expressions of regret were not enough to convince women that they cannot compete with the contributions of men, there is a third form of persuasion employed by many prestigious academics. This approach has at its centre the *implication* that the words of women have been examined by expert and reasonable men—and found wanting. This is the approach which presents a male cast of thousands in the canon, the curriculum, and the establishment, and encourages the belief that if any explanation is needed for women's absence, it is because their *writing* is not up to standard. Credibility is lent to this particular approach because women are allowed some achievements: Because it is often said that Jane Austen, Charlotte Brontë, George Eliot, and Virginia Woolf *dominate* the novel (although such an assertion is an instance where women's .001% is seen as more than a fair share), then clearly men cannot be accused of refusing to let women in. Of course, the inherent inconsistency in this approach is completely overlooked: The fact that women are held to dominate the field, while at the same time the good woman writer remains the rare exception, is another example of the operation of the double standard. As with the spoken word, the apparent contradiction is resolved when it is realised that a woman who enjoys the same recognition as a man is perceived as getting too much and can be held to "dominate" the area.

Among the men who have used the more sophisticated ploy of presenting women's relative absence from the world of letters as a product of women's poor performance, is Ian Watt. In his classic text, *The Rise of the Novel: Studies in Defoe, Richardson and Fielding* (1957) he includes one sentence which reveals that most eighteenth century novels were written by women. But because he does not expand on this, because he gives no indication of who these women were or what they have written, the message he transmits is that the work of these writers is not worth bothering about. So unobtrusive and understated is his dismissal of the *majority* of the novels of the eighteenth century that even the most diligent reader could be forgiven for missing the reference; and certainly, the most doubting of readers could be forgiven for not suspecting that the body of work being "brushed aside" contained more than six hundred novels and comprised the work of more than one hundred writing women (see Dale Spender, 1986: *Mothers of the Novel*).

In the absence of even minimal acknowledgement of the quantity (and quality) of these women writers, Ian Watt is helping to construct the belief that there is nothing these women wrote that warrants study or attention. And because he is the expert, the authority, who claims scholarly impartiality and credibility for his judgement, within the literary community there has been no great suspicion about his findings or his motives.

But there should be. For in a few lines Ian Watt disqualifies all the eighteenth century women writers' contributions. And he does this without offering any substantiating evidence. This is one of the reasons that literary criticism has been brought into disrepute. Because under the guise of scholarship and the dogma of "objectivity" literary men have been playing politics, protecting their own power base by providing preferential treatment for their own sex. Within the field of literary criticism men are not even required to present a case that discredits the writing of women in order to prevent women's appearance in the canon. Rather, like Ian Watt, they can simply exclude women from consideration because they are women, while continuing to foster the fallacious assumption that it was the work, not the sex, which was found to be inferior.

One of the most blatant examples of the thesis that you don't have to read women's writing to know it's no good is provided by John Cawelti in his book *Adventure, Mystery and Romance* (1976), in which he states as his aim the analysis of the attractions of mass-market fiction. Now the biggest category of mass-market fiction—the form which has the greatest attraction—is romance, so one could expect to find a reasonable amount of space allocated to an explanation of romance's popularity in the marketplace.

But no; any such expectation is doomed to disappointment. For *romance* barely even rates a mention. Without apology or explanation, coverage of this vast, versatile, and vital category is virtually non-existent. As Margaret Jensen (1984) has pointed out, John Cawelti "deals with romances in one and a half pages, the same amount of space that he devotes to the discussion of alien beings" (p. 22).

Were John Cawelti to have subtitled his book "Categories of Popular Fiction which Appeal to Men," I would have no quarrel with his content or his conclusions. But what I do object to is his "sleight of hand" strategy, which gives the impression that even when it comes to mass-market fiction, women's contribution is beneath consideration and does not deserve discussion. The implication that the popular fiction associated with men—thrillers, westerns, tough spies, and private eyes—is intrinsically more significant than the popular fiction that is associated with women, is just another manifestation of the double standard which presumes men are better but which offers no supportive evidence for the view.

Were John Cawelti to even tackle the issue of his particular space allocation—to make a case for giving most of the space to men's fiction and to explicitly defend his judgement that 1 1/2 pages was, for women, a fair share, I would be less critical of his contribution. But what I cannot abide is the way his work reinforces the idea that when men concern themselves with only men they are engaged in scholarly, honourable, and admirable activities of universal significance, whereas women who concern themselves with women are branded as partisan, political—polemical—and confined to issues of minor importance and interest.

What women are encountering in these circumstances are much the same stereotypes about language that flourish in relation to the spoken word. You don't have to hear men and women talk to know that men do it well while women are woeful, and you don't have to read men's and women's writing to know that men are the masters, the great authors, while women lack "thrust," "guts," "genital congestion," and all the other qualities the sensitive artist requires.

Norman Mailer, of course, knows this: He doesn't need an in depth analysis to know that women's writing lacks force on just about every dimension. Just one sniff is sufficient to confirm his suspicions:

> The sniffs I get from the ink of women . . . are always fey, old hat, Quaintsy Goysy, tiny, too dykily psychotic, crippled, creepish, fashionable, frigid, outer Baroque *Maguille* in mannequin's whimsy or else bright and still born. (Norman Mailer, quoted in Elaine Showalter, 1984: p. 3)

Since women started writing they have been up against men's beliefs about what is proper, appropriate, and *womanly* in a writing woman, and to this day the problem persists. Men have a *mindset* about the literary efforts of women, and because it is derived from their construct of woman and not from a study of women's writing, it doesn't actually matter whether these qualities are or are not present in women's writing.

That men are by definition the major writers and women the minor ones was a lesson that the writer Mary Gordon was meant to learn early in her literary life: She comments that

> . . . there are people in the world who derive no small pleasure from the game of "major" and "minor". They think that no major work can be painted in watercolors. They think that Hemingway writing about the boys in the wood is major: Mansfield writing about the girls in the house is minor. Exquisite, they will hasten to add, but minor . . . (Mary Gordon, 1980: p. 28).

It becomes almost superfluous to add the information about the category to which Mary Gordon found herself consigned.

> . . . I have been told by male but not by female critics that my work was "exquisite," "lovely," "like a watercolor." They, of course were painting in oils. They were doing the important work. Watercolors are cheap and plentiful; oils are costly: their base must be bought. And the idea is that oil paintings will endure . . . (Mary Gordon, 1980: p. 28)

Even if a reliable study of the written word were undertaken, I have no doubt that it would provide no more evidence to support the thesis that "men are better" than studies of the spoken word have supplied. There are no grounds for the belief that men engage in the interesting talk, while women "gossip," and no grounds I suspect for the belief that men are the oil painters and the great writers, while women dabble in watercolors and produce trite little romances.

But, if there are no empirical grounds for such beliefs, there is persuasive evidence that suggests these beliefs play a powerful role in programming perception. When society believes man to be better, its members are prepared to project this belief on to everything from man's interests and experiences to his values and his language. As Margaret Mead has said:

> Men may cook or weave or dress dolls or hunt humming birds but if such activities are appropriate occupations of men, then the whole society, men and women alike, votes them as important. When the same activities are performed by women, they are regarded as less important. (Margaret Mead, 1971: p. 157)

Mary Gordon (1980) looks at the high status granted to male writers and the encouragement given to aspiring young men to explore their *masculine* experience and contrasts this with the devaluation of women writers and the dismissal of their *feminine* interpretation of existence. She deplores the operation of one (negative) rule for women and another (positive) rule for men. Commenting on her own introduction to this double standard she says:

> . . . It was alright for the young men I knew . . . to write about the hymens they had broken, the diner waitresses they had seduced. Those experiences were significant. But we were not to write about our broken hearts, about the married men we loved disastrously, about our mothers or our children. Men could write about their fears of dying of exposure in the forest; we could not write about our fears of being suffocated in the kitchen. Our desire to write about these experiences only revealed our shallowness; it was suggested we would, in time, get over it. And write about what? Perhaps we should stop writing. (Mary Gordon, 1980: p. 29)

So persistent and so pervasive have been the practices designed to prevent women from being proportionately represented in the literary heritage that one of the questions which can be asked is why nothing has been done about this long-standing injustice: Have there been no protests?

Objections have been registered, of course: But if it is easy enough to discredit women's literary offerings, it has been even easier to discredit women's "sour grapes" protests and challenges to the academy. Because this strand of "resistance writing" has also fallen victim to the double standard that disallows the value of women's contribution, it is often not appreciated that there has been a long line of women critics who over the centuries have been interpreting, evaluating, discussing—and theorising—about the efforts of women (and men) in a society where men have the upper hand.

When women engage in critical activity it is—predictably—called by another name: Literary biography, sociology, history, memoirs, notes, thoughts, opinions—in fact, almost anything but literary criticism. Yet since women have been writing—and publishing—they have been protesting about the unjust pre-eminence of men, in both the world, and the world of letters.

In the seventeenth century Katherine Philips, Margaret Cavendish, Aphra Behn, Anne Finch, and Mary Astell all concerned themselves with the nature of literature and the achievements of women; Mrs. Delany, Elizabeth Carter, Catherine Talbot, Elizabeth Montagu, Hester Chapone, Mrs. Thrale, Hannah More—indeed all of the bluestockings—were passionately concerned with literary criticism. There was Clara Reeve, who in 1785 wrote *The Progress of Romance through times, countries and manners; with remarks on the good and bad effects of it, on them respectively, in the course of evening conversations* (2 vols), and Mary Hays and Mary Wollstonecraft (and her daughter Mary Shelley) who made their own marks on the literary landscape. Joanne Baillie, Elizabeth Inchbald, Fanny Burney, Maria Edgeworth, Anna Laetitia Barbauld, and Elizabeth Barrett Browning were all contributors to women's traditions of literary criticism with Ann Thackeray and George Eliot bequeathing an impressive legacy to literary understandings. This century Dorothy Richardson—and all the modernist women writers, "H.D.," "Bryher," Amy Lowell, and Djuna Barnes to name but a few—(Gillian Hanscombe and Virginia Smyers, 1986), as well as Virginia Woolf and others are among some of the women who have written reams about women, the word, and the power of men. When they are brought together, not only do these writings provide an extensive record of women's achievements in the face of men's opposition, but these works comprise an elaborated alternative tradition which encodes a very different version of literary history.

There are numerous reasons why this different historical perspective should be reclaimed and made available: Apart from the need to set the record straight—to show how, what and why women were writing, and with what effect—from the point of view of women there is the particular need to establish that women's protests about men's power and protection policies in literature have a long and laudable history. The point made by Erica Jong about the systematic discouragement (and punishment) of women is the one that other women have been elaborating, at least since Anne Finch (1661–1720) wrote those now famous words

Alas! A woman that attempts the pen
Such an intruder on the rights of men . . .
(Joan Goulianos, 1974: p. 71)

While it might not have been until the 1970s that the term *feminist literary criticism* appeared, the activities undertaken now in its name are not new but have been going on for centuries and it is important that feminist literary critics (along with women writers in general) should also be aware of their antecedents, and able to benefit from the analyses and insights of the past.

Think of what it would be like to be able to go to numerous volumes of women's lit-crit from across the centuries. Think of what it would be like for the woman writer to be able to see the routine dismissals of men exposed and denounced by women critics. Think what it would be like for the woman critic to have her views and values confirmed—and her confidence boosted—by such a repository of accumulated wisdom.

Women literary critics currently face many of the same problems women poets, playwrights, and novelists have encountered: All are the victims of the patriarchal silences and interruptions described by Adrienne Rich (1980), which can undermine women's sense of purpose and instil deep and destructive doubts. As Joanna Russ indicates:

> . . . When the memory of one's predecessor is buried . . . the assumption persists that there were none and each generation of women believes itself to be faced with the burden of doing everything for the first time. And if no one ever did it before, if no woman was ever that socially sacred creature, "a great writer", (or a wise literary critic), why do we think we can succeed now? (Joanna Russ, 1984: p. 93)

Women are underrepresented in the canon, but they are also underrepresented—if not unrepresented—in the critical curriculum. Few, if any, are the women who are numbered among the rigorous, intellectual, and critical thinkers in the world of letters. Even contemporary women critics are more likely to be the objects of contempt and derision rather than figures of respect as Annette Kolodny (1986) and Elaine Showalter (1986) have pointed out in their studies of some of men's ugly responses to feminist literary criticism.

But there is method in the male madness: Intimidatory tactics can work. They can keep women out of the influential literary circles and the literary curriculum. For centuries men have been declaring that because women are women they cannot be good or great writers—which is why, on average, less than 10% of the writers included on college course lists in Britain, North America, and Australia are women. Despite the documentation of gross injustice and foul play, despite the challenge thrown out by women's research and literary scholarship, it could be claimed that influential male academics have shown not the slightest intention of opening the doors to women. Let women be students (and tutors and teaching assistants) by all means; let them sit at the feet of great men's literature; let them learn that it is men who have made the memorable contributions to the literary landscape and who deserve praise and prestige. Let women be consumers—the more the merrier—but let them not be the makers, the producers of literary culture. Let the priorities, the perspectives—and the politics of men—prevail.

Shocking stories abound of the way male academics have excluded women from the literary hierarchies and the heritage; stories about hiring and firing that are so discriminatory and disgraceful that if retribution is not forthcoming, all faith in affirmative action programmes and equal opportunities departments has to be lost. Without apology or explanation, outstanding contemporary women writers and critics are bypassed when it comes to appointments, grants, honours, and recognition. On the grounds that individually they are not up to standard and that collectively they will lower the standard, outstanding women writers and critics of the past are simply omitted from academic courses. And yet students—and the wider community—are not informed that this particular offering is but the best education that men can provide by, for, and about men. Instead they are asked to believe that is is *the* best education and that there is nothing partisan or petty about the influential men who are responsible for the provision.

At one stage, because I thought I was strong enough, I wrote to a number of women who work in the literary realm and asked them for accounts of the strategies used by men to discredit women and their writing. The response was extensive—and astonishing. And while it would give me great satisfaction to publish the details of some of these appalling incidents—and to name names, the law of libel preempts this. (Perhaps the lawmakers could have forseen the dangers of feminism—which is why they found it necessary to pass a law that made it an offence to deprive a man of his good name.)[1]

Among eminent literary men it seems that it is still common practice to assert that they would like to appoint a woman but there simply isn't one who is qualified—who comes up to standard. And while such an admission is an indication of significant ignorance, it must also be noted that it is a clever strategy which has proved to be extremely successful in keeping women out.[2] It continues to work. And the men who advance such an argument continue to be credible. While at the same time all the evidence that has been amassed about the limited and ludicrous nature of such an assertion continues to be "overlooked."

Stereotypes about women and their language appear to have just as much currency among academic men as among the lay community. Few academic men seem to have read any literature about the treatment of women and their work and in the best traditions of the male-dominated academy they are prepared to assert—as Elaine Showalter (1986) has indicated—that they are against feminist literary criticism and consequently have not read any (p. 126). Without being embarrassed by the gaffes they are making or the power-ploys that they reveal, there are men in English Departments who continue to state unequivocally that the reason there are no women—or so few women— on their reading lists is because during the particular period being studied women did not write anything—or that what they wrote was without literary merit.

---

[1]Some of the responses are to be found in Appendix, on page 195.
[2]For further discussion of the strategies men have used to exclude women, see the excellent coverage provided by Barbara Rogers, 1988.

Such a stance constitutes one of the greatest "con" tricks ever perpetrated in the academy: It continues to pass as "truth."

There is one example—raised by a number of literary women—which would help to suggest that no matter how much evidence women accumulate about the dimension of self-interest in men's pronouncements it will not cause them to abandon their practices. When it comes to the eighteenth century there have been—in the last few years—at least four volumes that have been designed to challenge the exclusion of women from the canon: Mary Anne Schofield and Cecilia Macheski (eds), 1986, *Fetter'd or Free? British Women Novelists 1670–1815*; Jane Spencer, 1986, *The Rise of the Woman Novelist: From Aphra Behn to Jane Austen*; Dale Spender, 1986, *Mothers of the Novel: 100 Good Women Writers Before Jane Austen*; and Janet Todd (ed), 1984, *A Dictionary of British and American Women Writers 1660–1800*. For my own part I can state categorically that it was partly because I was tired of the tenets that the novel was invented by men and that the male sex dominated the literary scene in the eighteenth century that I determined on the title and the contents of *Mothers of the Novel: 100 Good Women Writers Before Jane Austen*. But like so many other women I naïvely (and erroneously) believed that all that was necessary to dislodge the male myth was the evidence that women had written, and written well—so well, in fact, that during the eighteenth century there were complaints about men's use of female pseudonyms in the attempt to obtain publication (see Dale Spender, 1986).

But "proof" and persuasion in a patriarchal society are not so simple. I have to keep reminding myself that if it were just a matter of finding and presenting the evidence of injustice and inequality, the struggle between the sexes would have long since been resolved and there would be no need for feminist literary critics. What we must contend with however is the double standard which has built into it the means of discrediting the views and values of women: So whether it be four or forty texts that outline the significant nature and stature of women's contribution to fiction, the entire enterprise can be discounted in a male-favoured society where circular arguments have currency and where women's words can be dismissed on the grounds that they are the words of women.

It is all very well to suggest that men may unconsciously favour their own sex, that they may in all innocence believe men to be better and remain oblivious to the implications of their preferences for women and their contribution (as some apologists are wont to do), but these same men who are supposed to be sincere when they daily discredit women—often in the most derogatory of terms—hold their positions and their prestige and their pay on the presumption that they are reasonable, impartial, and the *best* informed members of the literary community.

Their rhetoric does not match reality. Unlike Virginia Woolf (1929) who was prepared to "excuse" male critics for their unconscious preference for their own perspective, I find it difficult to draw the line between innocence and intention:

> . . . when a woman comes to write a novel, she will find that she is perpetually wishing to alter the established values—to make serious what appears insignificant to a man, and trivial what is to him important. And for that, of course, she will be criticized; for the critic of the opposite sex will be genuinely puzzled and surprised by an attempt to alter the current scale of values, and will see in it not merely a difference of view, but a view that is weak, or trivial, or sentimental because it differs from his own. (Virginia Woolf (1929), 1972: p. 146)

Of course I think this statement of Virginia Woolf's is a superb summation of the operation of the double standard in literature. Where I disagree with her is in her surmise that male critics are *genuinely puzzled* about the different scale of values of women. It's not just that I think the possibilities of sexual difference and the double standard are simple precepts that could be readily understood by literary men if they so wanted, but that some of the attacks on women writers are so excessive—and so "convenient"—that I find it hard to accept that the entire arrangement is the product of naïve unconsciousness.

There are good grounds for my suspicions: More than two decades ago when my own university education in literature began, I accepted the assurances of my male teachers, who led me to believe that there were no great women dramatists, poets, or critics—just a few women novelists who had managed to document the finer detail of the *domestic/relationship* realm. And while I was overjoyed, for example, to discover Aphra Behn—arguably the leading dramatist of the Restoration period, the first novelist, and a powerful poet (see Dale Spender, 1986)—I was also angry: Angry at my tutors for misleading me and angry at myself for not being more cautious, more questioning, more suspicious of the claims made by men about the greater achievements and value of men.

When I found that Aphra Behn was one of the many women dramatists of her own period (Fidelis Morgan, 1981) and one of the very many from that period on, I was even more upset. And when I found that there was an extensive but suppressed tradition of women poets, and an alternative but different tradition of women critics, I was determined to be even more wary in the future. So when I am asked to accept that today's male academics and critics who scorn women's writing are acting innocently or unconsciously and are motivated by sincerity, I have good reason for entertaining my doubts.

My own reading of the present situation is that there are men in the literary establishment who feel threatened, who fear that women's contributions are about to overwhelm them, and who are therefore making a last ditch stand to defend what they hold as their territory. And yes, they can deny the reality and the legitimacy of feminist scholarship and the work of women writers while at the same time they can perceive this "energy" and "enthusiasm" as a challenge to their power. On the one hand they can repudiate the feminist research that has reclaimed hundreds of women writers and that is calling for those writers to be reinstated in the canon and the classroom, but on the other hand they are aware of all this activity on their doorstep, and can be prepared to take desperate measures to discredit—and disperse—the protesters.

Currently a state of crisis prevails. There are women making demands and there are men who are engaged in several forms of resistance which at times can be quite savage. There is a *backlash* and it is possible that things are even worse for women in the literary community now than they were before the concerted calls for change began. So while I would not want to suggest that the women's movement and feminist literary criticism have been an unqualified success, neither do I want to play into patriarchal hands and deny women's achievements of the last twenty years. Certainly with all the women writers reclaimed—and reprinted—there has been a success story but there has also been resistance, a counterattack in the face of the feminist challenge. This is why I agree with Carolyn Heilbrun (1986) when she points out that it is precisely because the literary establishment is frightened by the threat that women's writing represents that there has been an escalation in the intimidatory tactics intended to keep women from trespassing on male territory.

And, according to Carolyn Heilbrun, these fears are not without substance: There *is* evidence that women are claiming—and could be attaining—a greater (though not necessarily an equal) share of the power and influence in the literary establishment.

> Men's fears are palpable. Men have long been members of a profession whose masculinity can, particularly in our American society, be questioned. I suspect that the macho attitudes of most English professors, their notable male bonding, can be directly attributed to the fear of female dominance. Now comes the additional threat of the profession being feminized. More students are women. The pressure for studying women authors and hiring women professors increases. Those in power in Departments still safely male dominated close their ranks. These male fears are profound, and no less so for being largely unconscious. Meanwhile the old familiar habits of male dominance and scorn of female interests in the profession make these attitudes appear natural and right. (Carolyn Heilbrun, 1986: p. 24)

3

Publishing: Damned if You Do, and Damned if You Don't

The premise that a new literary era is about to be ushered in is supported by some of the changes that are taking place *outside* the academic community, as well as those that are occurring within it. For one of the most dramatic developments on the literary landscape over the last decade has been the birth—and the growth—of women's publishing—to the predictable point where there are those who are prepared to declare that the pendulum has now swung the other way and that it is women who are getting more than their share of prominence in the marketplace.

Leaving aside this assertion for a while (because it is dangerous to make assumptions about the relative share accorded to women), what can be claimed with credibility is that there are now specific publishing houses which are controlled/directed by women who have taken as their brief the task of providing outlets for the words of women. And there is considerable evidence that they have been extraordinarily successful in achieving their aims. Not only are there women's presses in many areas—in Australia, Britain, France, Germany, India, Italy, New Zealand, North America, Scandinavia for example—but a whole new industry has developed around them in the form of women's bookshops, women's periodicals, even women's book fairs and festivals, not to mention courses, conferences, schools of criticism, and societies (such as Women in Publishing and Women in Libraries in Britain).

However, while there is cause for celebration, there is also cause for caution: Publishing is such an unresearched and under-professionalised area that there is little reliable data which can serve to clarify some of the claims made in its name. Parallels can be drawn between publishing and the field of language behaviour *before* studies were undertaken on the actual conversation patterns of women and men, so stereotyped prejudices and perceptual fallacies could well abound: Which is why there is a pressing need to do some sifting, to establish a context in which questions about publishing and the relationship between the sexes can be raised.

But before a start can be made on whether women really are in the ascendancy in the world of print, it is necessary to address a few basic questions about publishing and its contemporary significance. Historically, those who have controlled the printed medium have also exercised power—hence the existence of a variety of forms of subversion, of censorship and propaganda. But what has been the pattern of the past is not necessarily that which prevails in the present: clearly, the *information revolution* which is currently in progress could well be challenging much of the received wisdom about the place and power of print—and women's position within it.

The importance of print is not a peripheral issue but a crucial consideration in any contemporary analysis of the role and relationship of literature. Lynne Spender—who has written a book on women's *unpublished* heritage, (*Intruders on the Rights of Men*, 1983), and who is an "expert" on the many means that have been used to discredit women's writing—is of the opinion that with the advent of the technological-information-revolution, print has lost its place as the powerful medium and that this has significant implications for women's publishing. "The printed word is . . . being challenged in its role as primary source and recorder of information and knowledge" (p. 116) she states, so if there are more women in print now—particularly of the protesting feminist type—then we have to entertain the possibility that such a presence is permitted because it doesn't challenge the power of men. It is her contention that

> . . . the feminist movement and its close association with print has been allowed to re-emerge because they do not currently present a threat to male power. If, as present trends indicate, print is being replaced as the primary form of communication, then gatekeeping over print can be relaxed and controls can be moved to protect new areas of power. (Lynne Spender, 1983: p. 115)

While women's studies has generated a huge demand for women's books (a demand that has often been met by "authors" from within women's studies), the success story may not be all that it seems. If such an area is considered inconsequential, then the growth of women's publications—and women's publishing houses—may amount to a hollow victory.

The case is convincing: It is one which draws on insights about sex and status in relation to other media. There is radio, for example, and women's relative success within it—once television made its appearance. That radio is now frequently represented in terms of personnel and programming as "a women's medium" is taken as an indication that men vacated the area to pursue the more prestigious and potent attraction of television.

It is plausible, even probable, that a comparable shift in power is taking place in the world of print and this is therefore the background against which we should be assessing any expansion in women's publishing. As men follow the increasingly influential computer screens, women are left with more space in the less-valued realm of print. This certainly takes the gloss off any claims of women's victory. But such an interpretation is in keeping with conclusions provided by other examples where women have been allowed entry to areas men no longer consider desirable or necessary: So women are the major users of public transport while men take the car, women's access is to the postal system while men transmit their messages via computers and FAX machines.

And these similarities are not the only sources of supporting evidence: Many are the "coincidences" which lend credence to the claim that the printed word no longer has priority.

There is a paper shortage, for example, and one could reasonably expect that this would lead to protests and predictions of chaos and catastrophe. The fact that so little consternation has been expressed could suggest that those who are in power won't find the increasing scarcity of paper an intolerable inconvenience. Perhaps—as Lynne Spender (1983) has intimated—it will be left to women and women's publishers to contend with this difficulty (p. 115).

Then too there is the issue of literacy levels, which are seen to be falling—just at the time that women are gaining influence in print:

> Even as a form of entertainment print does not have the same appeal today that it had in the past. For a large proportion of people, television, radio and film have taken over from print as entertainment and leisure activities and have undermined the value of reading and writing skills. The ability to use print is no longer essential for the maintenance of social and family communication. My own children [adds Lynne Spender] could make long distance phone calls long before they could write or read letters. (Lynne Spender, 1985: p. 116)

Despite all these supportive sources, the issue of whether women have actually moved into an area after the power has gone must remain primarily a philosophical one for there is surprisingly little reliable data available on this aspect of the medium. But clearly, the focus of power has shifted with the information revolution and it could well be that we are witnessing the demise of "the great literature era."

Gone are the days when an understanding of the great books was the pathway to power and influence in the community; gone are the old certainties about the value and worth of literary study, when the measure of a man could be taken by his familiarity with great works. Models of education no longer assume that the secret of life is to be found in the study of Shakespeare, Swift, or Milton; but rather look to DNA, technology, and "user-pays" as solutions. Traditional literary academics and publishers face, "whether they admit it or not, an enormous sense of loss, of lack of clarity in the purposes from which they speak; the old Arnoldian pride in literature has gone, and little has arisen to take its place" (Carolyn Heilbrun 1986, p. 25). And although these changes might not have been well documented, there is no doubt that they have occurred—and that they help to explain some of the attitudes of literary men and some of the developments in publishing.

There is no doubt that print has lost its primary importance, and literature has lost its primary status as the repository of knowledge. As a result the men who have traditionally derived their role and identity from the world of letters, are experiencing a crisis. And if this isn't enough, there's "the woman-question" as well; for it seems that women have taken advantage of this time of turmoil to carve out a space for themselves, to establish women's studies courses and women's presses which give even greater prominence to women's writing.

Not surprisingly these two issues can become conflated: That the presence of women in the literary enterprise is perceived to be on the increase at the precise time that the entire literary enterprise is losing its influence can—in the minds of many—become an issue of cause and effect. When it comes to the current decline in literary purpose and prestige, there are those who are prepared to argue that it's women who are at fault, that it's women who have "lowered the standards." With all this interest in the study of women's writing and with all these women's publishing houses there are now too many women in print. Such sentiments are being expressed across a variety of literary/publishing contexts and help to "explain" some of the sensational attacks on women's books.

In the attempt to untangle the prejudices and the perceptions, let us first deal with the basic premise that women now are getting more than their fair share of publishing opportunities. The question is—whether a *fair* share is an *equal* share, or whether it is the share that men think is fair to women in a male-dominated society.

While there are little reliable data that can be drawn upon in this area, there is some evidence which suggests that even though there may have been an increase in the number of women's books published during the last decade, it does not approach the number published by men. Women may be enjoying greater access to print but given their starting point this is not necessarily an impressive achievement: Anyone who suggests that women now have gone too far in the publishing industry provides a dramatic illustration of just how contained they think women should be.

Richard Altick (1962) calculated that between 1800–1935, the number of books authored by women hovered consistently around 20%. Tillie Olsen (1980) helped to add weight to these findings from her own survey which suggested that four to five books are published by men to every one published by a woman (see "One Out of Twelve: Writers Who are Women in

Our Century'' pp. 22–46). Joanna Russ (1954), Elaine Showalter (1978), and Lynne Spender (1983), all of whom have tried to provide reliable estimates of the publication ratio of men to women, have all been prepared to accept Richard Altick's data, and have been satisfied with the conservative figures that it is one woman to every four men.

However, there has been a more recent, detailed (but limited) study conducted by the British Women in Publishing association for their own book, *Reviewing the Reviews: A Woman's Place on the Book Page* (1987). In order to establish whether fewer women were being reviewed, they had to first establish women's publication rate, which was not a simple matter:

> In 1985, 52,994 books were published in Great Britain, but there are no statistics available on how many of those were by men and women. While the general statistic given for the average percentage of women-authored books is 20%, we wanted to try and check that for the year 1985.
>
> To do this a representative sampling was done of the *British National Bibliography*, a comprehensive listing of published books for 1985. This survey showed that about 18% of the books were written by women and 51% by men. (The remainder were unknown, mixed or group authors.) This average was further broken down into two categories—general books that you would expect to find in a reasonably stocked bookshop and specialist books that were academic. In this breakdown, women wrote 25% of general books and 5% of specialist books.[1] (Women in Publishing, 1987: p. 12)

According to this most recent survey, it looks as though women can still be classified as the authors of approximately 20% of the published books.

There does seem to be something of a contradiction here: Women writers are "swamping" men—yet women comprise only one fifth of the published authors. (The mind boggles at a half-share: How many more books would women have to produce and how many more complaints would be registered if women were to achieve such a publication rate?)

But this apparent contradiction in relation to women and the written word can be resolved in much the same way as the apparent contradiction in relation to women and the spoken word. If men are assumed to be the authors then the existence of even *one* woman writer can be problematic: Her presence can be noted and objections about women entering the area (and disturbing "the world order") can be lodged readily. In such a frame of reference it may take only four woman writers—Jane Austen, Charlotte Brontë, George Eliot, and Virginia Woolf for example—to lead to allegations that women are dominating the novel, even though there may be more than one hundred famous male novelists being promoted in the literary community.

Just as the woman who talks for more than 30% of the time can be seen to be talking too much (and to be lowering the conversation standards with her

---

[1]Further breakdowns and discussion are contained in Chapter Four on reviews.

"prattle") so can the women who gain a 30% (or even a 20%) publication rate be regarded as publishing too much—and lowering the literary standards in the process. Which is why it is possible for women to remain well below the level of one third of the published authors and yet to still be castigated for excessive publication rates.

Those of us who think that as slightly more than half the population, women are entitled to a *half* share in publications may well find current arrangements irrational and unfair. But those who believe that women do not count as much as men will find nothing inconsistent in the argument that women should stay in their allocated place and should be berated for going too far if they have the temerity to trespass on the territory of men.

For my own part I must admit that I still have my suspicions about the figure of 20% for women's publications, if only because I have been privy to some of the inner workings of the publishing industry[2] and have first-hand experience of the ways in which women's existence as readers and writers can be denied.[3] I never cease to be astonished at the number of times and the number of means that can be used to discount women's contributions, even when evidence to the contrary is overwhelming. So one look at the list of women, titles, and sales of fiction in the nineteenth—as well as the eighteenth—century is enough to arouse my suspicions about the 20% ceiling on women's publication rate. But then, of course, this is in the realm of fiction: Non-fiction provides a totally different picture with men dominating—almost to the complete exclusion of women—such categories as biography, economics, history, lexicography, literary criticism, politics, sermons, scientific and technical works, and travel. Men even appear to have the edge in gardening and cooking publications. What I don't know (and it doesn't seem that a lot of other people know either) is the ratio of published fiction to non-fiction. In the absence of such information I too have to be satisfied with the working figures of one woman to every four men in print.

On this basis it is not hard to accept that there has been a noticeable increase in the rate of women's publishing over the last decade; nor is it difficult to accept that one of the reactions to this discernibly higher profile for women writers should be backlash. (Backlash has sometimes been defined as a *response* to the erosion of power, but I suspect it can also be an intimidatory tactic employed *before* power has been taken and is meant to discourage aspirants from even trying, rather than a counter-measure resorted to after power has been seized.)

That there has been a negative response among some men to the pub-

[2]Founding editor of *Women's Studies International Forum* (initially *Women's Studies International Quarterly*), and the *Athene Series* for Pergamon Press; a founding editor of *Pandora Press* and of Penguin *Australian Women's Library*, as well as consultant for a range of publishers.
[3]This is not the case of course with women's publishers.

lishing success of women can be readily documented. One Australian male, however, would probably get the award for the expression of the greatest grievance: Confronted with the popularity of contemporary Australian women writers (and their visibility in *women's* courses), he complained publicly at a writers' conference that there was a conspiracy being orchestrated among women to buy women's books and that this was grossly unfair. He insisted that women were receiving advantageous treatment in publishing and reviewing (more on this in the next chapter) and that this was causing problems for men. But as Bronwen Levy (1987/8) has pointed out, apart from the fact that the protests of one man have made the headlines while those of countless women over the centuries have not even enjoyed a hearing, the empirical reality is, of course, that Australian men still get a great deal more space (and not just in publishing!) than Australian women. What this great and aggrieved writer was really objecting to was the threat that women's efforts represent, the challenge they constitute to the deeply entrenched—but unsupported—belief, that men are the genuine writers, readers, and subjects for study and that any legitimacy given to women is an alteration, an aberration, in the proper scale of values.

That for centuries the male-dominated publishing industry has conducted its business on the basis that its audience was men, is a practice which stands exposed by the very existence—and success—of some of the women's presses. Take Virago, for example, the first (and some would say the foremost) women's publisher in Britain: Its list began with reprints, with the republication of women's writing which had been rejected by the male-controlled mainstream. Presented with proposals for putting back into print some of the women who, in the past, had been on their own lists (and for whom they sometimes held the rights) many mainstream publishers had declined to reissue or reprint, on the grounds that there was no market for such material. It must be stated, therefore, that out of this *non*-market, Virago has managed to create a highly successful publishing business and has delivered a serious challenge to the entire literary/publishing edifice.

But both before and after the Virago revolution there were mind-set-male publishers who continued to behave as if books were meant for members of their own sex. No mainstream publishing houses that I know of have been seriously involved in research to establish which sex buys/reads books: However some of the bookselling agencies and some of the women's presses, periodical publishers, and bookshop proprietors have undertaken investigations to determine the nature of today's reading public (see Women in Publishing 1987, for further discussion). Not surprisingly the answer is that the market is mainly female.

Women buy more books than men, they even buy books for other people, a practice not common among men (see Dale Spender, unpublished). And women read more books than men (see Women in Publishing, 1987). Indeed, there is much evidence that suggests reading (and writing) are at the core of women's culture (in much the same way that football can be said to be at the core of men's culture), but because so much of women's experience has been "invisiblised" this aspect of women's existence attracts little research attention or social validation. So central, however, is reading to feminist reality that it is not unusual to find women acknowledging that a particular book "changed my life"; and so central is writing to feminist experience that it is not unusual to find a feminist defined as "a woman who writes" (this was one version that was put forward at the Women in Publishing Conference, London, November 1985).

This of course helps to explain some of the successes of the women's publishing industry. Once women became "organised" in their reading/writing and educational demands—as they did in women's studies courses—they supplied not only many of the authors, but an extensive and expanding audience, and a stimulus for even more books.

That women now may be the major part of the reading public in numerous areas might not be a new development however. It is possible that this was always the case, but that this aspect of women's behaviour has gone undocumented and undetected. Women today might buy more books in comparison with women of the past—because they have more money, because there are more books available, and because they have more opportunities for purchasing books than did their foremothers; but it could still be that, *vis à vis* men, women now and women in the past have bought more books and read more books, so that the premise that men were the proper audience was derived *not* from an accurate representation of their bookish habits, but from beliefs about the importance of their sex.

For all this evidence about the existence of the woman reader (evidence provided by women's successful publishing ventures as well as surveys) has done little to dislodge the premise in the mind of many a contemporary publishing man that males are the genuine writers and readers. Another case where women do not count, where the reality is not allowed to interfere with the patriarchal presumption or prejudice, where it is not the writing, the reading, or the buying, but the sex which determines the assessment.

In the publishing business, as in the colleges and universities, women's success story is inextricably linked with a pattern of male resistance and the present atmosphere contains many elements of tension. This is partly because this is one—if not the only—area where women have been able to set up an *alternative*, autonomous, and viable industry, and this has numerous implications for publishing, and for the power configurations of the sexes.

As Virginia Woolf has observed, because women are poor and lack capital (see *A Room of One's Own*, 1929) there are few women's publishing businesses that are financed solely by women; but this factor does not seem to have caused undue interference in the control women have exercised over their product. And no doubt this arrangement will persist while ever women's books make a profit. (Many are the satisfying stories that circulate within the women's publishing community in relation to mainstream publishers who some years ago were persuaded to finance a subsidiary women's press division and who now find that the "subsidiary" has the greater turnover—which raises crucial questions about which is the mainstream, and which the ghetto?).

The reasons behind women's establishment of an *alternative* book industry (as distinct from an extension of influence within an industry) are not hard to find. While men insisted that there was no market for women's books (which in good circular fashion was why there were so few in print!) there was no point in trying to convince them that reprinting "lost" women would be a good publishing move, so women faced the fact that if they wanted women in print—in appreciable numbers—they would have to do the printing themselves. But having elected to publish books for which men declared there was no demand, women publishers soon realised that if they couldn't get their books out to their women readers, men's predictions about poor sales could quickly prove to be true.

Some of the women who founded women's presses, particularly in Britain, realised that this was only the first stage in the process of getting women into print (see Women in Publishing Newsletter—*Wiplash*—for a fascinating record of the development of the women's book industry). It was pointless publishing women's books if they simply stayed in the warehouse: An extensive distribution system—controlled by women's publishers—was needed if the books were to get to the buyers and readers. Sales representatives, booksellers, reviewers and review space, promotion events—all were necessary if women's books were to reach their desired destination.

In Britain, for example, Virago led the way and confounded the critics by creating a popular (and profitable) autonomous business: On the basis of such success the industry expanded and The Women's Press, Sheba, Pandora, Battle Axe Books, and more came into existence along with professional associations (Women in Publishing, Women in Libraries, Women in Heritage and Museums (WHAM), etc.), a chain of women's bookshops, and a series of women's publications which gave review coverage to women's books; in 1984 came the culmination in the form of the First International Feminist Book Fair in London. It was extremely popular—its success outstripping even the most positive predictions of the organisers (of whom I was one). The inauguration of what has become an annual (national) and a bi-annual (international) event marked the maturity of the women's book industry: One of the slogans used at the Fair was *Women's Books Are Here to Stay!*

The value of this viable and vital woman-controlled enterprise should not be underestimated. To put it bluntly publishing is (still) a markedly influential medium and it is one where it is possible for women to go to women: While the process and the products may not always please everyone, at least this arrangement affords a better chance for women to get a fairer hearing—as women.

This achievement of women in publishing is not matched in any other medium. While there may be the occasional newspaper, radio station/television programme managed by women, there is no *industry* in which women are setting their own standards and determining their own terms—and this publishing venture must stand as a spectacular success in a male-dominated society! It sometimes seems to me that what women need in the other media (and in other institutions) is much the same *revolution* that has occurred with women's books: It may be a revolution which has too often been overlooked, one which has not even been fully acclaimed or analysed within feminism, but it has been a revolution, none the less.

This was brought home to me by an incident at the First Feminist International Bookfair. At a well attended seminar on male-bias in reviews (a sore point then and still, see next chapter) three men who had some form of responsibility in this area protested at the prejudices and the presentations of some of the women. And when these three influential men were asked how they would feel about submitting their work to a woman's press or a feminist literary journal they were exceedingly scornful and actually declared that it was obvious that as they were men, their work would never be published because the women would not give them a fair hearing.

When—after the guffaws and groans that the men were at a loss to understand—the chairperson Alison Hennegan attempted to explain that this was precisely how women felt about submitting *their* work to *men's* presses and *male* literary editors, the men could not be convinced of the validity of such a stance. They continued to insist that it was different; that *men* in reputable publishing houses and on respectable journals would act objectively and fairly, while women in (disreputable?) publishing houses and on feminist journals would act subjectively, would clearly be biased, and this was unfair.

This is "the writing or the sex" argument in a nutshell. It shows the positive value that men accord to men and the negative value they accord to women, regardless of the circumstances. And it also suggests the power that women have to subvert this system.

While there may be debates about how many women are now in print, how this compares with past patterns, and how important any gains might be in a declining medium, no one could seriously dispute the extraordinary success that the women's book industry currently enjoys. So impressive has its record been that one of the contemporary concerns (among women) can be that male publishers are now trying to muscle-in, so care must be taken to guard against takeovers and misleading competition: Almost all the major publishing houses have now jumped on the bandwagon and started women's lists which in many instances amount to but another version of male control of women's writing—in a way that few women have ever had control over men's.

Women in publishing are aware that the new power base cannot be taken for granted, that the very success of their venture has set them up as a "target" which can attract fire—and not just from male publishers who may feel that their own influence is being eroded. Because women's publishing has been able to overcome some of the distribution difficulties and to get its books to readers, a new generation of women has emerged, one which is familiar with a wide range of women's printed words and which has made good use of them. These women, reared on women's print, are creating all manner of difficulties throughout the literary establishment, and it is no wonder that academics and publishers who wish to preserve male preeminence should be disposed to be negative towards the writing of women and to the women's presses which are producing it.

One factor which has not received the attention it deserves is that there are now tens of thousands of women who have had access to a common female educational experience—who have read *Virago* classics, the *Women's Press* debates, the *Pandora* series reprints, the *Kitchen Table* criticisms, the *Sisters* analyses, the *Athene* Monographs, the *Feminist Press* resource materials; thousands of women who have shared a *common curriculum* of periodicals in which these books have been assessed, and shifts in emphasis outlined and explained. All these women have had access to a form of education championed by Virginia Woolf in *Three Guineas* (1938): It is the education provided *outside* the institutions which have been set up by men with the purpose of producing the best men.

There are many similarities between the women of the eighteenth and nineteenth century who were not allowed access to men's education, and who through the novel developed an educational medium of their own; and the women of the 1970s and 1980s who have had access *only* to men's education and who have developed an extracurricular medium of their own, which resonates the experience of women in a male-dominated society.

There is now a vast number of women on a variety of continents who have for years been regular readers of these books; and the failure of mainstream publishers, of the humanities and social sciences (particularly the discipline of education) to produce studies which chart the creation, characteristics, and current concerns of this group and the changes it has wrought, is yet another indication of the extent to which the mind-set of the male as *the* writer, reader, and student prevails.

Carmen Callil (one of the founders of Virago Press) in many talks and discussions has referred to Virago readers as "The Club"[4]: She knows that the women who read Virago books, who "demand" the thought-provoking fiction and non-fiction of women writers past and present, now share a certain frame of reference—though whether this is why they are attracted to the books in the first place or the result of their reading (or both) is a matter for conjecture. But it is likely that her terminology and her testimony would be incomprehensible to some men in the literary industry, many of whom are still perplexed as to why it is that women's books do sell and who haven't got the faintest idea who buys them!

However, throughout this "body of knowledge," which is published primarily by the women's presses, there are of course references to this new reading public and assumptions about its nature and its interests. Women writers are often acutely conscious that they are talking to other women, that they are providing resources for sustenance and survival in a patriarchal world. And the members of "the Club" show every sign of learning the lessons that so many women's books have to teach them. Whether or not they are aware of it, women publishers have produced a new breed of well-informed women who are causing a lot of trouble for some men: One major area of confrontation is the exclusion of women's books from the academic curriculum.

At the risk of going over old ground I think I must reiterate that more than two decades ago when I was "subjected" to a university literary education, I was readily led to believe the explanation offered for the absence of women writers on the course: Women were less than 2% of the authors studied because—generally speaking—women had not written, or what they had written was not very good.[5] And not only did I have then no reason to doubt the *authority* of my masters, I had no contradictory evidence that might have prompted me to think I was being misled. I didn't find rows of women's books in bookshops—books that made it abundantly clear women had indeed written and I had only to read their work to satisfy my curiosity as to whether they were any good. On the contrary, when at the age of seventeen I experienced an identity crisis and specifically went in search of "women in literature," I could find nothing that helped me to clarify my own position: Having decided that the fates of Anna Karenina and Madame Bovary were not for me, I also stopped short of accepting the destinies of Emma, Jane Eyre and Maggie Tulliver and Dorothea. It was because I didn't know any better that I accepted unquestioningly the judgements of literary men.

---

[4]This was one of the themes of her address to the annual conference of *Women in Publishing*, London, November, 1985.

[5]Susan Koppelman (1988) has labelled this widespread phenomenon as *epistemological solipsism*: "I have never encountered these good women writers, therefore they do not exist."

Like Erica Jong I believed that literature was the province of men: I too had to wait until the women's movement to know any better:

> . . . Poetry meant Yeats, Lowell, James Dickey. Without even realising it I assumed that the voice of the poet had to be male. Not that I didn't get a good literary education. I did. Barnard was a miraculous place where they actually gave you a degree for losing yourself in a library with volumes of Byron and Keats, Shakespeare and Chaucer, but the whole female side of the literary heritage was something I would have to discover for myself years later, propelled by the steam generated by the Women's Movement. (Erica Jong, 1980: p. 171)

For those of us whose education predates the rise of the contemporary women's presses[6] the discovery that there was a lost tradition of women writers was momentous—and invigorating. But it also helped to fuel our anger against the collaboration of the academic and publishing institutions that had misled us. As Louise Bernikow (1980) pointed out, when women writers were lost, *someone lost them*, and scores of women were determined to find out who had been responsible and to demand an explanation for their exclusion.

This is how women's presses contributed to the growth and development of a formidable pressure group: When they found and reprinted so many various women from the past, the presses produced the ammunition which could challenge the defences of literary men. The contribution of the women's presses created the awareness that women were the inheritors of a rich but buried legacy, and armed with their new understandings women not only challenged the old practices and prejudices, they experienced a new confidence and enthusiasm as the value and validity of women's literature was affirmed. Again Erica Jong comments on this reaction:

> . . . One of the most positive by . . . products of the so called second wave of the feminist movement was its discovery of a new audience of readers—readers both female and male—who came to realize that literary history as we previously knew it was the history of the literature of the white, the affluent, the male, and that the female side of experience had been almost completely omitted (except as seen through the eyes of the traditional victors in the war between the sexes—men). And this audience was suddenly passionately interested in dispatches from the center of the female heart which represented a sort of dark continent, a *terra incognito*, the exploration of which was necessary to a full understanding of human consciousness in all its permutations. (Erica Jong, 1980: pp. 177–178).

Once women were made aware of the existence of good women writers, they wanted more. They also began to ask awkward questions and wanted to

---

[6]In 1911, in London there was a Women's Press at Clement's Inn, and a Feminist Bookshop— and of course more than twenty regular periodicals of women: there were many comparable achievements too in other countries.

know why all these good women were kept out of institutions dominated by men. And the more women's books, past and present, which have found their way into print, the more pressure has been applied to literary men to the point where they should be shamefully embarrassed to offer the age-old pretext that women have not written—or that they have written nothing worthy of attention. Unfortunately, however, the self-serving and transparent nature of their case has not prevented some men from insisting (with ever-increasing intensity) that if standards are to be preserved, if established values are to be retained and respected, then a stop must be put to this infernal women's publishing business.

Some such calls for a return to the glorious days of "decent literature"—to the literature of the white, the affluent, the male, as Erica Jong so aptly phrased it—have come from academics who are on the receiving end of the demand to include in their courses a representative number of women writers who are *available*. But similar calls have come from some mainstream publishers too, who are emotionally and materially threatened by the growth of the women's book industry.

Clearly there are close connections between publishers and academics: There would be no literary academics without publishers and conversely, numerous publications would not exist without the services of academics as consultants, editors, even authors. Given these interconnections and overlaps it could seem surprising that so little research has been undertaken on the place of publishing in society (outside some women's studies courses)—if one were not a feminist with an appropriate explanation of course.

Such research could help reveal, for example, the way in which print legitimates knowledge, the means by which some knowledge is legitimated and some not,[7] as well as the significance of the printed medium in a computer-based society—and the strategies used by some members of the publishing community to resist change. What could then be documented in more systematic style is the state of flux within the publishing arena—and the lengths to which some men will go to maintain their influence.

For within publishing, the practice of using one rule for women and another for men is just as prevalent as within the academic community. And despite the profits that women's books may generate, there has been extensive and often bitter resistance to the publication of women's books. The basis for this antagonism is invariably associated with the sex, rather than the writing.

No better example of the double standard could be provided than the "no-win" situation that confronts women in relation to sales. Whereas publishers could once justify their refusal to print women on the grounds that they

---

[7]For further discussion see Dale Spender, 1981 "The Gatekeepers: A feminist critique of academic publishing."

would *not* sell, there are now publishers who are equally adamant that it is poor business practice to publish women—on the grounds that they have sold too well!

At various times I have been obliged to listen (and to keep my cool) when men have informed me that in the present circumstances it would be an unwise move to publish *more* women: So many women are now in print that the market has reached saturation point—and "the bubble is about to burst." And all this information given under the guise of well-researched and reliable data, the presumably professional expertise of knowledgeable men in the publishing world.

Presented with the sales figures which forced him to face the fact that it was women's books which kept his company afloat, one publisher was prepared to argue that this was precisely the reason no more women's manuscripts should be commissioned. *He* knew that the bottom was about to fall out of the market, that the boom was coming to an end, and *he* wasn't going to be caught with a warehouse full of books when the current fad for them had passed.

When men behave emotionally, irrationally, or even absurdly it is called something different: In this case, managerial responsibility.

It could be that some men are sincerely puzzled about the whys and wherefores of women's books. Because women's experience—and women's writing—are outside the male frame of reference, men may be at a genuine loss to explain the attractions (and the sales) of women's literature. Locked into the premise that men are the proper writers and readers, men may be confused by any information that doesn't fit into this framework—so that they find the success of women's books something of a mystery.

There are countless examples of the mistakes made by male publishers who have tried to apply to the literature of women some of the rules they have gleaned from dealing with the literature of men: For here, as in other areas, there is convincing evidence that the sexes have "a difference of view." But from questions about the marketplace to issues of literary value, male publishers have attempted to impose their standards on women's work—only to make some of the most asinine *faux pas* imaginable.

There is not enough space here for me to quote the long list of incidents of this nature that I have personally experienced, but there is one particular example which I cannot omit and which I think epitomises the attitude in question. Working as a consultant for a major publisher I had proposed the introduction of a women's series, and market research was duly undertaken by the company to test the "demand." But when the findings were presented I was astonished (and somewhat perturbed) to read that the researchers had concluded that there was no market at all for such material. My first response was to check my own sources of information and it was only after I had confirmed that there was a considerable need expressed for the proposed series that I began to query the credibility of the market research itself.

Then it dawned on me. I telephoned the individuals concerned and asked *who* had they polled in their study. The answer? Men, of course! Exclusively. 100%. Their standard, representative sample consisted of one hundred and eighty men on three continents: these men had been asked whether they needed, wanted, or would use or recommend the series of women's books. And the market research people had been satisfied with the totally negative reaction. I congratulated them on their perspicacity and their ingenuity in amassing objective statistical data that proved that women's books would never sell. But I fear they found even my sarcasm inexplicable.

If there is genuine perplexity about the popularity of women's books, there are also preconceptions about the nature of women and their writing, which help to perpetuate discriminatory practices. At the core of some of the attitudes to women's literature is the basic belief that women's books are a risky business. Because women writers, readers, and purchasers do not behave in the same way as men they are invariably perceived as unpredictable. And when publishers cannot confidently predict profits and sales, when in fact they have no way of knowing whether the product is valuable and no way of deciding for whom it is intended, it is not surprising that they should be hesitant: But while "when in doubt, don't publish" may be a good maxim for mainstream publishers, it does not bode well for women.

And, of course, it must be noted—yet again—that there are numerous publishers who share the premise that you don't have to read women's books to know they're no good, who don't even have to go to the trouble of analysing markets or manuscripts to know that dealing with women's books is quite a risk. In contrast to some of their colleagues in the academic community (who want to convey the impression that their dismissal of women's books is a result of an assessment of the text) there are publishers who are prepared to acknowledge (or proudly boast) that it isn't necessary to actually read the work of women to determine whether there is a demand for it. The sign of a good publisher is often that he has "flair,"[8] the professional expertise that instinctively allows him to know what the market requires, and it is quite remarkable just how many of these good publishers know that it doesn't require any more contributions from women.

The fact that this particular "prejudice" produced the proverbial "gap in the market," which the women's presses were then able to "fill" with such extraordinary success, has not been sufficient to cause some publishers to change their minds and to look for more than a gut reaction as a basis for

---

[8]See Lynne Spender, 1983: pp. 29 and 34 for further discussion of "flair" as a qualification for publishers.

market and manuscript analysis. So willfully "blind" have some publishers been that there are times when I believe that there are those among them who would continue to insist that the only real writers are men and that the primary audience is male—and that there was therefore no demand for women's books—even when 90% of presses, publications, and profits were the province of females.

Were women's books to be evaluated according to a single, rather than a double, publishing standard, the inherent absurdity of many existing practices would soon be made clear. For example, while it may be the received wisdom in mainstream publishing circles that women's books are a risky business, who ever heard the members of the circle suggest that there may be a ceiling on men's books, precisely because they are men? Who ever heard or read the argument that so many men have been published over the centuries that the market has now reached saturation point, that the interest in men's books has peaked and that this passing phase is coming to an end?

When men's books are judged by the same standards as those that have been applied to women, it is blatantly obvious that the critical issue is not about the writing, about the market, or about publication: It is about sex. Whether or not men's books sell is not the question: The premise is that they *should* and they are therefore seen as the desirable product and treated accordingly. And by the same token, whether or not women's books actually sell is not significant. The premise is that they *should not* so they are consistently treated as "risky business" with all manner of rationalisations required to maintain this reality. So deeply entrenched is this mind-set that it's the books of *men* which are "the real thing," that where women's books enjoy spectacular success, such an achievement may not begin to dent the belief in male supremacy; rather such a surprising success can be taken as a sign of the further unpredictability of women (who are not supposed to sell) and used to caution any publisher who may be contemplating the rash action of putting women into print.

Given the belief that women's books are a risky business it's not difficult to see why women should have enjoyed an average only 20% of the published authorship rate over the years. In the absence of women's presses, the path to publication was controlled by men, and they were not required to read the work of women before making their decisions about the number of women's books it seemed appropriate to print. If they talked only to men (and since the introduction of the printing press this appears to have been the predominant practice) then an allocation of 20% of the space to women, in their own terms could have been generous, an indication that they were not discriminatory but, on the contrary, gave (risky) women the benefit of the doubt.

But perhaps the women's presses of the past decade are changing this pattern. It may be that women writers are not just more visible—or even that there are more women writers of the past who have currently been reprinted:

It could be that women now are really writing and publishing more *vis à vis* men, than in any previous period. That women are now writing more fiction than men has been well established by the research of Women in Publishing: 58% of the fiction published in Britain in 1985 was by women (1987). But does this figure represent an increase?

There was a time when I might have been convinced that 58% constituted a breakthrough for women, but that was before I undertook my own research on eighteenth and nineteenth century women writers. Clearly in the eighteenth century women wrote more fiction than men (see Dale Spender *Mothers of the Novel: 100 Good Women Writers Before Jane Austen*, 1986): I am convinced that in the nineteenth century women wrote more fiction than men (see Dale Spender *Novel Knowledge: A Guide to the Woman's Novel of the Nineteenth Century*, forthcoming). So many "lost" women writers have been reclaimed and the statistics of the past are being so persistently challenged—and revised—that one wonders whether 58% of fiction constitutes any improvement at all. But if the actual ratios on the publications of the sexes are difficult to gather and interpret, this is not the case when it comes to commenting on the importance of contemporary women's presses, and the volume of women's writing. With women's success, it is the *myth* of male supremacy that's under attack, regardless of whether men are writing more than they did before. Numbers are only part of the game in determining the authority of women and men writers—which is probably just as well given that women comprise only 25% of the general writers, and 5% of specialist writers (see Women in Publishing, 1987: p. 12). Women's presses, women's books, women writers, women's courses, and women's bookshops[9] are now challenging men's right to be the primary writers in much the same way as men's right to be the primary speakers has been called into question. The size and the status of the male contribution has come under scrutiny and new issues are emerging—including those of perception.

That there are some men who *think* that there are more women in print—and that they enjoy more than their share of sales—is not difficult to establish. Witness the Australian male who accused women of a conspiracy to buy the books of their own sex; and while his sentiments may have been explicit they are by no means unusual. And that men have little evidence for the claim other than their own apprehension about the visibility of women is all too readily demonstrable.

Were it legally possible I would print here some of the many rejection letters that I have been able to collect (my own, and others) to show the extent to which some publishers in all seriousness have dismissed women's books on the grounds that as a category they do—or do not—sell. The incon-

---

[9]See Jane Cholmeley, "Silver Moon: Setting Up a Feminist Business in a Capitalist World" Unpublished M.A. Thesis, 1985. *University of Canterbury*, Kent.

sistencies are astonishing, often hilarious, but they are also convincing evidence that women authors are being rejected not as writers, but as women. Unfortunately, however, the sad fact is that those letters cannot be published without permission. And no permissions have been forthcoming from requests to print.

But this does not prevent me from paraphrasing "illuminating" contributions to the literature of women's rejection. While a modified version might not have the same authority as the original it can still serve to inform—and to illustrate—the means which have been used to keep women out of print.

The following is a typical example. In this instance I was again working as a consultant for a mainstream publisher; again I had done my homework and had recommended a series of reprints in an area where *not one* novel of a woman had been reissued. And again the publisher—who had absolutely no familiarity with the field and had not read a single work under discussion—decided to reject the list on the grounds that women had sold too well!

> I think the proposed series is too thinly spread. Clearly there is a lot of material there that could be published but the fact that it is there does not mean that it will sell. My own feeling is that the boom period has passed for this sort of women's publishing and all the women I have spoken to tell me that these days they don't buy everything that's printed but are much more discriminatory and go looking for quality not quantity. And if this is true in Australia it will be even more true in other countries. It seems to me that there is a real danger that we could overpublish in the area and that it's vital that we ensure that we only publish the writing of women that is really good—and not just what exists. (Letter from a Publisher paraphrased, October 16, 1986)

This man did not have to read one book to know that these women writers were no good ("too thinly spread"); he didn't have to do any market research to know that the boom had finished, and he didn't have to use any logic to warn against the dangers of over publication before even one book was reprinted. And it isn't just that he slates the achievements of women writers: He also insults the intelligence of women readers. As if women have ever been such foolish buyers as to be concerned with quantity rather than quality, purchasing their books by the mile!

But although this typical publisher's analysis of the marketplace may be riddled with inconsistencies and irrationalities, it must be emphasised that such standard judgements can pass as the objective, authoritative, and accurate expertise of the publishing fraternity. And because it is extraordinarily difficult to dislodge the mind-set that gives rise to such perceptions, the partiality of some publishers for the literary offerings of men is likely to persist.

The belief that women should not write has often been transformed into the conviction that women could not write—and there has been no need to read the writing of women to reach this conclusion. And much the same pattern of behaviour has applied in relation to women's books. The belief that women's books should not sell became the received wisdom that women's books do not sell—and it isn't necessary to consult the sales figures to obtain this information. And when women are considered to be inferior writers and their books are believed to be a risky business and to do badly—and all this without reference to the books or the sales—it is clear that the judgements are based on the sex and not the books.

Given the way women writers are dismissed before they even begin, it is not surprising that so many of them would want to deny the disqualification of their sex. Though whether this will be achieved by denying that they are women is quite another matter as Elaine Showalter has pointed out (Elaine Showalter "Women Who Write are Women", 1984). Women who want to get rid of the belief that women writers are deficient might be better advised to challenge those who are doing the disqualifying, rather than to insist that they are not women, but human.

But if women have been grossly disadvantaged by the discriminatory practices of the publishing community, the scenario is not entirely bleak. I suspect that it was partly because the obstacles to women's full participation and a fair hearing within the industry were so great that women elected to establish an alternative women-controlled business.

I suspect too that it is partly because publishing as a whole is under threat—that it is in a state of semi-chaos as a result of corporate takeovers (see Jonathan Raban, 1988) as well as its displacement as a medium—that women publishers have been able to make a niche for themselves, to provide such an independent (and subversive) service for women and to enjoy such spectacular success. The least surprising factor in this whole equation should be the non-substantiated accusations of conspiracy, foul play—and overpublication from those whose traditional power and influence is at risk.

4

Reviewing: The Little Women
Are Entitled To

The same old complaint that women writers are getting more than their fair share of space also surfaces in relation to reviews. Unlike some mixed-sex conversation, however, this is an area where women actually do report discrimination and where they are aware of a double standard in operation (see particularly Margaret Atwood, 1985). Despite the insistence of so many literary editors that all is fair and above board—and even favours the female author—women writers themselves have been prepared to assert that on the literary pages women are definitely not getting a fair deal. And because reviews have been accorded such an important place in the book industry, women have been prepared to back up their claims of "unfair reception." The result is that a number of studies on the nature of reviews and the treatment of the sexes have been undertaken by women over the last few years. These projects range from major research efforts (such as that of Women in Publishing in Britain—see their book *Reviewing the Reviews: A Woman's Place on the Book Page*, 1987) to market research surveys (such as that undertaken by the University of Queensland Press): from classroom projects (see Margaret Atwood, 1985) to writer-response reports and analyses, (see Marilyn French, 1984/85 unpublished) and the records of individual writers on their own reviews (see Andrea Dworkin, 1987; Zoe Fairbairns, 1987; Jill Tweedie, 1986a).

All of these studies reveal such a wealth of fascinating data and such scope for analysis and debate about literary forms and values, about the media and society, that one of the questions which (once again) arises, is why this crucial component of the world of letters does *not* receive systematic study (and surveillance) in literary departments. For not only does the area warrant interest in its own right—as well as for its contribution to the literary enterprise—but book reviews themselves throw up some of the most central and stimulating issues about the significance of sexism, and the maintenance of male authority in the literature of western society.

Given the interest among women in women's writing and its reception (see Bronwen Levy, 1985 and Joanna Russ, 1984, for example), there is no doubt that there would be considerable demand for courses which address some of the issues raised in this chapter. No doubt either that there would be ample scope for associated research projects along the lines of those currently being conducted outside the academy. (That no such "body of knowledge" ordinarily exists within the mainstream serves as yet another example of the way men's priorities are pursued within the institutions that they control, while women must invariably work outside them if they wish to explore a female oriented agenda.)

My own interest in reviews has been—of course—to some extent, self interest. Like most writers it seems, I have been on the receiving end of reviews which I have considered "fabrications" but against which I have had no form of redress. Not surprisingly, such blatantly false reviews motivated me to look more closely at the process of reviewing and particularly at the concept of accountability as it applied to reviewers. But when in 1982–3, in Britain, I embarked upon a six-month project (with Mandy Spry) to gather data on reviews of women, it was as part of my overall study on the silencing of women and not out of any sense of personal grievance. (I have pursued this cathartic exercise in other places, see Dale Spender and Lynne Spender, 1984).

For six months Mandy Spry and I were engaged in the intellectually demanding task of collecting "hard data" as we measured the column inches of review space allocated to women and men in a number of publications which professed a "general" readership: We sampled some of the quality national papers (*The Guardian, The Telegraph, The Times, The Sunday Times,* and *The Observer*) along with specifically literary publications (*Books and Bookmen, The Literary Review, The Times Literary Supplement*). The results of this survey were actually known to me[1] when in 1984, as part of the preliminaries for the panel discussion on reviews of women's books at the First International Feminist Book Fair, the opinions of literary editors of a range of publications were canvassed by telephone.

Six men and three women were contacted: They were responsible for the allocation of review space and the choice of reviewers and their responses revealed that all of the men and two of the women were under the impression that women's writing was very well represented on their pages. So confident were the editors that women received a fair share of the space, that six voluntarily stated that if indeed there had been prejudice against women in

---

[1]Details of this study were presented at a paper delivered at St. John's College, Cambridge, April 26, 1984 entitled "A Difference of View."

the past, the pendulum had since swung the other way and it was now "poor men" who were being penalised, who were being denied a fair share of review coverage.

This was basically the response I had expected. As all of these editors indicated they did not keep figures on the sex ratios of reviews at the time (and as some of them attested they would never waste their time on such petty considerations), I presumed their opinions would reflect the popular prejudices about the relative entitlements of women. What I did not entirely expect, however, was the downright rudeness of three of the editors who declared in tones of varying degrees of insult that *I* must have been bitter and twisted to even think of such things and to intimate that any form of bias could be found on their pages.

I must admit that I am still taken aback, no matter how often I encounter this phenomenon. An entire industry can be shown to wilfully discriminate against women and not a breath of scandal will be raised; but let a few questions be asked about the motives and means of the men who are perpetrating the injustice—and the wrath of the gods descends. While I understand, I certainly do not accept, that to criticise men—to reveal the operation of their self interest—is indeed a form of blasphemy in a patriarchal society.

But the "attacking defence" of these literary editors did not alter the fact that I knew that women, on average, had much less than 20% of the review space on their pages. I was well aware that one man who protested so much—who insisted that the pendulum had now swung so far the other way that one had to be female to be reviewed—was the editor who was responsible for allocating just under 6% of the review space to women, and for choosing only eight women out of every hundred reviewers to make a contribution!

Responses such as these, in conjunction with my own findings (later substantiated by Women in Publishing, 1987, and the surveys undertaken by Marilyn French) made it abundantly clear there was a problem here that warranted further investigation. While literary editors might blithely insist they conducted their business without fear or favour, the figures—and women's experience—told a very different story, and revealed once more the presence of a double standard. So—back to the drawing board again to examine the hypothesis that literary editors and reviewers, like publishers and academics, are influenced not so much by the writing as by the author's sex.

But if it is relatively easy to gather the "hard data" that women receive very little attention (and that not often flattering) while literary editors remain convinced that women receive far more attention than they deserve, it is much more difficult to amass the more complex "soft data" that helps to determine the significance of this form of discrimination. A context is required for the measurements on space, frequency, and positioning of reviews; for findings on language, tone, and sex of the reviewer; and for assessments to be made about the outcome of being included or excluded, of the consequences of good or bad reviews. And this is where the absence of systematic research studies and data makes the task more difficult. What must be taken into account is that although English studies have been part of the university scene for more than a century and have relied heavily on reviews, there is little material available which examines the place and the prejudices of this process. It would be interesting to compile an inventory of courses that encompass the challenge of reviews.

Few questions it seems have been asked within the mainstream about the status accorded to the review, past or present; few questions have been asked about the relationship of the review to literary insights—or to advertising and sales. In a field where "a good name" is the most prized possession, where "reputation" is proof of success, it does seem somewhat surprising that there are not courses, dissertations, books in abundance on the part played by the review in constructing—or denying—success. And it is surprising too that so few questions are asked directly about the value and nature of reviews. For there are certainly many which demand attention: Are reviews a form of journalism, for example, and subject to the imperative of "the good story"? Or are they an integral part of the more sober world of letters? Do they exist only in relation to the books they serve to assess—or are reviews an entity in their own right? Would reviews continue to be printed long after books ceased to be published, as some writers have satirically suggested?

Many and varied are the intriguing questions which can be asked about this form of writing; and some "answers" have to be found before any conclusions can be drawn about the fundamental problem—which is the nature and significance of the discrimination against women on the literary pages.

What can be stated at the outset is that reviews have always been taken seriously by writing women. The literary history of women is so replete with protests about unjust reviews that the topic stands at the centre of women's literary traditions and suggests how different literary history and literary criticism could be if women's version of experience had been equally represented. That the topic does not have such prominence in men's literary experience is no doubt because men do not feel victimised to the same extent as women, because men have no experience of being discriminated against on the grounds of sex in supposedly "general" review publications. (The picture changes dramatically, of course, when men are required to submit work to women's literary reviews!) This interpretation is lent support by the survey undertaken by Margaret Atwood (1985): She and her students wanted to know whether women and men writers believed that sex discrimination was a factor in reviews:

We wrote to ten female writers and ten male writers and asked them if they had
ever been the subject of sexual bias in reviewing. The results were interesting:
most of the men said no, in very brief notes or postcards. I would say three
quarters of the women said yes, and at length; they wrote letters, they sent
clippings, they gave examples. What that indicated to us was only that most of
the men thought they hadn't and a lot of women thought they had, and so
naturally we had to check on that. (Margaret Atwood, 1985: p. 151)

And further investigation revealed that the women writers were quite right
to feel aggrieved, and not just about the unfair nature of specific reviews, but
about the absence of a fair forum to register their protests in mainstream
literary circles. Another manifestation of the principle that if it doesn't
happen to men, it doesn't matter—it isn't a *real* issue.

But it's always been a real issue for women. Hundreds of them over the
centuries have protested strongly about the way their work has been valued
(or devalued) because it has come from a woman's pen: In the seventeenth
century there was the Duchess of Newcastle (1624–1674) who defended
herself against the charge of being Mad Madge (because she was a woman
who wanted to write); and too there was Aphra Behn (1640–1689) who in
popularity and profits mocked the literary men who would deny women an
education—and then insist that because women were not educated, they
could not possibly write! When they and their work were reviewed, these
women knew they were victims of a double standard.

Throughout the eighteenth century women continued to protest against
this sexual double standard and it would be a revised literary history—as well
as a wonderful book of readings—that incorporated the responses to reviews
written by Mary Brunton (1778–1818), Fanny Burney (1752–1840), Maria
Edgeworth (1768–1849), Sarah Fielding (1710–1768), Elizabeth Inchbald
(1753–1821), Charlotte Lennox (1720–1804), Lady Morgan (1778–1859),
Clara Reeve (1729–1807), Charlotte Smith (1749–1806), and Mary Wollstonecraft (1759–1797).[2]

And what about the nineteenth century? There are even some studies
available on sex bias against women in the reviews of this period. Because
some of the reviews of Elizabeth Gaskell's work (by David Cecil) are so false,
Anna Walters has declared that "we might well ask what the critic has been
reading?" (1977: p. 38). And there is some illuminating information about
how the Brontë sisters were received once the reviewers became aware that
they were not the Bell brothers (see Margot Peters, 1977 and Carol Ohman,
1986, for example). There is similar information about George Eliot—and
Frances Trollope and Anne Thackeray; and in the twentieth century—Virginia
Woolf. Together their words comprise a challenging (and subversive) alternative to the traditional literary history.

---

[2] For further discussion on all of these women see Dale Spender, 1986, *Mothers of the Novel*.

Women have written extensively about the unfounded and unfair review, about the toll it takes on their sense of self and their work. Women have even created characters who have suffered from poor reviews, in their attempts to explore and explain the shock that reviews give, and to elaborate strategies for survival. Not all have gone so far as that best selling nineteenth century novelist, Mrs. Henry Wood (1814–1887), the author of *East Lynne* (1861), who in her novel *Roland Yorke* (1869) created a character who died of bad reviews; one can only wonder about the details that informed this particular incident.

But it is no exaggeration to suggest that volumes could be written on women's response to men's offensive reviews. The Australian author, Katharine Susannah Prichard (1883–1969) has spoken for many members of her sex when she revealed how hurt and discouraged she had been by the pusillanimous reviews of an aspiring academic: "The debunking of K. S. seems to be a favourite pastime of Sydney University" she wrote dispiritedly. Later in the same letter she acknowledged some of the pain and the paralysis that were part of the reaction to the rancorous review:

> Seems, after all, my life's work doesn't amount to much! Just when one's ready to put all experience and technique into the job, the power's cut off. No matter! "She did what she could"—That's a good enough epitaph for your K. S. (Katharine Susannah Prichard, 1982: pp. 166–167)

Even Virginia Woolf was known to give way to despair after reading rotten reviews (tentative links have been made between malevolent reviews and her melancholy, see Phyllis Rose, 1978). So persistent has been this pattern of pejorative reviews of women by men, and so predictable has been women's response, that a pertinent question arises: Is the outcome intended?

In virtually any other context the behaviour of some reviewers would be quickly classified as sexual harassment.

When women have attempted to enter non-traditional occupations, (that is—to be more precise—areas of employment that men have appropriated for themselves and which they wish to defend), it is not unusual to find men engaging in intimidatory tactics in order to frighten off women. In countries where women have been granted the theoretical right to equal employment opportunity such harassing activities can be deemed illegal because they are directed against women on the grounds that they are women, and they are intended to prevent women from plying their skills as plumbers, pilots, engineers, and the like.

In this context, derogatory reviews designed to discourage women from writing—or to discourage potential readers from buying their books—can also be labelled as sexual harassment: They too can preclude women from practising their craft, from competing in an area which men may feel is reserved for their own sex.

Perhaps in the future we will see vituperative reviewers taken to court under anti-discrimination legislation and charged with trying to prevent women writers from working. There could be a test case which addressed the issue of whether it was the writing—or the sex—that was at issue!

Looked at in this light, the awful and often painful reviews of women that have been penned by men assume very different dimensions. If women were to be in charge of literary studies—both historical and contemporary—it would be nothing short of reasonable for them to give the role of the review high priority. Because it seems that the review plays an important part in the literary enterprise, in the *production* of literature—and in its *distribution*.

In any assessment of the overall significance of reviews, what needs to be taken into account is the extent to which the review is linked to advertising and sales. Given that the review is one of the primary means of advertising the publication of a book—of making it *public*, known, "interesting" and available—it is not surprising that publishers (and authors of both sexes), should take the process of review very seriously.

Not that this has prompted much systematic research. As Women in Publishing (1987) found, there are major publishers who do not keep records of how many of their dispatched review copies ever succeed in getting reviewed. And as to whether good reviews mean good sales—and bad reviews, bad sales—there are virtually no studies, and there is no agreement. About the only form of consensus that prevails is that *no* review is *no good*: It means that the reading public may not get to hear of a book's existence.

Of course, one of the "side-effects" of this arrangement in which the review alerts the public to the presence of a particular work is that it introduces an element of *dependency*: In the effort to get a book "out" to its audience, publishers and writers are in many ways dependent upon the review—and the reviewer. And this is one reason that the relationship between the reviewer and the reviewed is often so acrimonious.

Because writers *need* reviewers, the relationship between the two is not one of equals and is often regarded by authors as most unsatisfactory: Authors of both sexes have registered complaints about the power and irresponsibility of the reviewer. If above and beyond the ordinary limitations of the process an additional burden is placed upon women, then it is understandable that they should protest more—and with more cause. When the review constitutes yet another *gate* which the writer must pass through on the way to success, then women have every right to object to *gatekeepers* whose judgement is based not on writing, but on sex. Although there is convincing evidence that male literary editors and reviewers operate a double standard and inflict a raw deal on female authors, there is not a lot that women can do. Somewhat surprisingly perhaps, no matter how mischievous or misinformed a review, an author who wants to challenge a reviewer has few options short of a full-scale libel action or defamation suit.

How many retractions or apologies to misrepresented authors have ever been published on the literary pages? Precious few. And not because the crime of "misinformation" is not committed. On the contrary, most literary reviewers are subjected to much the same pressures as their fellow journalists who report *the news*: They are all influenced by considerations of "good copy," of "a good story," even a scoop, and such preoccupation can lead to distortion. Yet whereas the news reporter is bound by a code of ethics and professional tribunals, no such monitoring body oversees the reporting of reviewers. The right of reply seems not to extend to the literary pages of newspapers and only rarely to literary periodicals.

Sue Lloyd—the editor of the most recent edition of *Roget's Thesaurus*—is one woman who has learned the hard way that the writer has little redress for the fierce or false review. Having been the target of some harassing male critics—one of whom could not possibly have read her work to know it was no good as his review appeared in print *before* the publication of the book and when only the promotional blurb was available[3]—Sue Lloyd determined to tackle one columnist whose coverage of the *Thesaurus* was inaccurate, savage—and sensational.

Because she assumed that his caustic criticisms of her non-sexist editing style were legitimate, she questioned this reviewer about his reasons for his damning indictment of her work. But having apologised for any distress that his attack might have caused her, he proceeded to attempt to placate her with the reassurance that he—"had not meant what he had written"! He was simply after "a good story" which he argued was to the advantage of both of them!

Bad enough to be abused and berated for beliefs and behaviour that were non-existent; worse, to be obliged to be grateful for the ploy that was meant to promote interest, and to get readers in. Yet the reviewer who insisted that there was no point in writing platitudinous praise seems to have a case: Once he had concocted an issue and made the *Thesaurus* a topic of debate there was a definite response. For a while the publishers of the *Thesaurus* found themselves in the peculiar position of having on their hands a reference book that was a best-seller; in such circumstances they would be unlikely to register a protest about a base—and baseless—review.

Whether bad reviews sell more books (by attracting attention) is an issue which prompts debate, and one which can present many authors with a dilemma. For is it better to do battle with the personal pain caused by a vicious but highly visible review which could well help to produce better sales? Or would an accurate, and appreciative review—which attracted little or no attention—be preferable?

---

[3]For further discussion of this incident see Dale Spender and Lynne Spender, (1984, p. 36).

And if an author wants to challenge the writer of an unfair or inaccurate review, what is the best way to go about it? Authors may find some consolation in the private reassurance of reviewers who acknowledge that they didn't really mean all those dreadful things they said. But this hardly seems a satisfactory solution. The review still stands in the public domain and like other forms of sexual harassment won't simply vanish because the harassers declare that their words shouldn't be taken so seriously for they are just part of the review game.

One example of the reviews which fall into this category is that which concentrates on the *appearance* of the woman writer and uses this to disqualify the work. No one can undertake research on sex bias in reviews without becoming aware of the prevalence of this particular form of sex discrimination. Among the reviews of Casey Miller's and Kate Swift's innocuous *Handbook on Non-Sexist Writing* (1981) was the following evaluation— written by a highly esteemed (and highly paid) reviewer in a highly reputable British newspaper:

> From the photograph supplied of Mss Casey Miller and Kate Swift, I should judge that neither was sexually attractive . . . a sense of grievance can often bring out the worst in people, and there is no reason to extend our sympathy where the motives of these disgruntled feminist agitators is simply to make a nuisance of themselves. This would appear to be the inspiration behind Swift and Miller's *Handbook of Non Sexist Writing*.

This example reveals much more than the fears of the reviewer; it shows that there is one rule for women and another for men. No man has his literary credentials measured in terms of his looks—else this particular reviewer might find his own authority drastically undermined!

But for Casey Miller and Kate Swift there was no satisfactory means of calling this man to account. Despite the unwarranted personal attack and the malicious misrepresentation, they were not entitled to any "right of reply." Had they tried to register an objection by way of a "letter to the editor," assuming that their protests were published (and I suspect that most of the letters in this category are not), the exercise could still be completely counterproductive. For a woman's protest about injustice can be construed as the personal gripe of a carping woman rather than the genuine grievance about the unfair arrangements of a male-dominated society. This is one reason that women writers may prefer to remain silent rather than to add more grist to the mill and risk portrayal as narrow, irrational, and *complaining* women.

This has certainly been my own line of reasoning on occasion. When once I was confronted with a vicious review charging me with making the most crass and careless mistakes, my first reaction was to run and check through my work: I was disturbed when a quick reading did not reveal the errors that I was supposed to have made. But I presumed that the adrenalin flow (and the sense of mortification) were interfering with my search so I took more measured steps and set about enlisting the help of some post-graduate students who were given the assignment of locating the listed inaccuracies. My publishers also provided professional assistance: In the interest of eliminating errors from future editions of the work, they conducted their own examination of the text. And surprise, surprise: None of us could find these dreadful mistakes of which I stood accused (and condemned!) We were forced to conclude that the review was a "fabrication": The question was—what was I to do?

I had no confidence that the periodical which had published the review would have printed any protest that I might have submitted. And even if it did, I had even less confidence in the perception of my own credibility. It didn't require imaginative talent to be able to predict what the reaction would have been to the letter of a "suspect" feminist who charged a distinguished academic with fabricating a review: a likely story indeed!

So although this was undoubtedly the most perfidious review I ever received,[4] I registered no public objection. The (mis)representation of my work as glaringly and grossly inaccurate went unchallenged. Even the protest "letter to the editor," written by the post-graduate students who had tried to accomplish the impossible feat of locating the errors within the text, went unprinted. And it must be said that of all the many reviews this particular work of mine received (not all of which were derogatory by any means) it is this *false* one that is most frequently cited and that—ironically—tends to support the premise that even "bad" reviews are "good" reviews in that they attract more attention.

But even if it can be argued that there are benefits to be derived from bad reviews, there is a price to be paid as well. And it can be a very heavy price as countless women writers have testified. I assume that the absence of a forum for examining false reviews, and the failure of papers and periodicals to provide misrepresented writers with a right of reply, leaves all writers, but especially women writers, in a vulnerable position where they can readily be exploited by unscrupulous reviewers.

Of course, some writers have found their own solution to the review problem. Rebecca West, (1983) for example, was among those who were well aware of the pitfalls of the process and who took appropriate countermeasures for her own protection.

Reflecting on a lifetime's experience as author and critic, she informed me when interviewed[5] that she had lived to regret her resignation from the role of

---

[4]This statement no longer stands: I have since had a much worse review from an Australian feminist. Anyone who wishes to read it will find it in the September issue of the *Australian Book Review*.
[5]Interviews with Rebecca West were undertaken in 1982 as a basis for the book, *There's always Been a Women's Movement*, 1983.

reviewer when in 1916 she made the shift from journalism (on *The Clarion*) to literature (writing a study of Henry James). It was her contention that as a columnist she had always had a platform from which she could launch her own shafts, so she was treated by other reviewers with a healthy respect. But when she gave up her column and turned to more literary pursuits, there was a significant change in the commentary in the press about herself and her work. In her words, it was because "critics and reviewers tell the most extraordinary lies about me" that she had felt obliged to take up her reviewing pen again, and to defend herself against some of the "poisonous nonsense" that unchecked reviewers could spread (1983: p. 74). "One gets an entirely better class of review", she insisted, "when one can publicly hit back."[6] Unfortunately, however, this "remedy" is not readily available to all women writers who are reviewed.

And even where the opportunity to hit back *is* provided, it affords no guaranteed protection against awful reviews as Jill Tweedie (1986(a)) makes painfully clear. A prominent British newspaper columnist, her position did not prevent the publication of a "poisonous review" of her novel, *Internal Affairs* (1986(b)). However, it did allow her to take to task the reviewer who blithely and blatantly declared that Jill Tweedie was a depressing feminist, that she was definitely not a novelist, and that the kindest thing to do was to draw a veil over her efforts to write fiction.

But hitting back may be no compensation for the hurt and harm that such horrid reviews are capable of inflicting. Writing in her own defence, and on behalf of women writers who are subjected to the additional burden of sex-biased reviews, Jill Tweedie (1986(a)) documents the damage that the "short, brutish and obscure" review can give rise to. It forces the author "at whom it is directed to feel personally rather than artistically attacked," she says, and she tells of how her own "stomach went into spasm" when she read one man's crude and capricious criticism of her work. She gives advice to writers on how to recover from such reviews and in setting out her "golden rule" she shows just how far the process of reviewing has been brought into disrepute:

> (I tell them) . . . take no notice, pretend you don't care, they'll only get meaner if they think you mind—the sort of stock advice handed out to bullied children in school. (Jill Tweedie, 1986(a): p. 12)

Jill Tweedie is but one of the latest in the long line of women who have protested about the unaccountable and abusive nature of reviews in general, and about the misogynist nature of reviews in particular. This pattern of male disparagement of female contributions emerges with consistent clarity while the majority of reviews are written by men and the majority of works of fiction, for example, are written by women (see Women in Publishing, 1987

---

[6]Interview with Rebecca West, March, 1982, London.

for further statistical breakdown). All writers may have legitimate complaints to make about the review process, but for women writers the difficulties are exacerbated, and so routine and regular have been these attacks on women by men that the role of the review as a form of *sexual harassment at the workplace* must be taken into consideration. As a means of undermining women's confidence to the point where they may feel unable to write, as a means of dissuading women from seeking publication by presenting them with evidence of the derision to which they can be subjected, the intimidatory tactics of some reviewers could certainly qualify as sexual harassment which is intended to keep women out of an occupation regarded as a stronghold of men.

There are of course, no stipulated qualifications for reviewers—though maleness is undoubtedly a distinct advantage: Yet the position is a privileged one in that it allows the reviewer to wield considerable power and influence. It is not too much to suggest that with a stroke of the pen a reviewer can discredit, discount, even destroy, the creative/artistic work of a lifetime: In a society where the creative/artistic skills of women are considered suspect, even non-existent, the process would still be problematic to women even if half the reviewers were women (see Margaret Atwood, 1986 for further discussion). As research on language and sex indicates, women too can be "prejudiced" against the words of women, though women are not of course intent on preserving literary and reviewing territory as the province of men.

But given that the majority of reviewers are men, and that the reviewed have no established right of reply against their excesses, it is hardly surprising that women should have an enduring and healthy tradition of resistance to the unreasonable process of reviewing.

Part of this tradition is the common contemporary allegation that reviews and reviewers "go too far" in putting reviews *before* the books they are designed to serve. Some writers today argue that there are reviewers who no longer see their role as one of providing responsible commentary on the latest books, but rather as one of producing their own work which stands in its own right. According to this line of reasoning the review has become an independent literary form that allows the reviewer to indulge his own literary pretensions while the book—the ostensible object of consideration—is nothing other than a pretext for enhancing the reviewer's own reputation and earnings. Some writers would even be prepared to assert that so "disconnected" are reviews from the books that are ostensibly their raison d'etre, that were all publishing to cease forthwith, reviews themselves would continue to be printed![7]

---

[7]This was the contention of many women at the First International Feminist Book Fair, and it is an issue that has been raised at many meetings of Women in Publishing in Britain—including the 1986 Conference.

Whether they are indeed completely cut off from the books they are supposed to serve is a matter for speculation, but the fact that reviewers have obligations and loyalties that are distinct from—and maybe in conflict with—publishers and authors, is readily discernible. For reviewers are also authors: Reviewers are also paid writers. Not surprisingly they may have a vested interest in the paper/periodical that prints their work: Not surprisingly they may be interested in the success of their own publication. In these circumstances, were reviewers more concerned to do "a good job" for their employer, rather than "a good job" for a particular publisher or author, their motives and actions would be perfectly comprehensible. This is part and parcel of the pressure on reviewers—as publishers, authors, and editors are aware. Lynne Spender helps to clarify this issue:

> I went to a meeting of the *Editors*—a group of people involved in publishing—where the evening's discussion was based on reviews . . . There was quite a lot of talk about reviews as a particular literary genre—used to sell papers and magazines rather than the books reviewed. The idea of the reviewer being the selling point—rather than the author of the original work—makes the whole scene rather bizarre. (Dale and Lynne Spender, 1984: p. 57)

Bizarre though this concept may be, uncommon it is not. Many members of literary circles (such as the *Editors* or Women in Publishing) acknowledge that there are literary editors and reviewers for whom the books that they are reviewing are nothing other than "raw material" that can be conveniently "mined" to promote the paper/periodical in which they appear. When the purpose of the exercise is to secure provocative pieces which can become news and improve sales, the latest books can be reduced to pegs on which good stories can hang.

No wonder writers protest about their treatment at the hands of the reviewer: No wonder women writers frequently view the process as iniquitous—and frustrating in the extreme.

"He who pays the piper, calls the tune" and in contrast to *writing* books, reviewing books can be a profitable activity. The highly popular and prolific Australian writer, Kylie Tennant, pointed this out in her autobiography when she declared that she "could make more money by writing book reviews than by writing books" (1986: p. 139). Not that Kylie Tennant was ever an irresponsible reviewer: Quite the reverse. Her record is exemplary and reveals the contribution that constructive and lively criticism can make. But she identified with writers rather than reviewers, and she was concerned to document the pressures placed on reviewers to produce "good copy"—even at the authors' expense—if they wanted their reviews in print, and their pay in the bank.

But despite all these protests about the unsatisfactory nature of reviews, there has been little systematic or scholarly scrutiny of the practice. This is one reason women have had to start virtually from scratch in their efforts to critique the critics and review the reviews. Not that it is unusual for women to start from their own experience of a particular phenomenon and to end up questioning the arrangements of an entire institution, or even of society. But given that publishing and reviewing have been going on for quite a long time, it is extraordinary that there were so few studies of the review process and its deficiencies when the present generation of women began to conduct their own investigation into bias in the reviews of women's books.

As early as 1970–1971, the Canadian novelist Margaret Atwood was sufficiently uneasy about the treatment of women in reviews to undertake research on the topic at York University. Using her own experience as a framework, her hypothesis was (as mine is here) that there were cases where it was not the writing but the sex that was being rated in reviews. With her students she set out

> . . . to study "sexual bias in reviewing" by which we meant not unfavourable reviews, but points being added or subtracted on the basis of the author's sex and supposedly associated characteristics rather than on the basis of the work itself. (Margaret Atwood, 1986: p. 75)

As the first part of their survey, Margaret Atwood and her students proceeded to contact women and men writers and to ask them whether they believed they had been unfairly treated by reviewers. They found—as has been mentioned earlier—that while no man felt he had been the victim of sex-bias in reviews, half the women were convinced that they had been, and a quarter suspected that they might have been.

Given these findings, that the majority of women believed they were and the majority of men believed they were not subjected to sexual bias in reviews, the second part of the research project was initiated: Numerous reviews from a variety of sources were checked to determine the extent to which the different beliefs of the sexes were justified. This survey helped to suggest that for men, their sex was no disadvantage, whereas women had good grounds for their grievance.

For example, one aspect of the reviews which was analysed and which produced some dramatic results was in relation to language and tone: a comparison of the work of women and men in this area revealed the systematic operation of the sexual double standard. So *much* of men's writing was considered positive because the writers were men: So *little* of women's writing was considered positive because the writers were women.

Just as the language in general terms has a set of positive names which relates to men and a set of negative terms which relates to women (the phenomenon Muriel Schulz, 1975, described as "The Semantic Derogation of Women") so too does the particular language of reviews draw on a set of positive references for men, and negative references for women. Having detected this language of systematic disparagement of women in reviews,

Margaret Atwood goes on to name this phenomenon herself. She calls it *The Quiller-Couch Syndrome*:

> ... This phrase refers to the turn-of-the-century essay by Quiller-Couch, de-
> fining "masculine" and "feminine" styles in writing. The "masculine" style is,
> of course, bold, forceful, clear, vigorous etc.; the "feminine" style is vague,
> weak, tremulous, pastel etc. In the list of pairs you can include "objective" and
> "subjective", "universal" or "accurate depiction of society" versus "confes-
> sional", "personal", or even "narcissistic" and "neurotic". It's roughly seventy
> years since Quiller-Couch's essay, but the "masculine" group of adjectives is
> still much more likely to be applied to the work of male writers; female writers
> are much more likely to get hit with some version of "the feminine sensibility",
> or "the feminine style" *whether their work merits it or not.* (Margaret Atwood,
> 1986: p. 75. my emphasis)

This description of the written word parallels Cheris Kramarae's description of the spoken word (1977): Both Margaret Atwood and Cheris Kramarae
have sampled the assumption of a male-dominated society that men are the
strong speakers and the forceful writers—the very *masters* of the language—
and that women are the hesitant speakers and the weak writers. And it is not
necessary to hear the sexes speak, or to read what they write, in order to
know that this is how they are supposed to use the language. Such judgements are derived solely from "sex stereotypes" and may have no relevance
to the reality of women's and men's speaking and writing. But they have
considerable relevance for male power and its perpetuation. For in this context it can be stated with conviction that no matter what women write—no
matter how accomplished or competent it may be—their contribution can
still be rated as the work of women, which is assumed, *a priori*, to be inferior
to the work of a man. The evidence for the operation of this double standard
can be found in reviews.

It would be difficult to overstate the perniciousness and pervasiveness of
the assumptions which deny women's intellectual/creative competence in a
patriarchal society. As Margaret Atwood suggests, so negative is the connota-
tion of women in the "review code," it is the height of approbation to
describe a woman writer as *unrepresentative* of her sex. So loaded is the
language and so common these "paradoxical compliments" in reviews, that
she was forced to conclude that the very *existence* of the woman as writer
was at stake:

> When women writers were praised, they were likely to be praised in terms that
> deprived them of their femininity, as in "she writes like a man", "she thinks like
> a man", "she transcends her sex". I love that last one ... I don't think anybody
> has ever said in a review of a man's book that he transcended his sex. For a
> woman that's supposed to be a plus. (Margaret Atwood, 1985: p. 152)

Again Margaret Atwood has a term for this phenomenon: *The Lady Painter
Syndrome, or She Writes Like a Man.* As she explains, her labelling has its

origins in a discussion she had with a male painter in 1960: He said that when a woman was good she was called a *painter* (and granted honorary status as "the real thing") and when she was bad, she was called a *Lady* painter. Margaret Atwood expands her definition of the term:

> . . . "She writes like a man" is part of the same pattern; it's usually used by a male reviewer who is impressed by a female writer. It's meant as a compliment. See also "She thinks like a man", which means the author thinks, unlike most women who are held to be incapable of objective thought (their province is "feeling"). (Margaret Atwood, 1986: p. 76).

Margaret Atwood goes on to give examples of the constant use of the double standard which, on the basis of sex, dictates one response to the writing of women—and quite another to the writing of men. "A hard-hitting piece of writing by a man is liable to be thought of as merely realistic," she says, while "an equivalent piece by a woman is much more likely to be labelled as "cruel" or "tough"! (1986: p. 76). And she concludes:

> "Maleness" is exemplified by the "good" male writer; "femaleness", since it is seen by . . . reviewers as a handicap or a deficiency, is held to be transcended or discarded by the "good" female one. In other words, there is no critical vocabulary for expressing the concept "good/female". Work by a male writer is often spoken of by critics admiring it as having "balls": have you ever heard anyone speak admiringly of work by a woman as having "tits"? (Margaret Atwood, 1986: p. 76)

When in 1975, within the framework of linguistics, Julia Penelope (see Julia Stanley) attempted to define this phenomenon, she called it "negative semantic space" for women. It was her contention that the entire spectrum of positive semantic space had been appropriated by men with the result that there was no conceptual space in the English language to accommodate positive meanings for women: For praise about women's "femininity" is another paradoxical compliment in that it too marks a woman as *negative* in comparison to the positive connotations of "masculinity." And, of course, it's no good thing for a woman to be perceived as "masculine"—to think, act or write like a man!

As Margaret Atwood and many other women writers have discerned, within the constraints of the English language it is not possible to positively portray *woman* and it is this that is at the crux of the sex-bias in reviews of the woman writer.

In my own research on sexism in language and its implications for the woman writer, I encountered this problem in 1976, at a conference on Women in Literature in Bristol, England. I recorded the following comment, which I transcribed for publication in *Man Made Language* (1980)

> It's useless trying to say I'm a writer . . . and a good one. I nearly said "as good as a male". And that's what I'm talking about. By definition you can't be a good *female* writer, it's a contradiction of terms. And the more you try to establish

yourself as a writer the more you have to move towards being "as good as a male". That's exactly what I want to get away from. What happens if you are as good as a female? It's laughable, isn't it? It pisses me off . . . (mimics) . . . "Excuse me, I want a job on your paper. I'm an excellent *female* writer. I have all the *female virtues* . . . in abundance. I'm silly, irrational, irresponsible . . . " etc., you know the rest. You just can't capitalize on being female. That way no good lies, you have to show that you have *male virtues*, and then, of course, you're trapped. Because you are *not* a male. You're a substitute male. (Dale Spender, 1985: p. 21)

For much more than a decade, insights such as these about the negative nature of woman/writer as a category have been documented in disciplines other than literary criticism, but they have found little or no favour in critical/ review circles. Yet such considerations are fundamental to the practices of literary evaluation: Of what use are all the sciences of the text when the interpretive framework through which all "scientific" findings are filtered is so riddled with sex-stereotyped values that it could be hypothesised that it borders on the impossible to encode positive representations of the woman writer?

Even within the low status area of "kid's lit" a concerted attempt has been made to monitor and eliminate gross examples of sex-stereotyping, to portray female and male as they exist in the world in all their diversity, and *not* in the narrow way that patriarchal society decrees they *should* be. But while this much-despised enterprise has been mocked by many members of the more elevated and erudite branches of literature, their own critical essays and reviews have continued to include material that makes sex-stereotyping in children's books appear relatively innocuous.

Literary critics could learn a great deal from the elementary efforts of those who charted the sex-bias in children's books. When they met with widespread resistance (and ridicule) to their assertion that males were portrayed positively and females were portrayed negatively, they countered with a strategy of "reversal" to make their point. Comparable dramatic lessons can also be provided in relation to reviews, as Andrea Dworkin and other American women writers have demonstrated.

Angered by the language and tone toward women writers in that reputable publication, the *New York Times Book Review*, they determined to establish the significance of such systematic derogation:

> . . . At a meeting of the Writers Guild, Dworkin and colleagues selected "extraordinarily insulting" reviews of the works of eminent feminist writers such as Kate Millet [sic] and Adrienne Rich. *But*, when reading these aloud to the audience, they replaced the names of the women with the names of eminent male writers. The audience was stunned by the derogatory tone of the reviews and refused to believe that they had actually been written—until it was proved otherwise. (Women in Publishing, 1987: p. 83)

But, as Women in Publishing were quick to point out, "no action was taken." Not once it was realised that the victims were women. No doubt the sense of injustice was not so great when the audience—and wider community—were informed that it wasn't really celebrated male writers who were on the receiving end of this brutish and boorish criticism, but the much more suspect female writers who were prompted by a sense of grievance. And it is worth reflecting on the significance of this change in perception for it provides further and formidable evidence on the uses of the sexual double standard.

From outside the framework of literary criticism the documentation of the principle of "one rule for women and another for men" has proceeded with consistent clarity. Educational studies, for example, have suggested that when girls are treated like girls—particularly in relation to issues of verbal abuse and sexual harassment—the situation can be seen as so routine and ordinary that it may be difficult to get teachers to appreciate that such abuse is problematic. But if boys are treated like girls—well, this is quite another matter: In single sex boys schools it is common practice for a group of "psuedo-girls" to be created and these "poor boys" can be subjected to much the same abuse as are the girls in a mixed-sex educational environment. And when boys are treated in this manner—it is considered scandalous (see Katherine Clarricoates, 1978; Carol Jones, 1985; Pat Mahony, 1983; Michelle Stanworth, 1981). Research in media studies also lends support to the thesis that males are accorded more importance so the mistreatment of a male may be viewed as a more serious offence: So, for example, media reports on the abduction/abuse of boys (a much less common occurrence than the abduction/abuse of girls) may result in a much more outraged press response (see Kath Davies *et al*, (eds), 1987).

Now to this body of knowledge can be added some of the findings from (feminist) literary criticism. Thanks to the reversal-experiment of Andrea Dworkin we can see that within the traditional framework of literary criticism, it's not a problem for reviewers to treat women writers like women: This doesn't call for remedial action. But it *is* a problem, a problem of awful proportions, when men are treated like women by reviewers. The contrast is stark and the call for corrective measures is immediate: When men receive the sort of assessment which is routinely handed out to women, the evaluations are seen as disgraceful, even indefensible.

As many feminists have asserted—Andrea Dworkin among them—this is but another variation on the age-old theme of dominant groups, that subordinate groups don't feel the same pain!

But if the dominants don't want to come to terms with this very simple concept of the double standard, the subordinates are certainly committed to exposing and explaining its many ramifications. Margaret Mead (1971) could demonstrate in her anthropological studies that it was not *what* was done, but *who* did it, which determined the status and value of an activity. Margaret Atwood could show from her study of reviews that it was not the writing but the sex that was at the crux of positive/negative assessments. So men are positive and women are negative, no matter what they do or how they write: When men write about men's world they are reviewed as dealing with universal issues and when they write about women's world their efforts are taken as a sign of their imaginative genius. For women it is quite the reverse: When they write about women's world they are seen to be limited, and when they deal with men's world, reviewers find them unsexed, or unconvincing. Says Margaret Atwood:

> . . . when a man writes about things like doing the dishes, it's realism; when a woman does, it's an unfortunate genetic limitation. (Margaret Atwood, 1986: p. 76)

Yet why should this patently obvious and unjust practice persist? Clearly the principle of the sexual double standard can be readily understood and the evidence of its existence can be readily gathered—to the point where those *outside* the discipline can detect the discrepancies and the absurdities in lit-crit. Where it is not perceived as passé, boring, or irrelevant, the entire literary enterprise is being brought into disrepute by the failure of the discipline to put its own house in order.

Many women are aware of the current crisis (see particularly Annette Kolodny's paper presented at MLA, 1987) and they have attempted to analyse the causes and to suggest some solutions. Carolyn G. Heilbrun (1986) for example insists that literary studies are "in the doldrums" and that to this both teachers and students make a contribution. "Let us be blunt," she says, today's youth "no longer go to literature and what we used to call 'culture' as to the fountain of wisdom and experience." And this is partly because teachers wearily teach "'the same old stuff' or else dig their way into new theories that are concealed in a thicket of language so dense as to be virtually impenetrable." And the students? They "arrive unconvinced that literature holds important truths" with the result that they no longer see literary studies as a useful, attractive, or enlightening option (p. 21).

I would go further: I would suggest that students are not just "turned off" when it comes to English—but that they are positively disillusioned by an anachronistic "discipline" that refuses to monitor its own flawed assessment practices. Because the lay community often knows what the "experts" fail to take into account—namely that literary judgements are essentially personal/ political and *subjective*—it is the traditional literary critics who put themselves into an indefensible, and incredible, position.

But, of course, it doesn't have to be this way. In her essay "Bringing the Spirit Back to English Studies," Carolyn Heilbrun (1986) argues that "if students are to see literature as capable of informing them about any of the aspects of life, they must become convinced that literature is as capable of revolutionary exploration as their own lives are" (pp. 21–22) and to this end she calls for a feminist approach to literature, a critique of past practices, and a course which encompasses future concerns and considerations.

I completely endorse her stand. It is preposterous that so many of the burning issues and so much stimulating and illuminating research in literature should currently be conducted outside the discipline. For my own part I have at least twenty possibilities that I want to pursue in relation to literary judgements, perception, and the sexual double standard: And it is untenable that a few influential men should decree that these issues are not the legitimate considerations of a discipline they want to continue to dominate.

One of my first projects would be associated with the concept of romantic fiction—and whether it is a classification that is based upon the writing—or the sex: I have long wanted to place a D. H. Lawrence novel between the covers of Harlequin/Mills and Boon, and to test its status when seen in this light. And I am convinced that students would see the point of such an exercise and would not need to be persuaded about the importance of English studies in this context or the relevance of literature to life.

At the moment, however, those who query the very process of assessment—who raise the awkward questions about criticism and reviews—generally find themselves defined out of the literary framework. Which is one reason that such events as the Feminist International Book Fair—and all its associated activities—is so astonishingly successful: There is no established institutional base that allows for such vital discussion and encourages such valid challenges to entrenched literary practices. This is why events at the Feminist International Book Fair are over-subscribed and why women's supposedly alternative sessions attract bigger audiences than the mainstream meetings at conferences: This is why associations like the British Women in Publishing finance and print their own research on the issue, and why women writers in North America formed a pressure group to monitor the sex bias in the *New York Times Book Review*. That these problems of such central importance should have to be addressed *outside* the discipline is an indictment of the paradigm of "literary criticism": In the light of Thomas Kuhn's arguments on the transformation of paradigms (see *The Structure of Scientific Revolutions*, 1972) it seems that English no longer enjoys credibility and that it is therefore likely to undergo quite a dramatic shift. Then such surveys as the one undertaken by Marilyn French (and other North American women writers) could become the logical and legitimate concern of "literary studies."

Despite the documented sense of grievance that exists among women

Table 4.1. Breakdown By Sex of Authors and Reviewers in the
New York Times Book Review—9/30–12/2/84

Date of Issue	Front Page Auth		Rvwr		Full Page Auth		Rvwr		Partial Page Auth		Rvwr		In Short Auth		Rvwr	
	M	F	M	F	M	F	M	F	M	F	M	F	M	F	M	F
9/30	1	1	1	1	4*	3*	4	1	11	3	10	3	9	2	8	3
10/7	1	0	1	0	4	0	4	0	10	4	8	4	10	0	9	3
10/14	1	0	0	1	5	1	4	0	12	3	12	3	9	2	7	4
10/21	1	0	1	0	4	1	4	1	8	6	11	3	9	3	5	6
10/21 (Bus)	1	0	1	0	2	0	2	0	5	0	3	2	13	5	11	5
10/28	1	0	1	0	6	0	5	1	11	5	11	5	5	5	5	5
11/4	1	0	1	0	3	2	2	2	11	5	11	3	10	2	5	6
11/11	1	0	1	0	4	0	3	0	13	1	11	1	7*	4*	6	4
11/11 (Child)	1	0	1	0	1	0	0	1	7	6	4	7	—	—	—	—
Totals	9	1	8	2	33	7	28	6	88	33	81	31	72	23	56	36
%s**	90/10		80/20		83/17		82/18		73/27		72/28		76/24		61/39	
11/18	0	1	0	1	4	1	5	0	10	8	10	7	10	1	6	2
11/25	1	0	1	0	3	1	3	1	12*	4*	11	3	12	1	10	3
12/2	—	—	—	—	2	0	2	0	6	1	4	1	—	—	—	—

*Joint male-female authorship   *(continued)*
**Percentages rounded to the nearest whole

with regard to reviews, there is a dearth of hard data available on this form of discrimination. Yet any attempt to systematically evaluate the nature of sex-bias in reviews requires a great deal of background information. Margaret Atwood (1985, 1986) has done an admirable job in extending understandings about sex bias in review language and tone, but there are many more dimensions that demand examination: Most crucial among these are the measurements of selection and space, issues about which women writers get selected for review and how much attention they receive. And how does this compare with the treatment accorded to men?

Concerned to answer these specific questions, a group of prominent North American women writers recently conducted one of the most impressive monitoring and follow up exercises that has been undertaken—and their target was nothing less than the reputable *New York Times Book Review*. The initiative for this project was taken by the well-known and highly esteemed author, Marilyn French, who had been sufficiently motivated to keep her own records on the representation of women in the *NYT Book Review* from September 30 to November 11, 1984. So disturbed was she by her findings (see Table 4.1) that she contacted other women writers who had a vested interest—who could be candidates for reviews or for reviewing—and suggested that they mount a campaign to promote change.

The first and significant fact that Marilyn French put forward was just

Table 4.1.
(Continued)

Poetry				Children's				Front Page Essay				Inside Essay				Bios			
Auth		Rvwr		Auth		Rvwr		Wrtr		Subj		Wrtr		Subj		Wrtr		Subj	
M	F	M	F	M	F	M	F	M	F	M	F	M	F	M	F	M	F	M	F
4	0	2	0	1	0	0	1	1	0	—	—	0	1	—	—	1	0	1	0
1	0	1	0	1	1	0	2	1	0	—	—	1	0	—	—	2	1	3	0
—	—	—	—	0	1	0	1	1	0	1	0	2	0	—	—	0	1	1	0
—	—	—	—	0	1	0	1	1	0	—	—	—	—	—	—	2	2	1	3
—	—	—	—	—	—	—	—	—	—	—	—	0	1	—	—	—	—	—	—
—	—	—	—	0	1	1	0	1	0	—	—	—	—	—	—	1	1	2	0
—	—	—	—	1	2	1	2	0	1	—	—	1	0	—	—	0	1	0	1
3	0	1	0	—	—	—	—	1	0	—	—	3	0	1	0	1	0	1	0
8	0	4	0	3	6	2	7	6	1	1	0	7	2	1	0	7	6	9	4
100/0		100/0		33/67		22/78		86/14		100/0		78/22		100/0		54/46		69/31	
1	0	1	0	1	1	0	2	1	0	—	—	—	—	—	—	2	1	2	1
0	3	0	1	0	1	0	1	1	0	—	—	—	—	—	—	2	0	2	0
2	1	1	0	—	—	—	—	—	—	—	—	2	1	—	—	—	—	—	—

how few reviews women received: a seven weeks survey of the *NYT Book Review* yielded the following figures—

Table 4.2.

Type of Coverage	Percentage taken by men
Front Page Reviews	90%
Inside Page/Full Reviews	53%
Inside Page/Partial Reviews	73%
'In Short' Reviews	76%
Poetry	100%
Total of Men's Reviews	86%

The only area where men did *not* receive the predominant share was that of children's books, where their contributions were confined to 33%.

Clearly men get most of the review space, but this is not the only dimension on which they dominate. Men also get many more opportunities to write reviews—about men.

"Essays" in the *New York Times Book Review* were examined and revealed the predictable pattern of male preference. Of seven front page essays, six were written by men; of nine inside, seven were written by men; of the thirteen short biographical pieces, nine were devoted to men—although only seven were written by men.

Women writers had known that the situation was bad: They had not realised that it was appalling. The twenty-five women authors who were first confronted with the findings of Marilyn French's simple survey, determined to do something about it and a protest "Letter to the Editor" was prepared and circulated among an even wider audience, for signature. Well over 100 women writers endorsed the objection that was forwarded to the periodical, along with the breakdown of women's review representation. The result was a meeting of editors/writers and an agreement that steps would be taken to reduce the discrepancy and for the periodical to reflect the full range of writers and writing.

While there is no evidence that the staff of the *NYT Book Review* pleaded extenuating circumstances—"that they really would have liked to include more reviews on/by women but unfortunately there weren't any who were up to standard"—this could have been because the pressure group preempted such a response. The women writers were prepared to wait and watch for improvements in the representation of women in reviews but they also took precautions to ensure that the periodical had plenty of opportunities to select qualified women.[8]

In March 1985 all the women signatories were asked to contribute further to the campaign in three specific ways:

1. To forward their own suggested topics for essays to the editor of the *NYT Book Review*—and if they had not written for the publication before, to include samples of their work in essay form.
2. To write to the editor informing him of their availability (and expertise) if they wanted to be considered as reviewers.
3. To make a list of recent publications of interesting books by women which the *NYT Book Review* had not covered—and to recommend current publications that warranted attention.

And, stated the organising committee, they would continue to monitor the reviews and to note any improvements in the position of women.

Given that more than one hundred of the most distinguished women writers in North America were asked to participate in this campaign, one could confidently conclude that the staff of the *NYT Book Review* received many communications about women writers and reviewers. And for a brief period it seemed as if the effort put into the campaign would pay dividends: For three months from March 1985 there was an increase in the representation of women, but for the following three months (from June to September, 1985) there was a decline in the number of women's reviews (see Table 4.3).

So Phase II of the campaign was implemented. Once more the women authors were asked to renew their efforts, to write to the editor with sugges-

---

[8]Women in Publishing, 1987, encountered this "explanation" when they questioned literary editors about the small number of women reviewers, see p. 58.

tions for essays, with offers to review, and with a list of recommended books worthy of attention. And a new (and most impressive) delegation of prestigious women writers met with the editor to make the point, once more, that women's writing was not obtaining a fair hearing in a publication that took pride in its record of presumed impartiality.

While I would not for one minute want to detract from this admirable effort to expose the bias against women in reviews publications, I do want to suggest that even this campaign helps to highlight the limitations of the review system. While the women were able to keep up the pressure they could influence the outcome, to some extent, but as soon as the pressure was decreased—so too was the representation of women. With no built-in mechanism of accountability, no guaranteed form of redress or right of reply, it can be "back to normal" again once the abnormal emphasis on the position of women no longer applies: It can be back to the overwhelming predominance of men once women cease to skew the statistics on the representation of women.

Sadly there is no evidence to suggest that campaigns like the one centred on the *NYT Book Review* result in long-term gains for women. Confronted with the empirical data on their enormous sex bias in favour of men, some literary editors who wish to *appear* balanced, just, or even "liberated," can be sufficiently shamed to want to put their own house in order—for a short period, anyway. But what must be recognised is that such policies require effort: That to provide women with a greater share of review space, "goes against the grain." Just as men may be embarrassed by their dominance in conversation and some may consciously try to give women more space, so too they may think it politic to stand back to permit women more space in reviews. But for women this is not a right, it is a privilege, and granted by the powerful: It is a privilege that can be readily withdrawn or fall into disuse once the powerful feel no obligation to bestow it. Then we are left with the same old ratios again—where two thirds of the conversation and review space is being taken up by even "informed" men.

And the women who continue to complain? The women who in 1985 and 1986 and 1987 and 1988 continue to object to the unfair representation of women in reviews—what happens to them? The fact that they have a genuine grievance can soon be overlooked: Like the women who try to get a fair share in the conversation, they are soon discredited. They are regarded as unreasonable, pushy, bitter, and twisted, as definitely difficult and disagreeable. As the survey coordinated by Marilyn French makes clear, it's hard to "crack the system" of reviews: Indeed it seems that like women's publishing, the only way to *ensure* that women's work is fairly treated is by setting up women-controlled sources of review—such as *The Women's Review of Books*.

But the existence of such valuable publications as *The Women's Review of Books*—and numerous other women's periodicals and magazines—does not

Table 4.3. Breakdown By Sex of Authors and Reviewers in the
New York Times Book Review—4/7/85–9/22/85—25 weeks

Date of Issue	Front Page				Full Page				Partial Page				In Short			
	Auth		Rvwr		Auth		Rvwr		Auth		Rvwr		Auth		Rvwr	
	M	F	M	F	M	F	M	F	M	F	M	F	M	F	M	F
4/7	1	0	1	0	2	2	2	1	6	2	5	2	10	2	5	7
4/14	1	0	1	0	2	2	3	1	14	5	15	4	11	2	6	7
4/21	0	1	1	0	5	0	4	0	13	2	10	3	9	2	7	4
4/21 (Sci & Tech)	1	0	1	0	1	0	1	0	5	1	5	1	14*	1*	7	7
4/28	1	0	1	0	3	1	3	1	11	3	9	4	10*	4*	6	6
5/5	0	1	0	1	3	0	3	0	15	2	14	2	9	4	8	5
5/12	0	1	1	0	3	0	3	0	9*	3*	8	2	11	2	5	8
5/19	1	0	1	0	3	1	2	2	13	3	9	5	10	2	4	8
5/26	1	0	1	0	3	0	1	2	7*	4*	8	2	9	2	8	4
6/2	—	—	—	—	—	—	—	—	11	4	9	6	20*	13*	3	2
6/9	1	0	1	0	2	0	2	0	13*	0	8	3	10	3	5	8
6/16	2	0	2	0	3	2	3	1	12*	3*	11	3	11	2	7	6
6/23	0	1	0	1	3	1	2	1	9	4	10	3	9	4	4	9
6/30	1	0	1	0	6	—	6	—	9	2	7	4	8	5	4	9
7/7	1	0	0	1	2	—	2	—	9	3	7	5	10*	3*	5	7
7/14	0	1	1	0	2	1	2	0	12	5	10	7	10	2	6	6
7/21	1	0	1	0	4	2	2	0	8	4	7	3	8*	6*	7	5
7/28	0	1	1	0	5	0	4	0	12*	2*	9	4	10	2	7	5
8/4	2	0	2	0	1	0	1	0	10	3	10	2	9	4	9	4
8/11	1	0	1	0	1	0	1	0	11	2	9	4	8*	5*	7	6
8/18	—	—	—	—	4	1	4	0	10**	5**	7	5	9	3	7	5
8/25	1	0	0	1	5	1	5	1	7	4	7	3	9	3	6	6
9/1	1	0	1	0	2	0	2	0	5	4	5	4	8	4	7	5
9/8	0	1	1	0	6	0	3	1	10	3	7	5	8	3	5	6
9/15	1	0	1	0	3	3	3	1	15	3	11	6	10	3	6	7
9/22	1	0	1	0	6	1	5	1	14*	4*	14	2	10*	3*	8	9
Half-year Totals	19	7	22	4	80	18	69	13	270	80	231	60	260	89	159	156
Half-Year %@	73	27	85	15	82	18	84	16	77	23	79	21	75	25	50	50

Comparisons
%@ 6 + months before women's group spoke to TBR

	84	16	72	28	82	18	78	22	74	26	73	27	75	25	55	45

%@ 3 months after women's group spoke to TBR

	75	25	92	8	79	21	77	23	80	20	75	25	77	23	50	50

%@ 6 months after women's group spoke to TBR

	73	27	85	15	82	18	84	16	77	23	79	21	75	25	50	50

*Joint male–female authorship; ** = two such works   (continued)
@Percentages rounded to the nearest whole

alter the fact that mainstream review sources which purport to cover the range of books in print, practise routine discrimination against the writing of women; and they give no indication that they are disturbed about their ethics or determined to change their ways.

Recent studies by women in different countries have revealed much the same pattern of representation as the one which emerged from the survey of

Table 4.3.
(Continued)

Poetry				Children's				Front Page Essay				Inside Essay				Bios			
Auth		Rvwr		Auth		Rvwr		Wrtr		Subj		Wrtr		Subj		Wrtr		Subj	
M	F	M	F	M	F	M	F	M	F	M	F	M	F	M	F	M	F	M	F
1	3	0	1	0	1	0	1	0	1	1	0	1	0	—	—	1	2	1	2
—	—	—	—	1	0	0	1	0	1	—	—	2	0	1	0	1	1	1	1
—	—	—	—	2**	4**	0	1	1	0	—	—	—	—	—	—	2	0	2	0
—	—	—	—	—	—	—	—	—	—	—	—	2	0	1	0	—	—	—	—
3	0	1	1	1	1	0	2	0	1	0	0	1	0	1	0	1	1	1	1
1	0	0	1	1	0	0	1	1	0	0	0	1	1	0	0	1	1	2	0
1	0	1	0	1	1	2	0	1	0	0	0	1	0	0	0	0	1	0	1
0	1	1	0	0	1	0	1	1	0	0	0	1	0	0	0	2	1	1	2
0	3	1	0	0	1	1	0	1	0	0	0	1	0	0	0	1	0	0	1
—	—	—	—	0	1	1	0	—	—	—	—	2	1	0	0	1	1	1	1
—	—	—	—	2*	1*	1	1	1	0	0	0	0	1	0	0	3	0	2	1
1	0	1	0	2	1	0	2	1	0	0	0	1	1	0	1	3	0	2	1
2	0	1	0	0	2	1	1	1	—	1	—	—	1	—	—	1	1	1	1
1	0	1	0	0	4	0	1	1	—	—	—	—	—	—	—	3	0	2	1
—	—	—	—	—	—	—	—	1	—	—	—	1	1	—	—	2	1	2	1
2	0	1	0	1	0	0	1	1	—	—	—	1	1	—	—	—	1	—	1
2	1	1	0	0	2	1	1	1	1	—	—	1	—	1	—	1	—	1	—
—	—	—	—	—	1	—	1	—	1	—	—	1	—	—	—	1	1	—	2
1	0	1	0	0	1	0	1	1	—	—	—	2	—	1	—	1	—	—	1
1	0	1	0	0	1	0	1	—	1	—	—	1	—	—	—	2	—	2	—
1	0	1	0	1	0	1	0	1	—	—	—	—	—	—	—	2	1	1	2
—	—	—	—	0	1	0	1	1	—	—	—	1	—	—	—	2	0	2	0
3	0	1	0	1	0	1	0	1	—	—	—	1	—	—	—	3	0	3	0
—	—	—	—	1	0	1	0	1	—	—	—	1	—	—	—	2	0	1	1
—	—	—	—	0	1	1	0	1	—	—	—	1	—	—	—	1	1	1	1
—	—	—	—	1	1	0	2	1	—	—	—	—	—	—	—	2	1	2	1
20	8	13	3	15	26	11	20	18	6	2	0	23	7	5	1	39	15	32	22
71	29	81	19	37	63	35	65	75	25	100	0	77	23	83	17	72	28	59	41
77	23	77	23	33	67	30	70	84	16	100	0	76	24	86	14	65	35	70	30
50	50	63	37	45	55	33	67	70	30	100	—	76	24	75	25	67	33	58	42
71	29	81	19	37	63	35	65	75	25	100	0	77	23	83	17	72	28	59	41

the *NYT Book Review*. For example, Richelle Van Snellenberg (1986) monitored the reviews in the Canadian *Globe and Mail* for March 1986 (five editions) and found that it was misleading to refer to the numbers of women and men reviewed: This was because of the popular practice of reviewing women writers en masse, a strategy which boosted the numbers but did not accurately reflect the space allocation. She cited the coverage for March 15, when there were fifteen books written by women and twelve by men in the reviews; but five of the women's books were reissues of Agatha Christie, five more were in a series on writers, and one was in the section "Book Briefs"— and ten out of the fifteen were at the bottom of the page!

In most studies of the reviews, comments are made on this practice of lumping women together as an undifferentiated mass or a specialty interest. No survey has yet found a headline "Men's Fiction" at the bottom of the page.

For Richelle van Snellenberg, positioning on the page was an important indicator of sex-bias in reviews. Her survey revealed that there were approximately ten headlines in each review edition and that in four out of the five issues studied, women received only one headline (on one occasion women received two). Women writers were generally featured in "Book Briefs" or "Paperbacks" and at the bottom of the page. And despite the emphasis on women's appearance in reviews there was only one photograph of a woman to every four of men.

In all, eighty-one books were reviewed by the *Globe and Mail* in March 1986. Twenty-nine were by women, fifty by men, and two were coauthored by a woman and a man. And the men consistently received more column inches than women with only 26.86% of the review space going to women.

In Australia, during March 1986 Lynne Spender kept a record of reviews in *The Sydney Morning Herald, The Australian*, and *The National Times* and concluded that less than one-third of the books reviewed were by women and that—because of the practice of placing women writers together—less than 20% of the column inches went to women. She found that men were the primary reviewers, that they got the prime space—and that there was more than a pronounced tendency for some of them to be hostile to women's books.

A brief survey of some of the same publications in March 1988 suggests that there has been no improvement: Indeed, if anything, the position is worse.

The findings of all these small and individual surveys are given greater weight when they are added to the data gathered by the British association, Women in Publishing. Disturbed and dissatisfied from their inception with the state of women's reviews, the association determined to be well informed when they confronted literary editors with allegations of sex-bias. By March, 1986, the Book Review Monitoring Group had been set up with the brief to survey the treatment of women as authors and reviewers in a cross-section of magazines and newspapers. Funds were raised, a research assistant was engaged and the task begun: By mid-1987, the results of the survey were published (see *Reviewing the Reviews: A Woman's Place on the Book Page*).

There is no substitute for reading this fascinating report in full, so only a few of the more salient and salutary findings are presented here. But what this report provides is indisputable evidence of the overwhelming bias

Table 4.4 Publications monitored by Women in Publishing* (12 issues of each publication during 1985: All issues of quarterlies and bi-monthlies. For *School Librarian* the figures are based on reviews featured in the section for 11–15 age group. Circulation figures taken from Benn's Directory)

	Circulation	No. of Reviews Seen
LITERARY		
Fiction Magazine	—	39
Literary Review	7,000	436
London Review of Books	15,000	350
The Times Literary Supplement	28,833	650
EDUCATION		
School Librarian	5,000	138
The Times Higher Education Supplement	15,285	325
NEWSPAPERS		
Daily Telegraph	1,156,304	266
Financial Times	251,554	135
Guardian	524,264	197
Mail on Sunday	1,616,860	28
Observer	778,207	453
Sunday Times	1,149,116	293
The Times	471,483	160
GENERAL		
City Limits	27,415	127
Listener	33,277	140
New Society	23,013	135
New Statesman	28,375	171
Punch	65,041	66
Spectator	25,636	107
SOCIALIST		
Marxism Today	7,500	73
New Socialist	24,232	53
WOMEN'S		
Company	207,860	76
Cosmopolitan	391,533	76
Good Housekeeping	351,655	64
Options	225,974	112
She	210,935	162
Spare Rib	30,000	63
Woman and Home	568,938	93

*All findings available in Women and Publishing, 1987 *Reviewing the Reviews*, Journeyman Press, London.

against women in *general* publications which purport to provide *general* reviews. (If these publications were to state that they were *male*, they would not attract the same criticism.)

Twenty-eight publications were reviewed (see Table 4.4): seven women's magazines and twenty-one "general" publications. But as Women in Publishing comment

... Out of these 28, it is in the women's magazines, and the women's magazines only, that the female author is the star turn. On the review pages of these
seven publications, the spot light is turned on her. In all the other 21 publications she is left in the shadows while the male author takes centre stage.
(Women in Publishing, 1987: p. 9)

The same story all over again: It's men who get the lion's share of reviews.
These twenty-one general publications may encompass a diversity of political
positions and literary purposes but they share a common denominator when
it comes to the status of males in their reviews. They all have a clear preference for the male author:

... whether they are to the left or the right of the political spectrum, a quality
Sunday newspaper or a literary magazine, devoted to humour or education,
their book sections are concerned mainly with reviewing books by men. They
may be aimed for a general (i.e. mixed sex) readership, but to some extent all of
the 21 could be called "men's" publications. (Women in Publishing, 1987: p.
10)

Calculating review width to within one-sixteenth of an inch, and review
length to one quarter, the Book Monitoring Group found that no matter
which dimension they focussed on, in the twenty-one 'men's' publications,
women got precious few reviews. They got less space overall, and less space
than their publication rate warranted.

As has been noted earlier, one of the thorny problems which Women in
Publishing addressed was that of ascertaining the relationship between
women's rate of publications and women's rate of reviews. In her communications with the *NYT Book Review* Marilyn French acknowledged that a
cursory examination of publishers' catalogues (March 1985) revealed that
men's publications outnumbered those of women, the ratio being approximately 65% to 35%: One of her complaints was, of course, that as women
did not receive anywhere near 35% of the review space, the *NYT Book
Review* was helping to construct even greater underrepresentation of women
in literary circles. But Women in Publishing took this line of reasoning further
when they tried to establish the overall publication rates for the sexes, in
Britain in 1985. Their representative sampling of the *British National Bibliography* for that year revealed that 18% of the published authors were women
and 51% were men—(the remaining publications were written by those of
"unknown sex").

Of *specialist* books, 5% were written by women; of *general* books women
wrote 25%; and when it came to fiction (12% of the books published)
women were the *major* writers—with a rate of 58%. (Men wrote 38% of the
fiction published in Britain in 1985; again, 4% of the books were authored by
those whose sex is unknown.)

These figures are extremely useful because they provide a basis for assessing the bias against women in reviews, in relation to the number of women's books printed. So, for example, while a 5% review rate of specialist books could represent a fair and proportionate coverage given that women are the authors of only 5% of specialist books, a 30% review rate in fiction would represent an unfair and disproportionate coverage given that women are the authors of almost 60% of the fiction.

And, of course, as Women in Publishing discovered, women writers don't begin to get close to realising such extensive coverage in either specialist fields, or fiction. "Women may write more fiction than men, but this is not reflected in an overwhelming majority of the 'men's' publications," comment Women in Publishing. "Instead," they continue, "remaining true to their favourite author, they run more reviews of men's fiction" (p. 28).

But even with this enormous bias against women in reviews of fiction, the cruel irony is that women writers of fiction are more likely to be reviewed than women writers of non-fiction. The smallest space (at times to the point of non-existence) is allocated to women who do not write fiction—and this leaves women's non-fiction as the biggest loser in the reviews. While the *Sunday Times*, for example, prefers to review non-fiction (60%)—it also prefers male reviews (just on 70%): Where women are reviewed it is almost always as writers of fiction. As Women in Publishing note, "This is one male-oriented newspaper that has pigeon-holed women authors into a fiction slot" (p. 29) and which "leaves the female writer of non-fiction even more marginalised" (p. 29).

Given all this information on the massive sex bias against women in reviews—and the data are clear, comprehensive, and highly provocative—one of the issues that arises from these fascinating findings is the nature of the response of literary editors and reviewers. And this is where the report of Women in Publishing returns to the point at which this chapter begins—with the perceptions of "a fair share" for women in a society that accords preferential treatment to men.

In *Reviewing the Reviews*, Women in Publishing found that the editors whose pages reflected the greatest sex bias were often the ones who were most emphatic about the fairness of their own practices—and the ones who were most convinced that any examination of these practices was not only impertinent, but absurd. The literary editors of some of the major "general" publications—which they declared were directed towards a mixed sex readership—were not only at times the greatest offenders but the ones who were adamant that no sex bias could be found within their pages, that they were interested only in good books and in satisfying the needs of their audience—and that any suggestion to the contrary was simply churlish. It was this marked discrepancy between philosophy and practice that led Women in Publishing to further exploration—and explanation. As they comment:

... It was not particularly surprising, for instance, that the *Financial Times*, which might be expected to have the most specialised readership of all papers, did in fact come near the bottom of the table of women authors (15%). But for all their specialised readership (and awareness of bias!) they still featured more female reviewers than the *Sunday Times* or the *Guardian* and more books written by women than the *Mail on Sunday*. David Holloway, the literary editor of the *Daily Telegraph* who stated quite blithely, "At a guess I should have thought I use as many men as women reviewers ... but I am certainly not going to bother to count", comes out with a score of 21%. (Women in Publishing 1987: p. 58)

As is so often the case in a male-dominated society, any space allocation of up to about one-third (in an area which men want for themselves) is judged as being "a fair share" for women, and any questioning of this arrangement is righteously resented. But there are no groups which have immunity from this sexist bias: Indeed, it is sometimes those who could have been expected to be the most "liberated" who turn out to be the most unreasonable and insist on their distorted perceptions.[9] And I'm not just referring to "loving husbands" or Marxist men—although both categories may be well represented within the realm of reviews. In the British newspaper world, the *Guardian* is generally accepted as being the most "progressive" national daily and the one which could be presumed to be committed to the principle of sex-equality, but as the Women in Publishing report reveals, it would be very misleading to assume that this is what happens on its review pages:

The *Guardian*, surprisingly, reflects probably the greatest discrepancy between philosophy and reality. Their fiction is reviewed by a regular panel which includes one woman and three men who review on a rotational basis. They firmly believe that there is no discrimination and, what is more, if there were they would hear about it.[10] In fact, only 18% of the books they review are by women and they foot the table of reviewers with only 9% women. (Women in Publishing, 1987: p. 58)

There is no evidence that the position is changing: not even that it's under review. On the contrary there is a growing conviction among some literary editors that women are now getting so much more than their fair share that tough measures are called for if men are to *regain* their proper place on the literary pages!

Clearly there is an enormous amount of work yet to be done in relation to women's reviews. There is a demonstrable need for further research, and, as the evidence of the existence of inequality is not in itself sufficient to promote change, there is a further need to form pressure groups, to conduct

---

[9]Claire Tomalin was the literary editor of the *Sunday Times* at a period when its bias against women writers was very marked.
[10]They have certainly heard about it from me and from numerous other women over the last five years.

campaigns—and to establish woman-controlled review publications where women's books can obtain a fair hearing. For, as Women in Publishing conclude:

> Our research shows that the number of books by women reviewed across the whole range of publications covered—does not necessarily reflect the percentage of books written by women published, that books by women are treated erratically (depending on the nature of the publication and, more significantly, the literary editor's view of his or her readership), and that they are not subject to the same criteria for evaluation as books by men. (Women in Publishing, 1987: p. 49)

One persistent problem which I have not pursued here, however, is that of which sex does the reviewing, and with what consequences for the reviewed, and the primary reason for this "omission" is the abundance of conflicting opinion on the topic. Of course it is clear that men in the main are the reviewers, and it is equally clear that if this situation were reversed—so that male authors were likely to be assessed by female reviewers—men would be the first to mount an indignant protest against the injustice of the arrangement. Which is why women can insist on the necessity of a *single standard* and argue that the goose should enjoy the same advantages as the gander. But this raises another perplexing issue—of whether women authors should find it preferable to be assigned women reviewers.

Such a practice would at least eliminate some of the emotional diatribes delivered by men who are trying to protect what they see as their property from a "takeover" by women, but it wouldn't necessarily usher in a more equitable era for the woman writer. Women too are products of the male-dominated society: Women reviewers have been schooled in the very same institutions and in the very same values as men and can be just as "prejudiced against women" as Philip Goldberg (1974) suggested. And—bitter though the acknowledgement may be—feminists also have to come to terms with the fact that there have been feminist reviews and feminist critiques that have been predicated on one rule for women and another for men—and where it hasn't been the women who have benefited.[11] As Margaret Atwood has said:

> . . . I believe there is still a tendency for reviewers of all kinds—including women and even feminists, to be somewhat harder on women writers. I think that feminists sometimes expect more from women: I mean from men, what can you expect? (Margaret Atwood, 1985: p. 152)

And this is by no means the end of the problem. There are women writers now who object to the classification *woman writer* on the grounds that their work is ghettoised in such a frame of reference (see particularly Elaine Showalter, 1984, "Women Who Write Are Women"): Think how intensified

---

[11]This is one of the underlying premises of *For The Record*, (Dale Spender, 1985).

their protests would be if a movement to have women writers reviewed solely by women were initiated! As there are also literary men who would be delighted to have women's writing kept separate, to have it excluded from their territory (even contained on a "woman's page") there is some justification for the stand that the position of women would not be improved if women writers were assigned exclusively to women reviewers—no matter how helpful such a strategy was intended to be. As Margaret Atwood has said of her own experience—and research:

> The books written by women that were reviewed were more likely to be assigned to a female reviewer. I think that in the seventies some editors assigning reviews thought it was a gesture in the direction of the women's movement to have women reviewing books by women, but it had a ghettoizing effect sometimes. I am often asked to review books, and for a while I was never asked to review a book by a man. Finally I had to say: "What is this? Am I supposed to be incapable of reading books by men?" I think it should go both ways. (Margaret Atwood, 1985: p. 151)

When it comes to reviews there are no simple solutions: From the process to the prejudices practised, the system is a source of much dissatisfaction. But one of the claims that can be made is that the area is underresearched despite the fact that it is of great influence and interest. Were "literary studies" to be extended so that they encompassed not just an appreciation of "great books" but an analysis of how they were made great, and by whom, there is no doubt in my mind that the discipline would soon be revitalised and would assume importance and relevance for many students.

Such a discipline could even begin to "deconstruct" some of the distortions it has generated about the authorship of women. One of its first priorities could be to look at how and why so few women's books become the subject of review, how and why women's books are allocated so little space. No doubt research in this area would reveal that the literary editors who selected so few women's books to review didn't have to read the many women's contributions submitted—to know they were no good.

5

Education: Learning
Literary Housework

So far, the primary focus of this study has been the extent to which males have been disproportionately successful as the professional writers, critics, and reviewers: So far, information from a variety of sources suggests that the success of males in these areas is not necessarily a measure of their writing skill, but part of the projected pattern of male supremacy. And, of course, it would be both convenient and convincing if, across the range of social institutions in which writing ability is relevant, the principle which operates is—"males do it better, no matter what they write."

But it seems that no such claim can be made. For there is one context in which the established pattern of male writing supremacy is fundamentally challenged. It is in *education*—where the success rates of the sexes are dramatically reversed: In educational institutions in the western world, it is girls who are routinely rated as the better writers.

The educational truth is that from primary school pupils to post-graduate students, it is females who are considered more competent writers—and readers (see Janet White, 1986), and it is this seemingly extraordinary educational reality which gives rise to some fascinating questions. For how can educational truth be in such direct conflict with the social reality? As Janet White asks—why is it that females can do so well at reading and writing in educational institutions and yet so few of them "make it to positions of power based on the strength of their apparent giftedness, their facility with written language?" (1986: p. 561)

This disjuncture between educational writing and writing in the wider world, this complete reversal in the perceived aptitudes of the sexes, introduces a new set of interesting issues—some of them associated with the role and reliability of educational theory and practice. What does this discrepancy signify in relation to what we know about writing and gender: Why has this problem not been given greater prominence and attracted more research attention?

The starting point for addressing these new questions is to draw on some of the understandings already generated in relation to writing and gender—namely that of determining whether it is indeed the writing, or the sex, that is being measured in educational institutions. The fact that educationalists may regularly test the abilities of the sexes, and readily assert that females are the better students, does not automatically make it so: After all, another educational "truth" has just toppled in the light of this evidence.

For years, educationalists have blithely asserted that there is a high correlation between educational achievement and occupational level: But, of course, such a finding is based entirely upon the experience of men. For women, who perform unpaid labour in the home, or who have poorly paid, or part-time or "dead-end" jobs in the workforce—*regardless of their educational achievements*—the assertion that educational and occupational level are linked has always been patently false. Not that the fact that this assertion is but a *half* truth has inhibited its use in educational circles.

An exhaustive documentation of educational theories and practices which accord higher status to female readers and writers, hardly seems necessary: Anyone who has passed through the system is familiar with the extent to which females are depicted as the superior *scribes*. In her own study of primary schools in Britain, Janet White found that girls were considered so good at writing that it was their work which was literally—"the writing on the wall":

> . . . it is girls written work which is frequently displayed in books, or used to ornament the classroom walls; girls are the obvious choice when it comes to writing on blackboards, in registers, for copying letters or programmes for parents etc. (Janet White, 1986: p. 561)

Girls are held to be neater, cleaner, their work more legible: In terms of the technicalities of writing they are invariably awarded first prize. In contrast, the technicalities of reading and writing are presented as problematic for many boys. Not only is it rare for boys to be rated as "copperplate writers," they are not ordinarily expected to be voracious, versatile, or virtuoso readers: Boys are the majority of remedial reading students throughout the entire education system.

There is, of course, the question of whether even these crude measurements are accurate—or whether they are the product of sex-stereotyping and expectation. It is as well to remember the power of sex-stereotyping to distort language perception (see Cheris Kramer/Kramarae, 1977) so that males, for example, can be rated as more forceful speakers—*regardless of their performance*. If it is firmly believed in educational circles that it is more appropriate for girls to be engaged in sedentary activities, and that as a result they are better scribes, it is also possible for girls to be rated as better educational writers—*regardless of their performance*. That sex stereotyping and expectation play a crucial role in constructing the differing literary abilities of the sexes was a point made by Anne Lee (1980) when she found reading teachers transmitting their anxieties about boys' reading capacity and interests to their male students: Behaving as if boys would find reading difficult was almost guaranteed to produce reading difficulties in boys.

This is not to suggest that the writing skills of girls (or the reading deficiencies of boys) are all the figments of teacher imagination or the creations of teacher expectation; but it is to suggest that we know next to nothing that is reliable about the nature of sex differences in reading and writing. It is to suggest that in education—as in the wider world—it could be that teachers don't have to read girls' writing to know it's good, or conversely they don't have to hear boys read to know that they have problems.

But this would still not explain why teachers *reverse* the double standard— why educational writing and reading appear to be the only literary fields that afford female advantage.

However there is yet another area where education differs from some of the practices of the outside world—in its penchant for holding tests and producing statistics. Whereas in publishing and reviewing it has been necessary for women to start from scratch to determine the female success rate, educational institutions regularly release marks, grades, numbers, and the like, which attest to the superior writing ability of the female sex. But of course, even in this context the critical questions remain—*what* is being tested, and how reliable is the measurement?

For example, one of the most extensive projects undertaken on writing and gender has been that of the British Assessment Performance Unit: Since 1979, the writing performance of 11–15 year olds in England, Northern Ireland, and Wales, has been surveyed twice yearly, with approximately 4,500 pupils involved on each occasion.[1] There are multiple tasks, a dual system of marks (impression and analysis assessment), and the work is examined along five dimensions by a panel of practising teachers. To Janet White—who is working on this project to test the claim that girls are better writers—this multifaceted method of assessment is important:

> . . . I stress this point because it is sometimes assumed that judgements about the merits of a piece of writing are hopelessly clouded in subjectivity or at any rate, lacking an "objective criterion" . . . If one then goes on to claim that girls happen to do well at writing, the rejoinder can often be dismissive of the presumed lack of hard "evidence" . . . (Janet White, 1986: p. 563)

---

[1] 12,000 pupils have been tested each time across a range of language activities.

On the basis of this complex and controlled marking methodology we are informed that girls are better writers than boys, and after all the reassurances that have been given, I cast no doubts on the *consistency* of the findings. But I do want to know whether in this case (and most other educational examples) the markers knew the sex of the writers: Without such information I *do* cast doubts on the authenticity of the differences that have been documented between the sexes.

After all, when the ostensible sex of the writer was given, Philip Goldberg (1974) found that the writing attributed to John T. McKay was rated as much more impressive than that attributed to Joan T. McKay so that the sex difference was consistent: But as it was the same piece of writing that was being evaluated in each case, the sex difference was also empirically non-existent! And there's no reason to assume that the markers in the Assessment Performance Unit are any more immune from sex bias than the rest of society, or their counterparts in Philip Goldberg's sample. If the scripts in the British Survey were not sex-blind, the finding that girls are better writers than boys could well have little to do with the writing—and a lot to do with the writers' sex: The results could be more a measurement of the sex-stereotyped perception of the markers than an accurate representation of differences in the writing of the sexes.

Such a research failure, while astonishing, is not beyond the bounds of possibility for there have been many precedents. There have been many foolish and fallacious findings in education—particularly in relation to literacy skills. Margaret Meek (1977) for example, discredited the entire remedial reading industry and all its elaborate research procedures when she simply pointed out that it derived its knowledge of reading from studying those who could not read! By focusing on those who had problems—and in the process ignoring those who arrived at the school gate already able to read—she suggested that educationalists had constructed a mistaken and misleading body of knowledge. It could be appropriate to make comparable criticisms about studies or writing and gender: It would be equally absurd to conduct research on sex differences in writing without testing for the significance and status of sex.

But whether the sex of the author was or was not known in the British Assessment Performance Unit project, there are still serious issues to address: Either way there are implications for understandings about writing and gender. Because if the scripts *were* sex blind, if girls were getting a fair hearing and were *legitimately being judged as superior*, then the poor representation of women as professional writers, critics, reviewers, and the like is all the more significant. For this would mean that not only were women underrepresented in those areas which depend upon writing skill—it would mean that the best writers were being excluded.

While the data lend themselves to a variety of interpretations, we are still left with a fundamental problem: How can we explain the good grades that girls get for educational writing—and their poor positioning in the professional world? If the fault lies not in the measurement, could it be that there is something wrong with what is being measured? This question ushers in an entirely new set of considerations.

To argue that because girls do well at educational writing they should then do well at professional writing is to *assume* that there is a connection, if not an overlap, between these two literary forms. And, of course, such an assumption could be quite erroneous. For it could be that the sort of writing which is valued in educational institutions—and at which girls excel—might have no currency outside the classroom walls. There wouldn't even be a discrepancy between girls' performance inside and outside the classroom if this evaluation of educational writing were to be accepted.

And this evaluation of educational writing is not without its supporters. It's not hard to find allegations that "educational English" is a specialised and superficial language form where the emphasis is placed on presentational features—on neatness and technical correctness; and more, that these skills are the very opposite to those that are required and rewarded in creative literary circles. That girls' writing is "on the wall"—in Janet White's terms—is precisely because it is pleasing in its surface structure, that it looks good and meets the narrowly defined technical standards.

Just in case there are any doubts about the form of writing that is valued within education, Janet White quotes from the reports of examiners who set the literary standards and are responsible for the awards:

> . . . the problems were the same as ever. The use of commas in the place of full stops in the mistaken belief that long sentences look better than short ones; the muddling of plurals and possessives with a totally arbitrary use of the apostrophe; the switching of first to third person narrative; quite arbitrary changes of tense; poor punctuation of speech; indentation, as if for paragraphs, mechanically inserted after a number of sentences had been written but these paragraphs revealing no corporate theme but rather a multitude of diverse thoughts. (West Midlands Examinations Board, 1979, quoted in Janet White, 1986: p. 566)

Clearly, James Joyce—not to mention Dorothy Richardson, Gertrude Stein, and even Virginia Woolf—would be candidates for failure in educational English.

But if educationalists have now become overly concerned with the mechanics, and bogged down in the technicalities of literacy, so that there is little or no connection between educational literary success, and literary achievement in the wider community, this is not the way it has always been. Despite the repeated calls from some sections of society for a return to the tried and true methods of old, to the drilling of punctuation, grammar, and other forms of "correct usage," it seems that such separate and specific skills did not receive such central attention when the model of literary education was at its height. There was a time when "men of letters" were presumed to be familiar with "letters," in every sense of the word, when there were no great divisions between form and content: These men were expected to be technically competent with commas and apostrophes, for example, and at the same time highly creative and well read, as Janet Batsleer et al. (1985) have pointed out in their book, *Rewriting English: Cultured Politics of Class and Gender*. In it the authors argue that educational English as we now know it depends on the relatively recent distinction that has been made between *literature* and *literacy*, a distinction which would not have been understood in the eighteenth century, even though that period made a considerable contribution to the contemporary model of education. For when only a privileged few were provided with a "literary education" it implied training in literary process: It included familiarity with Latin and the works of Milton, Pope, and other "classical" authors, as well as ease of personal communication. But since that time, *literature* and *literacy* have been severed and have gone their separate and narrow ways, so that literature "has shrunk to its now severely contracted and specialised range of meanings" (p. 14), and is markedly different from the more technically oriented "literacy," the more common concern of temporary education:

> . . . By the twentieth century, literacy has come more and more to denote things like spelling, punctuation, simple grammar—the elementary rules and rituals of a standardized official language called "English." It has tended to become, too, a narrowly educational matter . . . (Janet Batsleer et al., 1985: p. 14)

And this is what girls are good at!

There is considerable evidence that educational English can be a much despised activity. But given its lowly status it is a language form in which girls are held to excel. And if it is a form of writing that does not count in the creative/professional world, there is no longer any puzzle about the pattern of women's literary employment. Despite their good grades at educational English, women are absent from those areas where it is presumed that creative writing ability is desirable or necessary—because they lack the job qualifications.

So there are few women to be found in the top jobs in academe, in publishing, literary criticism, or even journalism. Janet White states that the place of women in these literary occupations is not as writers, but as *helpers*, as secretaries, editorial assistants, copy editors:

> . . . Writing skills are also involved in advertising, but although women consumers are the target for the majority of advertisements, only about 1 in 6 account executives are women, and about 1 in 5, copy writers. Women are present as behind the scene researchers, and ubiquitous typists/secretaries in all these fields. (Janet White, 1986: p. 562)

And here's the rub. What if women are working at the precise occupations for which their education has fitted them? What if their "English education" has been to prepare them to be the handmaidens of literary men? Is it possible that women have been trained to excel in technical correctness so that they can do all the maintenance work on men's "creative" contributions? Janet White gets close to declaring that women have to perform all the literary "shitwork" which great and gifted men—in top jobs!—cannot or will not do.

> Considering the disparity between women's early achievements in literacy and their subsequent paid employment, we need to ask why it is that thousands of able girl writers leave school and go into secretarial jobs, in the course of which they will patiently revise and type the semi-literate manuscripts of their male bosses, or else return in droves to the primary classroom, there to supervise the production of another generation of penwise girls. (Janet White, 1986: p. 562)

Once again, the parallels with the spoken word are striking. In analysing the relationship of women to men in mixed sex speech, Pamela Fishman (1977) declared that women were supposed to be good at the art of conversation—where the art of conversation was getting men to talk. In analysing the relationship of women to men with regard to writing, it is not too much to suggest that women are supposed to be good at the art of writing—where the art of writing is putting a man in print!

It was Pamela Fishman, too, who argued that women were developing the conversational topics of men at the expense of their own, and again the parallels with literary practices are pronounced: Female secretaries, editorial assistants, copy editors, etc. are developing the contributions of men at the expense of their own. They are enhancing the reputations of their bosses, putting their energy into creating the image of male expertise, often denying their own needs, interests, and aptitudes in the process.

My own research on mixed-sex conversations has revealed the ever-ready willingness of women to "rescue" men whose speech is silly, sordid, or simply embarrassing (see Sally Cline and Dale Spender, 1986: pp. 7–16). Even when the men are strangers, women can still be prepared to sacrifice their own space and topics to "save the face of a man." Is this so different from the secretary who revises/rewrites her bosses' less-than-perfect, and sometimes illiterate correspondence and communications?

And what about the shitwork? This is the term Pamela Fishman used to illustrate the role that women were required to play in mixed-sex conversations. She drew on the understandings about women's place in the home—where women are responsible for the shitwork, all the routine and invisible chores that keep the home functioning—and suggested that women's place in conversations was not very different. In both contexts, she argued, women are expected to "service" men, and in the main, their workload goes unacknowledged and unappreciated. The only time their effort is noted is when they stop: Then the home ceases to function, the conversation comes to an end.

It is the energy and the skill of women which maintain conversations, Pamela Fishman insists, and her thesis can be readily substantiated (see Sally Cline and Dale Spender, 1986: pp. 7–16). Again the similarities with the secretarial role are striking. Women do the maintenance work on the scripts of men, the routine, invisible chores that keep communication flowing. Their work goes unacknowledged and unappreciated—but would be noted immediately if they stopped!

To place such an interpretation on one of the few areas of excellence that women have been allowed in education can be greatly discomforting. To entertain the possibility that women's education—including their writing achievements—have been but the perfect preparation for their subservient and servicing place in a literate society, can be even more distressing. Yet the implications cannot be avoided: The extent to which women's emotional and creative labour—as well as women's physical labour—can be appropriated by men, is discussed at length in the second part of this volume, particularly in the chapter "Polish, Plagiarism, and Plain Theft." But the extent to which education paves the way for this theft of women's intellectual and creative resources (see Katherine Clarricoates, 1978), is very much the subject of this chapter.

Feminist research suggests that teachers of both sexes (and of all class and ethnic backgrounds and all political persuasions) share much the same value system and practise much the same implicit "cultural code" as all other members of society. As such they help to "construct" the apparent supremacy of boys, and the secondary status of girls across numerous dimensions. While it is not possible here to undertake a comprehensive résumé of research in the area, it is possible to focus on salient findings, to provide an elaboration of the premise that teachers favour male students, and to give an indication of some of the repercussions of this practise.

* Teachers spend more time with boys (see Dale Spender, 1982(b) and forthcoming).
* Teachers know more about the identities and interests of the boys (see Michelle Stanworth, 1981).
* Teachers gear their lessons to interest and extend boys (see Katherine Clarricoates, 1978).

Understandably, there's not a lot of funded/mainstream research in this critical area. But since Mary Wollstonecraft wrote her brilliant treatise on women's education in 1792 (Vindication of the Rights of Woman) and Virginia Woolf wrote her illuminating exposé of men's education in 1938 (Three Guineas), women have been analysing the contribution made by education to the *creation* of sex inequality. The results are damning: And, as in so many other areas, the knowledge that women have generated challenges much of the received wisdom.

For example, given the widespread belief that males are reasonable rather than emotional, it is somewhat ironic to find women's research focussing on concern for the feelings of men as a major problem: Teachers ordinarily assume that boys are more sensitive! So it is more of an issue if a boy loses face, if his ego is bruised, or his feelings hurt. As in the wider society, the underlying consideration of much educational practice hinges on protecting male feelings and preserving a positive male image.

However, there is an enormous amount of ethnographic data available[2] which helps to reveal the double standard, whereby teachers set the scene for the development of the differential status of the sexes: Almost any record of mixed sex classroom behaviour can help to show the way that teachers "programme" girls to believe that they and their skills are secondary, and that boys deserve first place.

In education, as in other institutions, sex can dictate the allocation of resources, and there can be no doubt about the basic belief that boys are entitled to more of them. For example just as they get more *space* on the book pages, so too do males get more space in educational institutions: They take up more space in classrooms and they are granted more space in relation to playing fields. Just as they are credited with being the better writers in the wider community and attract more resources, so too are males assumed to be the better students and worthy of more support in mixed-sex educational institutions.

Even where boys do badly, the explanation can be advanced that the results belie their real abilities, that they were misjudged—or unlucky—but that future tests would vindicate them. Aware that it was not the mathematics *mark*, but the *sex* of the mathematician that could be the influential factor in determining assessments of ability, Elizabeth Fennema (1987) pointed out that a high price was being paid for the educational treatment of boys as "bright" and girls as "deficient."

In a mathematical equivalent to Philip Goldberg's study of the written word, Elizabeth Fennema looked at what happened when the *same* mathematics mark was given to the different sexes. That there was one rule for women and another for men was obvious when entirely different constructions were placed on the same mark, depending on whether it was that of a female or a male. Regardless of the mark, boys were presumed to be better. A good mark for a boy and all was well: This was affirmation of proper world

---

[2]Virtually any realistic description of mixed sex classroom practices or record of behaviour, can serve as such a data base.

order. A bad mark? Well, he would do better next time: Poor performance was not allowed to interfere with the premise that boys are more proficient.

And the same "good mark" for a girl? Well, it was likely to be attributed to luck, to be held to belie her *true* ability. No doubt she would be caught out next time—and turn in a poor performance. A bad mark for a girl was, of course, the right result, the one which affirmed the correct world order. By such means are females cast in the role of helpmeet to men. Even where there is empirical evidence of equality it can be used differentially to teach men to trust their own judgement, and to teach females to distrust theirs!

Whether the resources are psychological or physical, the rationale persists that boys should receive more of them; whether the boys' records are good or bad, they are used to support the claim for greater consideration for males. When they are poor achievers then clearly there is a need for more resources to help improve male performance—hence remedial reading programmes; when they are high achievers then clearly they deserve enriched courses—so that those who do best are entitled to the most education. The only rule which seems to apply is that no matter the case that is presented, the result is that boys are given more resources.

I have personal experience of this educational principle that boys are entitled to the lion's share—and more. When my own research in classrooms revealed that teachers spent significantly more time with the boys, the remedies suggested by some eminent male educationalists were almost enough to make me abandon all hopes of ever achieving equity (or witnessing reason) in the system. The explanation that these men offered for the fact that boys made too great a demand on the teachers' time was that boys had difficulties in listening: Remedial listening classes were recommended! So, confronted with the problem that teachers spent too much time with boys, the imaginative solution put forward by these educational experts was—they should spend more.

There's virtually no end to the evidence that exists of the sexual double standard that intellectually endows boys and robs girls. In 1980–81, for example, with Elizabeth Sarah, I undertook research for the Equal Opportunities Commission in Britain which was designed—among other things—to explore the issue of sex bias in teacher training.[3] Because education was seen as a means of promoting sex equality—and because teachers were assumed to be the agents who would accomplish such a change—it seemed logical to assess teacher aptitude for transformation. As one of the many "exercises," trainee teachers were presented with a report card which was deliberately

---

[3]See Dale Spender and Elizabeth Sarah, 1981, "An Investigation of the Implications of Courses on Sex Discrimination in Teacher Education," Unpublished, Equal Opportunities Commission Report.

ambiguous, not just in relation to English ability, but also in terms of mathematics and science: While it was the same report, however, half had the name *Jane* Smith on them, and the other half were ostensibly reports on the performance of *John* Smith. The trainee teachers were then asked what "career" advice they would give to the student on the basis of the report card.

And the response revealed that it was not the rating but the sex which dictated the career advice.[4]

The following is the entry for English that the report card contained:

Shows aptitude. Obviously reads texts and benefits from it. Comes to terms with basic issues. Could pay more attention to detail—instead of broad sweeps. (Dale Spender, 1984(a): p. 135)

On the basis of this (and comparably ambiguous assessments in other subjects) the difference in the advice handed out to Jane and John is quite astonishing.

Underlying the comments that the trainee teachers made about Jane was the implication that poor performance was her fault. There were statements about the need for her to work harder and to be better organised. Career recommendations included public relations and secretarial work, and most respondents made reference to Jane's need for social contacts and the opportunity to talk to friends. Some concluded that she probably wouldn't stay long at school.

But no one saw Jane as having a future career which utilised mathematics or science, even though the report-card entry was open to the interpretation that she had ability in these areas.

The response to John is striking in contrast. First of all, the comments are much longer—they take up more space as trainee-teachers (of both sexes) spend more time on the boy and show more concern for his success and his future career. Secondly, and very interestingly, poor performance can be perceived as the teacher's fault, particularly in mathematics and science. So John needs "extra help," some "personal attention"; the ambiguity in the statement of his abilities has been interpreted to mean that he has potential but "suspect his teachers don't understand him."

And whereas the conclusion can be reached that Jane could soon leave school, the same report supplies the evidence that John has a great future, to the point where he "would probably do very well in the Civil Service." Even his language ability puts him on a higher plane than Jane: That *he* gets on well with people takes him into the Civil Service to manage personnel, but that *she* gets on well with people takes her into receptionist work where she can chat with her friends.

---

[4]This study has been written up as Dale Spender, 1984(a), "Sexism in Teacher Education" in Sandra Acker and David Warren Piper, *Is Higher Education Fair to Women?* pp. 132–142.

But of course the greatest concern is reserved for John's achievements in mathematics and science where the assumption is that he is "bright," "able," and "could do anything," providing that he gets the proper education to develop his potential.

What to do? As far as I know, there is no extensive or impressive body of literature in existence which systematically explores the *effects* of this theft of girls' ability—but then it isn't necessary to be a genius to have some idea of the contribution that it makes to the construction of sex inequality—and the belief that when boys put their hand to it, they are the more talented writers. If, regardless of the empirical evidence, teachers believe that boys are brighter and can do everything better—including writing, publishing, critiquing, and reviewing—then education can be said to be preparing girls to provide supportive services for men. In conversation and creative activities, Katherine Clarricoates certainly thinks this is what teachers and education are doing.

In her interviews with primary school teachers in the North of England, she recorded the following comments which help to suggest just how much more able teachers believe boys to be:

> . . . I like doing subjects like geography and I do find that this is the area where the lads do come out . . . they have got the scientific facts, they've got some geographical facts whereas the girls tend to be a bit more woolier in most of the things . . .
>
> They (girls) haven't got the imagination that most of the lads have got. I find you can spark the boys a bit easier than you can the girls.
>
> Girls have got their own set ideas, its always " . . . and we went home for tea" and "Mum and Dad were there" and "we all lived happily ever after . . . " whereas you can get the boys to write something really interesting and there's nothing like " . . . and we all went home for tea . . . " you know this sort of thing . . .
>
> Boys seem to want more exciting projects to do than girls, whereas girls will fall in with most things . . . (Katherine Clarricoates, 1978: p. 357)

The conviction of literary critics and literary reviewers, of publishers and academics, that males are the genuine audience, that their views and values are inherently more interesting and that it is only fair that they should enjoy greater recognition, is one which could well have been cultivated within educational institutions. And it is one which continues to be taught. So even where females make a major intellectual/creative contribution, their efforts are devalued or denied on no other grounds than that they are the works of women.

Katherine Clarricoates found that there were many teachers who discounted the competency/correctness/creativity of girls. She encountered teachers who readily volunteered the information that girls could not be

given credit for getting certain things "right" because after all, it was expected of them and was no great achievement (1978: p. 358).

Many of the teacher comments I have recorded (and customs I have observed) reflect the same value system. Again and again I have had teachers
discount neatness/presentation/care with detail, in the work of girls, yet be
delighted to award more marks to boys when they think have made a minimal
effort to be neat. When I have questioned this double standard, I have almost
always been told that it's *easy* for girls to be neat, to spend a lot of time on
their assignments and to hand in artistic projects, and it's not appropriate to
praise work which is relatively effortless. But—as with writing and reading—
it's much more difficult for boys to produce neat, tidy, well-planned and
presented assignments, so it is important to give them every encouragement:
Because they find such tasks so hard, they should be rewarded for the
slightest effort.

Katherine Clarricoates was outraged by such an attitude: She insisted that
this teacher denial of the "capacity of girls to be better behaved, more
conscientious, cleaner and neater in all aspects of work and conduct" was
nothing other than "the wholesale theft of true intellectual development in
favour of boys" (1978: p. 358). I completely agree. But I see no simple way of
putting an end to this pernicious form of discrimination. For not only is it
firmly entrenched and blatantly practised but many members of the teaching
(and literary) professions can see nothing wrong with it when confronted
with the evidence that they routinely behave in this manner.

I thought it was bad enough when in regular classroom observations in a
mixed-sex Inner London Comprehensive I found two teachers (one female,
one male) who explicitly gave boys more marks for "neatness" while un-
ashamedly acknowledging that the work of the girls was obviously much
neater. But when both then went on to award more marks to the untidy but
creative work of boys, I was stunned. I pointed out to these teachers that
either way, boys were getting better marks—whether their work was tidy or
untidy. But they found nothing problematic in my description of their
marking standards, and were quite perplexed as to what I was on about. The
following were among some of the "justifications" they gave for their professional practices—all freely delivered without a hint of embarrassment:

> But you can see with this one—it's not just untidiness as you call it. It's about
> his ability. His pen just doesn't keep up with what he wants to get out. Now
> compare it with this one (the girl). Yes, it's tidy, all very neat, but nothing else.
> It's got no depth to it. His is worth much more than hers, though you're right
> hers looks good.
>
> This is the one. Look at the effort he's made with these headings. You can
> see he's really tried. And he's got the substance too. There's no doubt about it,
> when a boy decides to do it properly, he's streets ahead of the girl.

> Yes. It's good. So good it could have been copied out of an encyclopaedia.
> You can see those drawings are traced too. It's not original, that's all.

So boys' writing doesn't have to be neat to be good. It doesn't even have to contain direct evidence of quality to be accorded high status. Conversely, girls' writing doesn't have to be slovenly or careless, it doesn't have to contain evidence of "failure" for it to be considered substandard: Being the work of girls it is automatically suspect. Teachers too may have no need to examine the scripts of their students to know that those of the girls are no good.

And this facet of teacher behaviour, while apparently contradictory, is quite in keeping with the double standard that would penalise girls, irrespective of their performance. The fact that teachers may agree that girls are the better English students while at the same time they acknowledge that this is not to the girls' credit and has no merit, is not such an unusual stance to adopt in a male-dominated society. There is even a most appropriate precedent to be found in relation to the spoken word.

Peter Trudgill (1975) for example, found that in England females are the "better" speakers, the more polite and technically more correct participants, and he used this positive feature to discredit the talk of women. He has suggested that it is because women are better, more pleasing and polite, that they are less forceful and less respected speakers: It is because they are better at these things that they do not hold the influential positions in the workplace, which draw on speaking ability.

Is the written word any different? If he were to direct his research to writing, no doubt Peter Trudgill could find that it was because women were considered better, were rated as more pleasing and correct, that they were less respected and very much less rewarded for their "excellence."

Like the researchers who have made these double-standard judgements about the spoken word, these teachers who made double-standard judgements about the written word are not atypical. They are trained teachers, good teachers, who care about the welfare of their students, and who are conscientious about their own responsibilities. Yet they are teachers who routinely construct sex-inequality at an intellectual/artistic level; they are teachers who help to forge the image of males as the authentic writers and readers; they are teachers who have little or no trouble accommodating the apparent contradictions of the double-standard—who see no problem in girls getting the better marks, and having their achievement discounted in favour of males.

And I have no problem in seeing how this principle of penalising women can be transferred to the wider literary community.

I have no trouble in seeing how it is that the writing of boys receives the better marks—the greater recognition—in the culture and the literary curriculum. I can even see how it is that today male writers continue to be perceived as better and more worthy of study—while many gifted women writers fade into oblivion. It hasn't been necessary to find fault with the work of such outstanding women writers as Delarivière Manley, Eliza Haywood, Sarah Fielding, Charlotte Smith, or Maria Edgeworth, for example, to prevent them from having a permanent or prominent place in the literary canon. That in conventional courses women may never exceed 10% of the curricular provision in western educational institutions has nothing to do with the *quality* of their work.

Women writers are kept out of classrooms primarily because their presence would challenge the importance of men. Not necessarily in terms of the greatness of their literary achievements—we have already seen how easily women's contributions can be discounted. No, the challenge that women writers would present is much the same as the one personified by women talkers—that of taking away the focus from men, of diverting attention from male experience so that it is not so all-pervasive or central.

Anyone who has taught a mixed-sex English class knows the risk of trying to teach too many women, to men. In schools—where students generally have little choice about attendance—the dangers can be compounded. The introduction of a woman writer can be greeted with male grimaces and groans, and if these aren't enough to put an end to the unwelcome presence, disruptive tactics can be threatened, and then used. Teachers are only too aware of this problem.

> There's no point trying to teach boys anything that's associated with girls. They go bonkers, get abusive. Start shouting they're not a bunch of poofters or queers. It's not worth it. And if they get out of control too often you can lose your job. These days its not so easy to get another one . . . (Woman teacher, private secondary school, Australia).
>
> I can get away with teaching *one* novel by a woman in the sixth form. It's as though one is expected . . . you know, Jane Austen or Charlotte Brontë. George Eliot. The boys don't like it but they let me do it. But no more. Everything else has to be for them. Really men writing about men . . . And if I didn't get the boys in, if *they* didn't want to do English, I wouldn't be teaching the sixth form. It's that simple . . . (Woman teacher, State high school, England).
>
> I don't think guys get a lot out of the woman writers, and you know, that's understandable. They haven't a lot to offer. Guys need more action, more adventures and hero stuff if they're going to get into reading. And I reckon the girls prefer it too. (Man teacher, State primary school, United States).
>
> Make males the centre of the curriculum—or give up teaching. (Woman lecturer, teacher training college, England).

When asked who their lessons were aimed at, the overwhelming majority of teachers in mixed-sex schools in Australia and England readily admit that they gear their lessons to what interests the boys. Otherwise—many of them state—there would *be* no lesson at all. For as a general rule, when boys don't get what they want, when their interest is not engaged, there are likely to be discipline problems. Asked whether their lessons were conducted on the principle of avoiding male violence, forty-four out of fifty-four secondary teachers I interviewed in England said "yes."

The case for including an equal number of women writers on any literary course may be a good one, but the chances of implementing such a policy certainly are not. The dynamics of the classroom—and male resistance—make it next to impossible to change the ratio of writing men to women, no matter how good the women are! On numerous occasions I have come to see the folly of my ways when I have tried to redress the balance and increase the quota of women in the curriculum. From four-year-old males in an Australian preschool who refused to listen to a girl's story—who said it was sissy and silly—to middle-aged men in a British University who threatened to "report" me, if I continued to teach "so many bloody women," I have encountered fierce resistance when I have tried to reach a female rate of representation of more than 10%.

But if the power of the male students is not sufficient to police the poor presence of women, then teachers and those responsible for curriculum decisions can lend their support to the cause. If all else fails, the reason that can be given for their refusal to include women writers in significant numbers is—too many women will lower the standard! Mainstream courses which have more than about 10% of women writers in them can be seen as *dominated* by women—and as not to be taken seriously.

In a sense, such assertions are accurate. In a society where women are considered secondary, without reference to the contribution or achievement, it is the case that a preponderance of women writers in a course will soon lead to accusations of an absence of academic rigour and respectability. Even studying women writers is perceived as a poor career choice. Elaine Showalter, Annette Kolodny and Cathy Davidson[5] are among those who have been told that they are "bright" enough to aim higher—to engage in research of more substance and greater significance. That is, they would have been better advised to study the *real thing*—the *men* of letters. And this, I suspect, is at the centre of the so-called "standards-strategy."

Quite simply, for the notion of male superiority to persist, males have to be seen systematically as superior: Male experience has to be perceived as more important, as more comprehensive. And one of the easiest ways to achieve this end is to make male experience the legitimated substance of the curriculum and the sanctioned social meanings. Then to be male is to be authoritative, to be the knower.

Ideally, women's voices should be silenced. But as women cannot be kept entirely out of the conversation or the curriculum or the canon, they must

---

[5]See Appendix for further details.

necessarily be contained. Women's voices cannot be completely excluded—partly because such a tactic would be seen as tyrannical and incompatible with a just society, but partly too because women have always been able to use devious practices to get around such rules (such as using male names to get published): So the next best thing is to minimise their presence, and their message.

I believe it is the very existence of women's knowledge that poses the fundamental threat to male superiority: It is knowledge derived from women's different position in society, a position which men do not share, and which develops a very different view of the world. Women know things men do not know; because of the way women relate to men, women know things about men that men may not know about themselves. And this view of the world—and of men—is powerfully inscribed in women's literature and presents a threat to men's knowledge and explanations. Women's writing, like women's conversation, is often a testimony to what men have left out—and why!

The representation of women in the world of letters is not just an issue of quantity; it's also about quality. Were women and men writers to be completely interchangeable, the argument of the presence of 50% of women writers on any course would be of an entirely different order. But it's the fact that women can write about a realm *outside* male experience which poses the challenge to male universality and supremacy. It's the fact that women can encode different priorities, perspectives, and problems (and even solutions!) that is at the root of men's time honoured practise of excluding the voices of women.

Not that the reasons for such exclusion are stated in terms of danger; more often they appear in the "standard's guise" whereby the different experience of women is branded as deviant, deficient, and substandard simply because it is *not* the experience of men! It is as Virginia Woolf has said, that the experience of men is taken as the norm—as the established values; and when women alter those established values they are not seen as creative in their own right, but as having failed to meet the male standard (see Virginia Woolf, 1972: p. 146).

This is why there is so little room for the views and values of women *as women* in great literature; no room for women's care, conscientiousness, or correctness. Room only for the contributions of superior men. And in the educational and professional world of letters, it is not necessarily the writing that is the "great" achievement.

Much of literary criticism and educational theory has been constructed in retrospect; both bodies of knowledge can be regarded as rationales constructed after the event with the aim of realising and legitimating the superiority of men. So whether the male has a neat or a scrawly hand, whether he does or does not make use of codes of grammatical correctness, his achievement will be accorded positive status; whether the male draws on only half the experience of humanity, whether he does or does not assume the comprehensive and normative nature of male experience, his contribution can be accorded universal significance and warrant lasting credit. It is in this context that women writers—and the ideas, explanations, and insights that have been forged in relation to their work—pose an enormous threat to male power.

II

WOMEN'S JUDGEMENT OF LITERARY MEN

Part I was concerned with analysing the behaviour of literary men—*on their own terms*. From within the traditional framework it examined the way men exercise their self-interested judgement to prevent women from having a primary or prestigious place within the world of letters.

Part II is based on *women's terms*. It is an exploration of the conditions under which women have lived and worked—have spoken and written—in a male-dominated society. It looks at the pressures which women confront as women, which are part of the writing process, and which serve as a starting point for an explanatory framework for women's writing. Part II also examines what happens to women and their writing in a system they do not control; it exposes some of the ways in which men have exploited and appropriated women's lives and work, and for which they stand judged.

6

Women's Work and Women's Criticism

WORKING OUT THE SILENCE

One of the first tasks that has to be undertaken when constructing a body of knowledge based on women's experience is to set out what that experience is. While over the centuries women have come from every stratum of society, and from every set of personal and political circumstances, they can still share a common experience of being women. At the crudest, broadest level, all women know what it's like to be non-men, they know what it's like to relate to men as women (to be "interrupted") and this in itself is a significant source of common experience. Women also know what it's like to be women—to have been socialised as a female, to have been required to do women's work, to have been treated as a member of the second sex, to be threatened by male violence and rape. And in varying degrees, women know about the biological aspects of being women—of menstruation, birth control, childbirth, menopause. While some of these experiences of women have changed over time, and have had different interpretations placed upon them, it is still possible to assume a common core of meanings for women.

What is problematic, however, is the *documentation* of this common—and diverse—experience of women. For one of the consequences of women having taken second place is that little is known about their lives. Men have dominated the talk; they have dominated the spoken and the written word, so that too often when we go looking for the experience of women, we find that it has been swamped—sometimes to the point of invisibility—by the overweening experience of men.

The public stage and the public records have been the province of men and it can be an exercise in futility to try and trace some of the nuances of women's lives from these sources. And of course, by definition, the *private* experience of women has been protected from prying eyes—which makes research in this realm even more problematic.

But within the constraints of the private world, women have kept records; they have written journals, diaries, autobiographies, memoirs, and letters that have afforded the opportunity to set out the daily reality of their lives. While these sources are better than nothing, we cannot confidently map the boundaries of women's lives from such evidence—partly because we have so few of them. Given how long women have been keeping diaries—and how many of them there have been—it is quite extraordinary to find so few in print. One reason for this is that women's personal chronicles—like so many other aspects of women's writing—are perceived to lack authority and universality. Another case of it being not the writing—but the sex. So while Anne Fanshawe (born 1625) might write one of the most fascinating and illuminating accounts of the British Civil War—from the perspective of an insider[1]—her efforts sometimes are classified as personal, idiosyncratic, even confessional, and of interest to but a few; yet Samuel Pepys's account of the Restoration just a few years later—and from the point of view of an outsider—is classified as an authoritative historical document of immense significance to a nation. Hence the greater publication rate of men's diaries, although it seems likely that women have been much more frequent journal keepers.

Given that there's so little about women to be found in the *public* realm of history, and so little available from the private realm of diaries—where can we go to gather details of women's past? For, as Virginia Woolf has said, if we are to understand the nature of "writing woman" and the context in which she wrote, we need to know about the everyday circumstances of "ordinary" women's lives:

> The extraordinary woman depends on the ordinary woman. It is only when we know what were the conditions of the average woman's life—the number of her children, whether she had money of her own, if she had a room to herself, whether she had help in bringing up her family, if she had servants, whether part of the housework was her task—it is only when we can measure the way of life and the experience of life made possible to the ordinary woman that we can account for the success or failure of the extraordinary woman as writer. (Virginia Woolf, 1972: p. 142)

Limited though the resource may be, there is however one form of documentation that can provide some information on the substance of women's lives: It is women's published writing, particularly fiction. In countless novels across the centuries numerous women writers have portrayed women's "private" world and conceptualised many of the realities of women's lives: These representations can help to suggest some of the conditions under which women have lived, worked—and written.

---

[1] Her husband, Richard Fanshawe, was Secretary of War to the deposed Prince Charles.

But novels are by no means "perfect" accounts of women's circumstances, partly because of the limitations of individual writers, partly because they are *transformations* of "raw data" into fiction. And partly because they are women's voices in the conversation controlled by men.

In looking to women's fiction to provide insights into women's existence, what should be kept in mind from the outset is that when women have written for publication, they have been required to meet the rules laid down by men. Men have been in charge of the discourse: They have determined the topics and the terms in the public/published realm. And in the world of printed fiction, women have been just as constrained in what they may speak and how they may speak it, as they are in mixed-sex conversations in contemporary society. There are so many topics which have been taboo, which have been precluded from discussion in the presence of men. They are often the topics which are specific to women, which are of deep significance in women's lives, and which are beyond the first-hand experience of men.

These omissions and gaps in the encoded records of women's past form a starting point for an explanatory framework for women's writing. For as so many women writers/critics have acknowledged, women's silences can be as meaningful as women's utterances (see particularly Mary Daly, Tillie Olsen, Adrienne Rich, and Virginia Woolf). So if we are going to have a body of knowledge about women's writing which originates with the experience of women rather than that of men, then we may as well start with what women are not allowed to say in their work. This is another variation on the theme that women have been obliged to develop the topics of men at the expense of their own—even in fiction.

One of the most startling omissions is, of course, that of childbirth and its associated repertoire of meanings. Given the number of novels in which childbirth is of central significance it is staggering to find that the event itself is virtually invisible. Women labour between the lines, children are born outside the pages, and rare even is the record of women's response to such a momentous occasion. Fear, pain, post-natal depression—anger? Little can be learned about these aspects of women's relationship to childbirth from women's fiction. And this cannot be because of the infrequency of the occurrence, the superficial nature of the physical/emotional involvement, or the inherent lack of dramatic interest in such experience. Clearly another explanation is called for.

What we have in our male-dominated society is a literature that dwells on the experience of men. From their birth to their death (and after) we are regaled with stories of their aspirations, their doubts, their struggles, and their strengths. We are even made privy to their stretched emotional state when, for example, on the eve of battle, they have believed themselves to be risking death. But what about the thousands, millions, of women who, on the eve of giving birth have faced the very same fate? Why such a resounding silence on

this topic among women writers? All those women through all those centuries who have known that they are about to endure pain, to risk death, and
who have been forced to contemplate the awful possibility of the vulnerable
children they would leave behind? What about their anguish—and their
bravery? Where are the testimonies to the constancy and courage of these
ordinary women?[2] Is it that in mixed-sex discourse such statements about
female endurance and strength are not allowed?

Perhaps even more noticeable in its absence is the record of women's
feelings towards the men who have been responsible for their state, to the
men who have "contributed" but who do not have to take the consequences.
Apart from Mary Wollstonecraft's heart-rending account in *The Wrongs of
Woman* (1798) I know of no other sustained analysis of a woman's resentment towards her spouse—who made her pregnant against her will. (Sparse
too are women's accounts in literature of their response to the rapist—to
pregnancy and progeny.) Yet many, many women there must have been who
not only dreaded the relationship which left them pregnant, but who must
have harboured hate towards husbands, and who must have despaired of
their own impotent, wifely state. But while we may know of the resentment of
the soldier toward those who give the orders, the bitterness toward those who
would plunge him into battle without heed for ordinary life, we know next to
nothing about the attitude of ordinary women toward men who have com-
manded their conjugal rights—without regard to the health or happiness of
their wives.

It seems that the insurrection of women has not been a topic in the presence of men.

But birth is not only or always about hardship or horror. The very fact that
the word "gossip" once referred to "a woman's female friend invited to be
present at the birth" (*A Feminist Dictionary*, 1985: p. 179) suggests that there
have been elements of contentment and comfort in the event. There has been
joy—and no doubt there has been humour too, for it is beyond belief that
women should have gathered together in such circumstances without at
times finding much to make merry about. Not that we would know this from
women's literature. In all the thousands of novels that I have read and all the
hundreds of diaries I have gone through, rarely have I come across a description of birth in a woman's terms, in relation to what it means to *her*. Much
more common is the representation of the woman as the bearer of a child for
a man—and even then she has to bear a son to warrant more than passing
reference.

---

[2]One of the few exceptions is in women's diaries—which were not intended for publication. A
very few women appear to have kept such accounts but among those that have been found are
the extracts contained in Cynthia Huff, 1987, "Chronicles of Confinement: Reactions to Childbirth in British Women's Diaries."

It is a tenet of women's research on the spoken word that men control the conversation topics and that they use this power to enhance their own image: It would not be difficult to transfer the same tenet to the written word, where the records show that some of the most significant experiences in the lives of women are allowed existence only in so far as they are relevant to—and reflect well upon—the lives of men.

Not even menstruation has an honourable mention: Many are the accounts of the young man on the brink of manhood, of the turbulence and trauma as he moves towards that unmarked state. But for the young woman who faces a physical as well as an emotional transformation, there is little or no resonance of her reality. No discussions of what it means to confront the recognition that one can now give birth: No discussion of what it means in terms of self, of relationships, of one's sex. No discussion either of the practicalities involved—of the preventive measures which need to be taken, of the tampons to be accommodated, the pads to be disposed of, and the inevitability of bloody accidents—and "embarrassments"!

It is one thing to read about such accounts in sex-education manuals; it is quite another to come to terms with such events through the medium of literature. But where can such literature be found?

For many years I taught English to adolescent girls. During that period I searched and I searched for sensitive, affirming, insightful accounts of the young girl who moves towards womanhood: I searched for understanding, I searched for joy, I searched for curiosity, philosophy, affinity—in all the sanctioned literature that the establishment permitted, I found nothing. Not even—heaven forbid!—an equivalent to A Portrait of the Artist as a Young Man.

Such a silence can be deafening.

Again, it must be appreciated that it is men who raise the topic of experience which is specific to women: It is indicative of the extent to which they control the discourse that their versions are taken as authoritative. So, as Elaine Showalter (1974) has wryly observed: We "encounter the myths of female sexuality as seen by Hardy and Lawrence, and the wonders of childbirth as seen by Sterne and Hemingway" (p. 319). In mixed-sex literary conversations women may only enter on the terms set by men.

While it is "woman's work" to give birth, this is not the only area of their labour which distinguishes them from men. Domestic work is no less significant—and is probably more intrusive and demanding—than the act of childbirth may be—and it should come as no surprise to find that this is another taboo topic in the presence of men. In women's conversations the issue of domestic drudgery may be constant and insistent but it has no place in the forum controlled by men.

Whereas the existence of women in "real life" is frequently interwoven with demanding and even demeaning domestic chores, the existence of women in fiction is almost entirely severed from such sordid concerns. So completely has this aspect of women's lives been excised from the "lofty" considerations of literature, that Marion Glastonbury (1979) refers to the silence on women and housework as one of the best kept secrets of the literary world. And she has no doubts about the reasons for this reticence.

Men don't want to have to admit how hard women have to work, argues Marion Glastonbury. It ruins their image as the chivalrous sex: It raises awkward questions about the ostensible weakness of women—and strength of men. And it certainly lends support to the premise that women have a genuine grievance. So "women and housework" is kept off the literary agenda—in so far as men can police it.

Marion Glastonbury goes to considerable lengths to dispel the myth that it is something about the nature of housework which renders it unfit for literary treatment. It is not the *work* but the response of men, she insists, that is at the root of the refusal to include the huge expanse of women's lives in the literary heritage. "Women fail to speak" in literature, she says, "not because they are personally disqualified, nor because the substance of their days is inherently intractable in its refusal to lend itself to literature, but because a direct view from the social position they occupy cannot be comfortably accommodated . . ."(1979: p. 172).

Men's work, no matter how menial, has found a place in the literary annals. (You should just read some of the Australian accounts of the man in the outback!) But the work of labouring women remains invisible. And there is no mystery about the reasons behind this. When an entire society—*and economic system*—is based upon the premise that men do real work and therefore deserve pay, it would be little short of treasonable to show women working harder—for no pay! (See Ann Oakley, 1974, *The Sociology of Housework*).

Housework, another topic which would hurt the feelings of men—which would challenge their image as reasonable and just. Another topic in fiction left "unsaid"—in the interest of men and at the expense of women.

Like Elaine Showalter, Marion Glastonbury is concerned with the effect of this absence upon writing and reading women. Men can turn to literature to help make sense of their world, she claims, but literature affords no such opportunities for women. Literature is the last place a woman would go to have her work—or her working conditions—elaborated or explained. And for Marion Glastonbury, this absence constitutes an enormous loss for women: Not only are they deprived of a way of interpreting the world, they are deprived of a way of discovering the realities of the women of the past.

Were women to be in charge of literature and its interpretive framework, these omissions and deficiencies would have a central place in such a body of knowledge. The invisibility of women's experience and the muted nature of women's voices in the forums controlled by men would stand as an indictment of male dominance and of particular literary men who have inhibited and invalidated the substance of women's literature. Where women have been able to talk to women, critics such as Annette Kolodny, Elaine Showalter, and Marion Glastonbury—to name but a very few—have already given some idea of the directions in which women's "unfettered" literary inclinations might go: Toward legitimating the full range of women's experience as women and as writers—toward making the links between women's lives and women's literature in a context of male dominance.

WOMEN'S LIVES, WOMEN'S LITERATURE

With so little information forthcoming about the lives of ordinary women from the public sources of fact and fiction, we must look to the lives of the extraordinary women—the writers themselves—to provide the parameters for our understandings about women and literature. As has been stated previously (pages 34–35) an alternative strand of women's literary criticism has existed over the centuries, even though it has been known by another name and has been left in isolated units rather than drawn together to form a distinct tradition. But women writers (and writers on women writers) have recorded and reviewed the patterns of their hours and their arts, and in bringing together their reflections, not only can we come to appreciate some of the conditions under which women have worked, we can begin to make some of the connections which are the substance of women's own literary traditions.

To suggest that women should construct their own autonomous body of knowledge about women's writing (and men's judgement as well as men's writing) is not to put to an instant end the old frame of reference provided by men. But it is to put men's meanings into a new perspective. It is to deny the *absolute authority* of men's lit-crit and to make it just one of a number of explanatory systems: It is to take out the element of "supremacy" so that women's and men's criticism can enjoy equal status, and coexist. With access to both frames of reference, and the comparisons they encompass, we will then have access to a greater range of understandings about the sexes, society, and literature.

While the full details of the working conditions of ordinary women may continue to elude us, we do know enough about women's position in society to realise that women lead very different lives from men. And we do know that different material circumstances can produce different world views, different forms of consciousness and frames of meaning. We can look to the commentary of women writers to pin-point some of these differences, and to elaborate on their significance.

Take for example, the very different attitudes of the sexes towards the "private" realm, and its contribution to the world of letters. It has been the traditional and male-decreed tenet that it is the text which is of paramount importance and that great works could and should be assessed without reference to the personal circumstances of the author. Critics such as W. K. Wimsatt (1970), Northrop Frye (1957), and Roland Barthes (1977) are but a few of the many men who have insisted on the independence of the text and who have proceeded to build a body of knowledge which proscribes all considerations about the private origins of public letters.

For women, however, the private realm has been an entirely different matter and their knowledge on the relationship of the personal/political adds a new dimension to literary criticism.

The fact that some men may have been able to insist on the exclusion of the domestic arrangements of the author from the study of his work, may say more about men's privileged existence, than the context of writing. Men may not have wanted to know if an author was married, had children, was responsible for hearth and home, but all this reveals is that such concerns have not been relevant to men's writing. Whereas for women, they have been more than relevant; they have been vital!

Husbands, homes, children, domestic responsibilities of any sort have often determined whether women would become writers: Indeed, whether a female author has been a wife or mother has often been the deciding factor in whether she has been able to produce a text to study. So, understandably women critics have been centrally concerned with the domestic circumstances of the author, and not just with the text itself. Within the traditions of women's criticism reference has generally been made to the nature and extent of domestic demands and the pressures on women to meet them. And it is this primary difference in priorities and perspective which has helped to brand women's criticism as "low status" and which has led to the labelling of women's commentary as "sociology" or "literary biography," rather than "pure" or "proper" literary criticism.

Men have had few domestic responsibilities in their role as spouse or parent, so it's not surprising to find that they have been able to keep "housework" out of both their creative and critical writing. But this has not been the case for literary women. Not only have they frequently been required to do a mammoth servicing job as spouse or parent before they can even begin to take up their writing, but assessments of their literary worth have often been tied to their domestic and womanly success. This is another example of the sexual double standard which emerges when women's criticism is allowed a hearing.

It has been a common practice among literary men to keep a decent distance between creativity and domesticity, a luxury which most women artists have been denied. Men have not been called to account as artists on the basis of their willingness to meet family responsibilities. On the contrary, the man who abandons or repudiates the traditional masculine role is likely to have his artistic reputation enhanced. Whereas a woman who sacrificed her family for the sake of art would risk condemnation, it could be taken as a sign of great commitment in a man who determined to put art before personal obligations. This was George Bernard Shaw's stance: "The true artist will let his wife starve, his children go barefoot, and his mother drudge for a living at seventy, sooner than work at anything but his art," he argued in *Man and Superman*.

Women may well wish to judge men, and art, by a different standard.

For women writers, art and domesticity have been inextricably linked. Women's commentary on literature abounds with references to the conflicting demands which confront the female who wants to be a writer: From Charlotte Brontë to Mary Gordon, women have been enjoined to be proper women rather than to be serious about being writers.[3] The list of women who have been counselled to *do* domestic work (instead of writing about it) is almost as long as the list of extraordinary women who have made their way into print. So, while men may be able to exclude the domestic realm from their writing—and in the process keep art clean—for women it has been virtually impossible to sever the personal from the professional commitments: This is one of the fundamentals of the writing woman's working conditions.

Terry Lovell (1986) has suggested that in our society art and literary production are not perceived as manly activities and although I take the point that in some circles the "creative" man may not enjoy quite the same status as the macho one, I think this is little more than a perturbation on the pathway to acceptance for the male. There are manly compensations too in the creative process and the prestige as Kate Millett (1972) has pointed out in relation to such leading literary lights as D. H. Lawrence and Norman Mailer. But for women, the conflict between sex role and artistic commitment goes much deeper: The successful woman is—almost by definition—the one who sacrifices her *self*, her creativity and intellectuality, who puts them into personal (read "male") and not professional (read "competition") commitments.

A well-developed body of women's criticism could start with the testimony of women writers (and the records on them—including biography) on the conditions under which they have worked and written. It could bring together the knowledge that women have generated about the problems of trying to reconcile the demands of the woman with those of the writer: It could compile a list of the strategies that have been used to prevent women from entering the literary community. And unlike the evidence of ordinary

---

[3]See Chapter two of this book, "Literary Criticism: Making It for Men."

women's existence, this information is not difficult to gather. For me the hardest part of this exercise has been to choose the few from the many experiences of literary women, which can suggest the nature and scope of women's working conditions—and women's criticism.

Because marriage has so often been a full-time occupation for women, with little or no opportunity for writing, one of the first questions a woman has had to ask is whether she could marry—*and* write? And she was often forced to conclude that while she might have one or the other, she could not have both: And this has been a difficult issue to resolve. For it is not unreasonable for a woman to want marriage *and* career (a reality taken for granted by most men), but literary women have ordinarily been required to *choose* and no matter what the decision, it has often been accompanied by a sense of loss.

Well aware of the way in which marriage (and children) have prevented women from being writers, Tillie Olsen (1980) has focussed on the women who opted for the profession, despite the personal price.

"In the last century," she writes, "of the women whose achievements endure for us in one way or another, nearly all never married (Jane Austen, Emily Brontë, Christina Rossetti, Emily Dickinson, Louisa May Alcott, Sarah Orne Jewett) or married late in their thirties (George Eliot, Elizabeth Barrett Browning, Charlotte Brontë, Olive Schreiner). I can think of only four (George Sand, Harriet Beecher Stowe, Helen Hunt Jackson, and Elizabeth Gaskell) who married and had children as young women"—and to this list, Tillie Olsen adds a footnote: "I would now add a fifth—Kate Chopin—also a foreground silence." And, comments Tillie Olsen on this group of women—"All had servants" (1980: p. 15).

"In our own century, until very recently, it has not been so different," she continues, as she goes through the list of women writers. "Most did not marry (Selma Lagerlof, Willa Cather, Ellen Glasgow, Gertrude Stein, Gabriela Mistral, Elizabeth Madox Roberts, Charlotte Mew, Eudora Welty, Marianne Moore) or, if married, have been childless (Edith Wharton, Virginia Woolf, Katherine Mansfield, Dorothy Richardson, H(enry) H(andel) Richardson, Elizabeth Bowen, Isak Dinesen, Katherine Anne Porter, Lillian Hellman, Dorothy Parker).[4] Colette had only one child (when she was forty). If I include

---

[4]This list is by no means exhaustive: Contemporary writers without children have been omitted—for example, Simone de Beauvoir, Anita Brookner, Germaine Greer, Kate Millett. And literary women from the past have also been left off the list—such as Anne Finch, Margaret Cavendish, Aphra Behn, Mary Astell, Elizabeth Inchbald, Ann Radcliffe, Mary Hays, Maria Edgeworth, Lady Morgan, Geraldine Jewsbury, *etc.*

Sigrid Undset, Kay Boyle, Pearl Buck, Dorothy Canfield Fisher, that will make a small group who had more than one child. All had household help or other special circumstances . . . " (1980: pp. 15–16).

That there have been few if any changes in this pattern over the century is for Tillie Olsen, no surprise: Despite the rhetoric of liberation (even of "post feminism"), women still have now—as women have had in the past—the primary responsibility for hearth and home, no matter what "extra" duties they may assume. And until the revolution, and a single sexual standard, there seems to be little likelihood of a solution. Unless it takes the form of a *natural* release or disaster:

"It took family deaths to free more than one woman writer into her own development," Tillie Olsen wryly states, and she goes on to cite George Eliot, Helen Hunt Jackson, Kate Chopin, Lady Gregory, and Isak Dinesen—and her list is by no means comprehensive. She also quotes Ivy Compton-Burnett and her explanation for the emergence of a substantial number of women writers in England after the First World War: When marriage and men were unavailable women had the opportunity to write. "The men were dead, you see," Ivy Compton-Burnett confided, "and the women didn't marry so much because there was no one for them to marry, and so they had leisure and, I think, in a good many cases they had money because their brothers were dead, and all that would lead to writing, wouldn't it, being single, and having some money, and having the time—having no men you see" (Tillie Olsen, 1980: p. 17).

The case for the removal of men in the interest of promoting women's writing could hardly be stated more starkly.

Some women have of course decided that they can combine marital and literary commitments, only to find that their lives can be extraordinarily, even impossibly difficult. Vera Brittain (1893–1970) was one determined woman writer who opted for marriage and career, and who explained in her autobiographical writing that the solution she adopted to make life manageable was not socially acceptable.

A promising English writer, Vera Brittain upon her marriage, like so many women "followed" her husband to his new appointment in the United States in 1925, only to find that the move virtually put an end to her literary career. And in this case, not necessarily because her domestic duties left little time for writing.

"In England I had been regarded as a promising young writer whose work dealt with subjects that mattered," she wrote in *Testament of Experience* (1981), "but in the United States I was less than dust" and this was in marked contrast to the success her husband met with. "Whereas G. (her husband) was now happily contributing to *The New Republic*, *Harper's Magazine*, *Current History* and several academic publications, I had failed to place one article in an American magazine. I could not even persuade some minor periodical to appoint me as its representative at the coming League of Nations Assembly" (p. 37).

The only fate that Vera Brittain could see awaiting her was that of the "faculty wife," of putting her talents into her man—and of becoming "increasingly depressed, frustrated, embittered" (p. 38) in the process. It was a fate she did not fancy: She sought "a compromise."

Vera Brittain elected to have a "semi-detached marriage" and returned to England (and life with Winifred Holtby, who more than shared the domestic responsibilities) to pursue her writing career. In so doing she was seen by many to be rejecting her womanly duties so that she could embark upon a selfish life: *She* felt criticised by others, she admits to "punishing" herself for having made such a choice. Yet for women who want to write, such difficult decisions invariably have to be made—often repeatedly. For the problems involved with "following" men are not the occasional ones which confront the woman writer: They are the context in which women writers are obliged to work and which are the legitimate focus of women's literary criticism.

This is why Sydney Owenson (1778?–1859) for example thought long and hard about marriage when, against all odds she carved out for herself a literary career and managed to achieve a measure of fame along with financial independence. When Charles Morgan offered to make her his wife it was not coyness or coquetry which made her hesitate. Sydney Owenson was aware that marriage could put all her achievements at risk: In the event of (many) children, it was possible that she might never write again. So her decision was not just about love, fulfilment, romance: It was about work, pay, and identity!

She was not to know that there would be no children. What she did know was that the options available to her as a woman were not in the same class as those available to creative men. "Few literary men have even lived with their children" comments Marion Glastonbury, caustically: "the poor, like Rousseau sent them to the foundling hospital, the prosperous like A. A. Milne, consigned them to the nursery" (1978: p. 36).

The recognition that marriage and maternity could mean the end of literary aspirations is one which runs right through women's commentary and reveals their regrets—and their resentments. Michele Murray (1980) was but one contributor to this painful record.

Born in 1933, she was a self-acknowledged victim of the "feminine mystique." She wanted to be a warm, wonderful woman *and* a serious writer, and she found that she had to compromise—with *both*. In her diary (March 12, 1956), she recorded the way her determination to be a writer forced her to modify her ideals as wife and mother.

Along with my commitment to writing, she stated "is the corollary abandonment of plans and dreams held for so many years they had become part of my life. This is not easy to do—it means, for one thing, that I was wrong about many things and for another, that part of my personality, part of my dreams, is gone. We will never have a large family and live in a big house in the country where I play the classic role of wife and mother" (p. 73). Yet at the very same time that Michele Murray discloses the cost of giving up the classic role of wife and mother, she insists that the classic role in itself could never be enough for her.

> I made a great effort to turn myself into a wife–mother type, like the majority of girls, because I do believe this is the best way to be, but I wasted my energy, because I can *never* be like they are. I love David (my husband) and being with him, I love cooking, and although I don't like routine housework, I can do it with toleration. Yet this is not enough. (Michele Murray, 1980: p. 73).

Marriage and motherhood with all their inherent demands have been the material conditions of most women's lives and—as Adrienne Rich (1980) has suggested—they form the root of women's consciousness and are reflected in the substance of women's writing. Commenting on the period in her own life when she had the care of young children as her primary consideration, she says "I was writing very little, partly from fatigue, that female fatigue of suppressed anger and loss of contact with my own being; partly from the discontinuity of female life with its attention to small chores, errands, work that others constantly undo, small children's needs . . . " Such conditions, insist Adrienne Rich, sap the creative process and curtail women's capacity to sustain imaginative effort—to write poetry. She continues:

> . . . For a poem to coalesce, for an action or character to take shape, there has to be an imaginative transformation of reality which is in no way passive. And a certain freedom of the mind is needed—freedom to press on, to enter the currents of your thought like a glider pilot, knowing that your motion can be sustained, that the buoyancy of your attention will not suddenly be snatched away . . . you have to be free to play around with the notion that day may be night, love might be hate; nothing can be too sacred for the imagination to turn into its opposite or to call experimentally by another name. For writing is renaming. (Adrienne Rich, 1980: p. 43)

But, adds Adrienne Rich, such working conditions are generally out of the reach of writing women, particularly those who are also wives and mothers: "to be materially with children all day in the old way" she says, "to be with a man in the old way of marriage, requires a holding back, a putting aside of that imaginative activity, and demands instead a kind of conservatism" (p. 43). Not that Adrienne Rich advocates that women should aspire to the same working conditions as those enjoyed by men: She doesn't find the conditions under which men have written all that desirable. "I am not saying that in order to write well, or think well, it is necessary to become unavailable to others, or to become a devouring ego" she hastens to add. "This has been the myth of the masculine artist and thinker, and I do not accept it. But to be a female human being trying to fulfil traditional female functions in a traditional way *is* in direct conflict with the subversive function of the imagination" (p. 43).

What women need are the working conditions which accommodate personal *and* professional needs, not conditions which make them mutually exclusive: A family context in which a woman can be available, as well as *A Room of One's Own*.

So extensive has the woman writer's commentary been on the connections between her circumstances as a woman, and the nature of her contribution as a writer, that it simply is not possible to adequately sample this literary tradition. There have been women writers who have protested about such gross injustice (see Aphra Behn), and women who have explored the issue in their creative work (Elizabeth Barrett Browning) and critical essays (Virginia Woolf). Some, like Jill Tweedie (1983) for example, have made the relationship between how they have lived, and what they have written, unequivocally explicit.

Finding herself unexpectedly the breadwinner, Jill Tweedie said:

> Writing was the only hope I had to earn a living and look after children as well, and writing had to take the form of journalism. Not for me the Shangri-la of fiction. The rewards, if any, would have been too little and too late, the bailiffs were at the door. (Jill Tweedie, 1983: p. 112)

Like so many other women from Eliza Haywood and Charlotte Smith, from Charlotte Lennox to Eliza Lynn Linton and Margaret Oliphant, Jill Tweedie joined the ranks of the writer, in order to earn her bread. But the *form* that her writing took was determined by *family* factors. Taking stock, in 1983, she said:

> . . . Now I am writing a novel, having put myself in training for the long distance haul with an earlier non-fiction book. There are amazing women who cope with children while producing books but, sadly, I am not one of them. My own writing efforts exactly mirror my various phases of motherhood. In my twenties and thirties, young children fragmented my attention span so much that I could only produce in short 2,000 word sprints, paid for immediately to bail out my always perilously low financial boat. My first book, the non-fiction *In the Name of Love*, coincided with a healthier bank account and the last child's arrival at the age of puberty and growing independence, giving me the chance to settle at my desk for longer periods and flex the flabby muscles of my concentration. With this novel the last child is nearly a man and I can afford to gamble at last. (Jill Tweedie, 1983: p. 116)

That men have had to sacrifice their art on occasion to provide family support has among critics often been cause for complaint: If only T. S. Eliot had had more time for writing, if only James Joyce had not been plagued by financial pressures. But the fact that women too have frequently had their art shaped by the necessity to support offspring—and even a spouse—is a point which is rarely conceded. On the contrary, it has readily been asserted that women are supported and so have no need to earn money from their writing—which is one of the means by which women have been represented as dilettante and amateur writers.[5]

While women can lament some of the limitations of women's lot, this should not be taken as an indication that they don't want to be women, or even that they don't want to meet some of the domestic demands which are placed upon them.[6] What it can mean is that they want a different "lot," improved working conditions which allow them to be writer and wife/mother. As Tillie Olsen has explained, many of the demands of motherhood can be rewarding and fulfilling and it is precisely because women want to willingly provide love and security for their children, that their writing efforts are undermined. (1980: p. 33).

When she comments on the interruptions and silences that have punctuated the life of the woman who seeks to be mother and writer, Tillie Olsen writes from personal experience: There can be few greater interruptions than the forty years which separated the draft of her novel *Yonnondio* in 1932 from its completion in 1973; there can be few more poignant glimpses of the plight of the mother/writer than that provided by her own admission that it was "no accident that the first work I considered publishable began: 'I stand here ironing and what you asked me moves tormented back and forth with the iron'"[7] (1980: p. 19).

One of the few references to housework in women's creative writing: It carries a wealth of meaning about women's lives.

Over the last few decades—with women's increased understanding about the personal, political and the part played by housework and child care in women's oppression—women have become more confident *about speaking out* on the topic of motherhood and artistic commitment. With the advent of women's publishing and women's periodicals, with formal and informal study of women writers in many countries and the astonishing growth in women's studies, women can now talk to women about some of these issues, without always having to think about the effect of their voices on men. Adrienne Rich and Tillie Olsen helped to start the conversations, which soon attracted many participants. Among them is the novelist, Anne Tyler (1980) who, in characteristic narrative style, has transformed the interruptions and responsibilities of motherhood into an amusing and significant literary story:

---

[5] See Ann Tyler, 1980, and Margaret Drabble, 1983, for further discussion of this particular double standard.
[6] Some women, of course, don't want to be labelled as low-status women writers, see Elaine Showalter, 1984.
[7] *Tell Me a Riddle*, 1976.

While I was painting the downstairs hall I thought of a novel to write . . . But it was March, and the children's spring vacation began the next day, so I waited.

After spring vacation the children went back to school but the dog got worms. It was a little complicated at the vet's and I lost a day. By then it was Thursday; Friday is the only day I can buy the groceries, pick up new cedar chips for the gerbils, scrub the bathrooms. I waited till Monday. Still, that left me four good weeks in April to block out the novel.

By May I was ready to start actually writing, but I had to do it in patches. There was the follow-up treatment at the vet, then a half day spent trailing the dog with a specimen tin so the lab could be sure the treatment had really worked. There were visits from the washing machine repairman and the Davey tree men, not to mention briefer interruptions by the meter reader, five Jehovah's Witnesses, and two Mormons. People telephoned wanting to sell me permanent light bulbs and waterproof basements . . . Then I wrote chapters one and two. I had planned to work till three-thirty every day, but it was a month of early quittings: once for the children's dental appointment, once for the cat's rabies shot, once for our older daughter's orthopedist, and twice for her gymnastic meets . . . By the time I'd written chapter three it was Memorial Day and the children were home again. (Anne Tyler, 1980: pp. 3–4)

"I knew I shouldn't expect anything from June," Anne Tyler continued. "School was finished then and camp hadn't yet begun. I closed down my mind and planted some herbs and played cribbage with the children" (p. 4). And when the children leave for camp, she heaves a sigh of relief and plans to resume her novel writing:

I was ready to start work again. First I had to take my car in for repairs and the mechanics lost it, but I didn't get diverted. I sat in the garage on a folding chair while they hunted my car all one afternoon, and I hummed a calming tune and tried to remember what I'd planned to do next in my novel. Or even what the novel was about for that matter . . .

I had high hopes for July, but it began with a four day weekend, and on Monday night we had a long distance call from our daughter's camp in Virginia. She was seriously ill. . . . (Anne Tyler, 1980: p. 5)

A drive through the night, a bedside vigil, a return trip with a sick daughter who needs nursing. But finally the daughter recovers—and is returned to camp: "The next day I was free to start writing again," Anne Tyler says, "but sat, instead, on the couch in my study, staring blankly at the wall" (p. 5).

These are the working conditions of *successful* novelist, Anne Tyler: They are the conditions common to many women writers. But in comparison to garrets and "the good life," they are conditions that are not commonly addressed in mainsteam literary criticism.

While women writers today might be more outspoken (and have a more autonomous women's audience) than their foremothers were prepared to risk, women of the past still made opportunities to record some of the conditions under which they worked. Another successful woman writer who "made light" of her liabilities was the nineteenth century novelist, Elizabeth Gaskell (1810–1865). Constrained by the conventions of the time which made it unacceptable for a wife and mother to withdraw and be unavailable, Elizabeth Gaskell wrote in the dining room: With three doors leading from it she was still at the centre of the household and able to perform her domestic duties:

"If I had a library like yours, all undisturbed for hours, how I would write," she declared in a letter to a male friend:

> . . . Mrs. Chapone's letters would be nothing to mine. I would outdo *Rasselas* in fiction. But you see, everyone comes to me perpetually. Now in this hour since breakfast I have had to decide on the following variety of important questions. Boiled beef—how to boil? What perennials will do in Manchester smoke and what colours our garden wants. Length of skirt for a gown. Salary of nursery governess and stipulations for a certain quantity of time to be left to herself. Settle twenty questions on dress for the girls. . . . and it's not half past ten yet. (Elizabeth Gaskell, 1966: Letter 384)

According to Virginia Woolf it was the specific working conditions of women which prompted them to write novels: "Fiction was, as fiction still is, the easiest thing for a woman to write," she stated in 1929, in her article "Women and Fiction." It is a form of women's writing which originates in women's living:

> . . . a novel is the least concentrated form of art. A novel can be taken up or put down more easily then a play or poem. George Eliot left her work to nurse her father. Charlotte Brontë put down her pen to pick the eye out of the potatoes. And living as she did in the common sitting room, surrounded by people, a woman was trained to use her mind in observation and upon the analysis of character. She was trained to be a novelist and not a poet. (Virginia Woolf, 1972: p. 143)

One assumes that the training is not everything, that women can go on to become poets and that men who do not have the advantage of the common sitting room and the management of relationships, can nonetheless go on to write novels. Virginia Woolf is not precluding such developments, only pointing out that the lives of women lend themselves to the production of fiction rather than other forms. Her thesis would make an interesting chapter in women's literary criticism: It would be a chapter to which many contemporary women writers could contribute.

Fay Weldon for example, would readily endorse the assertion that life in the common sitting room shapes the efforts of women writers. Describing her own life and art she has said "I often think I write such short paragraphs because I'm interrupted so frequently . . . It certainly sharpens the wits" (1983: p. 161). Nora Bartlett (1983) is another woman writer who has tried to find the commonalities between the pattern of her days and the pattern of her art: "My days were . . . like anyone's where children are involved," she has said, "a pattern of continual interruptions. I used to think of my novel as being constructed in bits, like a patchwork quilt" (p. 11).

But if there are those who would wholeheartedly support Virginia Woolf's premise that women have taken to writing fiction because it is the form which can most readily be accommodated within women's fragmented lives, there are those who would want to add their reservations. Toni Cade Bambara (1980) would be one of them; she believes that short stories are about all a women can manage, and that to a woman caught in the web of domestic duties the completion of a novel can appear an unattainable end.

After having achieved some recognition as a writer, Toni Cade Bambara acknowledged that she had "never fully appreciated before the concern that so many people express over women writers' work habits—how do you juggle the demands of motherhood etc? Do you find that friends, especially intimates, resent your need for privacy etc? Is it possible to wrench yourself away from active involvement for the lonely business of writing?" (p. 160). In short, many of the questions which would be at the centre of women's literary criticism and on which Toni Cade Bambara makes some interesting comments:

> . . . Writing had never been so central an activity in my life before. Besides, a short story is fairly portable. I could narrate the basic outline while driving to the farmer's market, work out the dialogue while waiting for the airlines to answer the phone, draft a rough sketch of the central scene while overseeing my daughter's carrot cake, write the first version in the middle of the night, edit while the laundry takes a spin, and make copies while running off some rally flyers. (Toni Cade Bambara, 1980: p. 166).

The short story was a cinch: But what about the novel? That was an entirely different matter:

> . . . The novel has taken me out of action for frequent and lengthy periods. Other than readings and an occasional lecture, I seem unfit for any other kind of work. I cannot knock out a terse and pithy office memo anymore. And my relationships, I'm sure, have suffered because I'm so distracted, preoccupied and distant. The short story is a piece of work, the novel is a way of life. (Toni Cade Bambara, 1980: p. 166).

And a way of life which Toni Cade Bambara found to be incompatible with domestic duties.

Almost as common as the commentary on the way that personal demands have prevented women from writing are the confessions of guilt over the way that writing has prevented women from meeting personal commitments. Women have felt guilty about being writers; they have felt guilty about being wives. Women have been ready to apologize for their success in the profes- sional world—and for their lack of it in the private realm. Not even women writers of the calibre of Virginia Woolf and Katherine Mansfield have been immune.

Marion Glastonbury (1978) is convinced that it was no coincidence that Virginia Woolf devoted so much time to the dining habits of women and men in *A Room of One's Own* (1929). The fact that she saw men as better nourished—in every sense of the word—was part of her personal/political analysis. Virginia Woolf was critical of the culinary advantages that men could command in public life—in the Oxbridge Colleges and restaurants for example: She was critical too of the culinary advantages they could command in their homes—in the form of the services of a wife. This is one area where women are the producers—and men the consumers—and where women are not paid for their work. Virginia Woolf felt the pressure placed upon her as a woman to conform—and cook—and according to Marion Glastonbury this was no figment of her imagination.

Good food—and where to get it—has been such a favoured topic among literary men, that as far as Marion Glastonbury is concerned, Virginia Woolf would not have been able to remain oblivious to its requirements: "When they write their memoirs," states Marion Glastonbury in reference to some of the most renowned men of letters, "they describe their ambitions, list their publications, and recall where the food was best. You did all right with Mrs Bernard Shaw; Mrs Wells; Mrs Bennet; Mrs Hardy; Mrs Mansfield. It was not so good when the woman of the house had artistic leanings of her own. The Woolfs lived austerely: Virginia struggled to suppress domestic guilt" (1978: p. 34).

So many women writers have dealt with the guilt along with the drudgery of the dinners—and the dirt. The guilt that they have not done their domestic duties, or that they have not done them *properly*: The guilt that they have not performed them with good grace. There could be few more illuminating examples of the double standard in relation to the working conditions of the writer than that provided by Katherine Mansfield in her journal (1981).

She and John Middleton Murry with whom she lived both aspired to be writers: While both needed "nourishment," it was she, not he, who did all the necessary domestic work. It was she who suffered from ill health: It was he who brought friends home and added to her workload. And it was she— not he—who felt guilty, and who apologised for her lack of good will! "Am I such a tyrant, Jack dear—or do you say it mainly to tease me?" Katherine Mansfield asks in her diary in the summer of 1913:

> . . . I suppose I'm a bad manager, and the house seems to take up so much time if it isn't looked after with some sort of method. I mean . . . when I have to clean up twice over, or wash up extra unnecessary things I get frightfully impatient and want to be working. So often this week, I've heard you and Gordon talking while I washed dishes. Well, someone's got to wash dishes and get food. Otherwise—"There's nothing in the house to eat." Yes, I hate hate *hate*

doing these things that you accept just as all men accept of their women. I can only play the servant with a very bad grace indeed. It's all very well for females who have nothing else to do . . . and then you say I'm a tyrant, and wonder because I get tired at night! The trouble with women like me is—they can't keep their nerves out of the job in hand—and Monday, after you and Gordon and Lesley have gone I walk about with a mind full of ghosts and saucepans and primus stoves and "will there be enough to go round?" . . . and you calling (whatever I am doing) "Tig, isn't there going to be tea? It's five o'clock" as though I were a dilatory housemaid. (Katherine Mansfield, 1981: pp. 43–44)

Women's working conditions—in a nutshell.

It's not just the inroads made into her time that pushes Katherine Mansfield to despair: It's the inroads made into her psyche; her sense of self, when she is torn between trying to be a "proper woman" and a professional writer. It's the sense of injustice, the recognition that one's work is demanded but not rewarded, that it is necessary and yet invisible, which can undermine the existence of women: Is there in men's experience any such pervasive and pernicious equivalent?

"I loathe myself today," Katherine Mansfield continues in her journal, "I detest this woman who 'superintends' you, and rushes about slamming doors and slopping water—all untidy with her blouse out and her nails grimed. I am disgusted and repelled by the creature who shouts at you. 'You might at least empty the pail and wash out the tea leaves!' Yes, no wonder you 'come over silent'" (1981: p. 44).

Even Katherine Mansfield cannot sustain the reality that she has a genuine grievance and that she is justified in her resistance. She abandons her judgement of men, and succumbs to their judgement of women who protest—as scolds, nags and, unattractive.

The wonder of it is that Katherine Mansfield was able to write at all, that despite all the obstacles she was able to produce the remarkable body of work that she did. Without all the handicaps no doubt she—and Elizabeth Gaskell and Tillie Olsen—could have written even more, but we should not lose sight of the great achievement that their work represents. They are women, and they are writers, and this is one of the celebratory aspects of women's literary criticism; for regardless of the discouragement and the disruptions women have faced, they have nonetheless created a vast and vital literary heritage. Paradoxically they have been able to use their experience as women to extend the boundaries of understanding in their writing.

In marriage and motherhood some women have found both the room and the rationale for writing. Antonia Fraser, for example, has been both mother and writer (as was her mother before her—Elizabeth Longford—and her daughter after her) and while she has found the combination difficult she has also found it desirable. Because both "add" to the other, she would not want to be without either dimension in her life (1986). Naomi Mitchison, the author of eighty books and mother, grandmother, great-grandmother extraordinaire, in earlier years had a special platform constructed on the handle of the pram so that she could push her babies—and continue to write.

Fay Weldon (mother of four), Margaret Drabble, and Sue Townsend (mothers and writers) have managed the demands of household and extensive literary commitments—and have managed to survive. Like Elizabeth Gaskell, Sue Townsend used to write on the kitchen table in the middle of family mayhem with a minimum of facilities and space.

One woman who has written movingly about her ambivalence, about the pressures and the pleasures of combining motherhood and writing, is Pulitzer Prize-winning novelist, Alice Walker: Her reflections on such an existence sum up the meanings of many women writers.

While she does not insist that maternity is a must for a woman writer, Alice Walker (1980) does suggest that motherhood can have its benefits, and that it may not be quite so disruptive as it seems. "Someone asked me once whether I thought women artists should have children," she states, "and, since we were beyond discussing why this question is never asked artists who are men, I gave my answer promptly."

> "Yes", I said, somewhat to my surprise. And, as if to amend my rashness, I added: "They should have children—*assuming this is of interest to them*—but only one".
>
> "Why only one?" this someone wanted to know.
>
> "Because with one you can move", I said, "with more than one you're a sitting duck". (Alice Walker, 1980: p. 121)

This evidence that (limited) motherhood and the muse can be combined is quite refreshing. While Alice Walker readily admits that it is not always easy, she also readily asserts that it's partly because there are so many myths about the *end* of women's creativity with the act of giving birth, that women can find the whole process fraught with difficulty. She awaited the expected challenge to her creativity when her daughter was born:

> Well, I wondered, with great fear, where is the split in me now? What is the damage? Was it true—as "anonymous"—so often a woman with distressing observations—warned: "Women have not created as fully as men because once she has a child a woman cannot give herself to her work the way a man can . . . etc etc?" Was I, as a writer, *done for*? (Alice Walker, 1980: p. 126)

Needless to say, Alice Walker is delighted to find that the birth of her daughter does not result in any permanent impairment to her writing. This is one insight which she has gained, and which she wants to share. Women's full creativity is not finite, and it is nothing other than a form of discouragement and dissuasion to suggest to women that the act of giving birth to a human being will inhibit the act of giving birth to the expression of ideas.

Discovering that there had been no damage done to her impulse for writing was not the end of the problem, however, as Alice Walker makes clear. After the birth, there was a daughter—a dependent human being who demanded a lot of time and attention. And Alice Walker admits that she found it just as important to learn that no damage would be done to her daughter by her own determination to write. "I feel very little guilt (most days) about the amount of time 'taken from my daughter' by my work," Alice Walker declares: "I was amazed to discover I could read a book and she could exist at the same time. And how soon she learned that there are other things to enjoy besides myself" (1980: p. 138).

But, *only one*, she warns: More than one and the burden of guilt would even be too great—as her poem reveals:

> Now that the book is finished
> Now that I know my characters will live,
> I can love my child again.
> She need sit no longer
> At the back of my mind.
> The lonely sucking of her thumb
> A giant stopper in my throat
> (Alice Walker, 1980: p. 138)

Part of the richness of Alice Walker's writing is contained in its complexity of views, in the extent to which it encompasses the various and contradictory aspects of the conditions of women's existence. Without detracting from the difficulties and the very real limitations under which women labour, Alice Walker has managed to add the positive dimensions of women's strength, inspiration, and joy. She balances the power with the powerlessness, the commonalities with the diversities when she suggests that women can be both enervated and energised by motherhood. Her insights stand at the very centre of women's literary criticism.

"For a long time," writes Alice Walker, piecing together part of the pattern of women's tradition, "I had this sign which I constructed myself, deliberately, out of false glitter, over my desk:

> Dear Alice
>   Virginia Woolf had madness
>   George Eliot had ostracism
>   somebody else's husband,
>   and did not dare to use
>   her own name.
>   Jane Austen had no privacy
>   and no love life.
>   The Brontë sisters never went anywhere
>   and died young
>   and dependent on their father
>   Zora Hurston (ah!) had no money
>   and poor health.
>   You have R- who is

much more delightful
and less distracting
than any of the calamities
above.
(Alice Walker, 1980: pp. 139–140)

HANDMAIDS TO LITERARY MEN

While women's experience as mothers is relevant to the study of women's writing so too is their experience as "wives." Women who have had to wait upon husbands, women who have had to meet the physical needs of their partners—like Katherine Mansfield for example—have often had little time to develop their own art—and have often lacked the inclination or inspiration to persevere after the demanding duties of their days. Nor have physical demands constituted the only form of discouragement. Men who have wanted to be masters in their own homes with no challenges to their limelight, have been able to make their own contribution to denying and decrying the talents and prominence of their wives. No doubt, there have been countless women for whom the going has been too hard, who have given up without making an entry in women's records.

But while there have been women who have believed it to be too difficult to pursue a literary career in their own right, they have not always abandoned their aspirations to lead—at least—a semi-literary life. And they have looked to literary men to provide them with a literary existence.

Given the values of society, this "solution" is not at all surprising. When it is believed that the members of one sex qualify as the genuine artists, while those of the other are granted but a secondary and supportive role (reinforced by educational processes) then it is predictable that these values will be reflected in heterosexual relationships. Like George Eliot's Dorothea, women can even aspire to be literary wives.

The final chapter of this volume deals with the way that women can have their efforts stolen by literary men, but before examining this area of women's work and criticism, it is necessary to acknowledge that men do not always need to steal women's creativity: Sometimes it is given to them. Just as in mixed-sex conversations, women can resource men at their own expense. So in mixed-sex relationships and in their role as literary wives, there have been women who have put all their energies into enhancing and consolidating the reputations of their men.

This is not to disguise or ignore the extenuating circumstances which account for such decisions: It is certainly not my intention to "blame the victim." But in literature as in life there are and have been women who have tried to make the best of their conditions with some form of compromise: Serving as handmaids to great literary men is just one of them.

Among the most famous real-life literary wives was Jane Carlyle. As Phyllis

Rose has said of her, "Until she decided to marry a writer, she wanted to be a writer herself" (1985: p. 32): There's no doubt she had the talent for it.

"At the age of thirteen she wrote a novel. At fourteen she wrote a five act tragedy, which Dr Welsh (her father) admired so much he sent on to a friend" (p. 31). By the age of twenty one, Jane was "a formidable prose stylist" (p. 36) and even when married to Carlyle, settled in London, and determined to develop his literary leanings at the expense of her own, there could be no concealing the capabilities of Jane Carlyle.

"Some people said that Jane was the cleverest woman in London . . . her friends had the highest estimate of her talents on the basis of her conversation and her brilliant letters. Dickens thought she would have been a great novelist and Forster agreed. She was a personage in her own right, George Eliot sent her and not Mr Carlyle copies of her first two novels" (Phyllis Rose, 1985: pp. 239–240).

But Jane Carlyle put her creative energies into ensuring that it was her husband who enjoyed conditions that were conducive to writing—even though it was by no means a simple or short-term task to meet his needs. What is surprising is that there was sufficient time left for her to write the lively and lengthy letters that testify to her own literary talent.

In her analysis of the Carlyle marriage, Phyllis Rose gives some idea of the division of labour between Tom and Jane. Mrs Carlyle, comments Phyllis Rose, joyously played—

> . . . the role of her husband's protector, slaying the serpents without so that he could concentrate on slaying the serpents within. That gaunt convenienceless house ran on Jane's spirit the way houses today run on electricity. Rather the house ran on servants, and the servants ran on Jane. She hired and fired them. She encouraged them to draw water, light fires, air bedrooms—to do whatever needed to be done. She also supervised repairs on the house, encouraging the workmen, while Carlyle escaped the uproar and retired somewhere else to write. She kept foolish people away from him, either putting them off with charmingly written excuses or, if that failed, by entertaining them herself. When they were called to account by the tax assessor it was, of course, Jane who went. At the last minute Carlyle had said that "the voice of honour" seemed to call on him to go himself. "But either it did not call loud enough", Jane commented, "or he would not listen to the charmer". For both the Carlyles the quintessential expression of Jane's role within the marriage was her continuing battle to protect her husband from the crowing of cocks. (Phyllis Rose, 1985: p. 242)

When wives can perform such valuable services for writers, it is understandable that some women writers might prefer to have wives[8] rather than to be wives!

---

[8]Gillian Hanscombe and Virginia Smyers (1987) point out that there have been women writers who have had "wives"—"H. D.", Amy Lowell, Gertrude Stein, etc.

Tom Carlyle showed little appreciation for the sacrifice made by his wife. According to Elizabeth Hardwick (1974) he "liked to say she had surrendered her own talents in order to help him have his great career" (p. 159) but his acknowledgement of her contribution did not go so far as to prevent him from forming a relationship with Lady Ashburton, though it was a friendship which was deeply distressing to his wife.

"After years of gratitude to her for having given up her self in his favour," comments Phyllis Rose, once Carlyle embarked on his relationship with Lady Ashburton, he started to wish that Jane "had more self—so she could leave him alone with his fantasies" (1985: p. 246). Ill, ignored, addicted to morphine, this was a tormented time for Jane Carlyle.

The critic Elizabeth Hardwick (1974) provides another revealing picture of the relationship of this particular writer to his work—and his wife: "Once when (Jane) told Carlyle that she had, at a certain moment, thought of leaving him, he replied, 'I don't know that I would have missed you. I was very busy just then with Cromwell'" (p. 173).

Marion Glastonbury (1978) has little patience with such an egocentric and blinkered response: While convinced that Thomas Carlyle took the services of Jane completely for granted and even expected them of right, Marion Glastonbury is also sure that Carlyle was "mistaken" when he declared that he would not have missed the ministrations of his wife. "He would of course have missed her as soon as he felt hungry, or needed a change of clothes," reports Marion Glastonbury, "But the master can afford the luxury of forgetting his reliance on the slave, whereas the condition of slavery can never be forgotten" (1978: pp. 44–45).

Behind every great man—are the resources of a woman! How many have there been like Jane Carlyle who have not only sacrificed themselves for their husbands—but who have been mocked and maligned for their efforts?

Like Jane Carlyle, Emma Hardy was married to a difficult man; like Jane Carlyle, Emma Hardy put much of her energy into helping her husband achieve success. Her contribution was not always domestic (the idea of a bohemian life appealed to her) but from the beginning of their relationship, Emma Hardy helped her Tom in his intellectual endeavours.

While she has been patronised, pitied, and pilloried for her own literary aspirations and efforts, Robert Gittings (1978) has pointed out that this has been the particular bias of commentators, and that Emma Hardy was certainly not without her own talent. "The tradition of her virtual illiteracy so universally stressed by Hardy's biographers, aided by his second wife, is simply not true," states Robert Gittings, and he quotes an example of one of Emma's published letters—"virtually an article"—which he judges to be "a well reasoned, direct, enlightened and admirable piece of writing" (pp. 63–64).

As so many other comments made by Robert Gittings on Emma Hardy are extremely harsh, his praise of her writing cannot be discounted on the grounds of partiality. But Robert Gittings believed Emma Hardy to have had ability, and Thomas Hardy to have benefited from her assistance.

Certainly she worked hard for her husband; when he embarked on his programme of self-education she proved to be an indefatigable note taker on his account. She copied his manuscripts for him and until the rupture of their relationship late in life, every novel he wrote was discussed in detail with her providing many suggestions for his work. With *Tess* for example, she was a contributor as well as a critic, for with this novel she helped her husband introduce an incident from her own unpublished story, "The Maid on the Shore" (see Robert Gittings, 1978: p. 63).

And of course as a wife, she provided other services as well. When Thomas Hardy was ill, he would dictate his novel to her, and there were times when he thanked her for working "bravely at both writing and nursing" (Robert Gittings, 1978: p. 23).

But if she put her energies into her husband, Emma Hardy did not reap what she believed to be her just reward. Thomas Hardy repudiated her religion . . . and went off with other women. Which brought an end to what Lord David Cecil described as her help in the form of "counsel, copious notes for references, and mutual discussion" (see Robert Gittings, 1978: p. 81).

Yet as she brought one chapter to an end, Emma Hardy started another. She recorded her resentment in her diary under the heading, "What I think of my husband." However, we cannot come to any conclusions about her literary skills on the basis of this contribution, nor can we add her insights to women's literary heritage: Her husband destroyed her diaries after her death.

All this is not to say of course that had Emma Hardy put her energy into developing her own talents, she would necessarily have become a great novelist. But it is to say that she put her not inconsiderable skills at her husband's disposal and that she demonstrably helped him in his own artistic development—and could at least be given credit for this work! And if he had done for her what she did for him . . . who knows? And on a more general level, if men had provided women with some of the support women have provided for men—how different would literary history be?

To Gillian Hanscombe and Virginia Smyers (1987) it is understandable that so many women writers have chosen to live with women—and not just because of the freedom of speech that such a context affords. In so many ways it has been easier for women to "support" women—even to play "the wife." As they point out, "Katherine Mansfield, for example, had to encourage Murry, rather than he her work, even when she was terminally ill; and for her own writing she called on her friend Ida Baker, whom she addressed as her 'wife'" (1987: pp. 244–245).

In 1971, Phyllis Chesler declared that if women wanted to talk they should talk to each other for they would get little opportunity in the presence of men (p. 179): To this we now appear to be able to add, if women want literary support they must turn to each other, for there is little evidence that they will get support for their work from men. These are the conditions of women's work, they warrant women's criticism: This is women's judgement of literary men.

7

Polish, Plagiarism and Plain Theft

ACKNOWLEDGEMENT OF THE PROBLEM

Jane Carlyle and Emma Hardy "gave" their emotional and physical resources to men without so much as a thanks for their troubles. But even had their husbands paid lip-service to the donations of their wives, and publicly acknowledged the nature and extent of their contributions, there would still be some problems left to address. For there is often much more to an acknowledgement than meets the eye, as an entry in *A Feminist Dictionary* makes clear:

> *Acknowledgement*: Before feminism, that portion of a book where authors acknowledged the ideas and intellectual contributions of males and the clerical and editorial assistance of females and where men thanked their wives for critically reading their manuscripts without asking for co-authorship (Cheris Kramarae and Paula Treichler, 1985: p. 28).

Many of the issues which have been raised within this volume are reflected in this definition; the sexual double standard which would have men as the intellectual beings, the gifted writers, while women are seen as secondary, as the source of servicing skills. And more; issues about literary values, educational practices, heterosexual relationships—and the way women are "ripped-off" in a male-dominated community.

This facetious—but fundamental—feminist definition of "acknowledgement" places on the literary agenda the male appropriation of female energy, intellectuality, skill. From the perspective of women, no judgement of men could be complete without some consideration being given to the means by which men have taken the resources of women. No discussion of the double standard would be adequate without reference to the extent to which men think they are entitled to the labours of women.

Through the centuries and across the creative spectrum, there have been countless cases of men claiming the credit for women's contributions. Fathers, brothers, husbands, sons, and lovers have all profited from the process. In her book *The Obstacle Race* (1979) Germaine Greer has suggested that one answer to the tedious question— Why no great women artists? —could well be that when women were good, their work was appropriated by men.

But if women of the past put up with these thefts, women of the present have been showing themselves to be much less tractable; the definition of acknowledgement in *A Feminist Dictionary* is indicative of a groundswell of protest against such patriarchal privilege. Mrs. Spock, for example, wife of the ostensible child rearing expert, Dr. Spock, is one woman who feels she has been particularly ill used.

In her article, "Holding the Pens," Marion Glastonbury (1978) focuses on the way men have exploited women in their literary work and she takes Mrs. Spock and her complaint as a typical example: "The reward of reflected glory was not enough for Mrs. Spock. She has left Benjamin protesting that her participation in the manual of Child Care has never been recognised," writes Marion Glastonbury reminding her readers of the international reputation of the husband and the relative obscurity of the wife. Yet according to Marion Glastonbury (and to Mrs. Spock) such disparity in visibility is by no means commensurate with the quantity or quality of the input.

"In my edition of the manual," continues Marion Glastonbury caustically, Benjamin states that "Jane Spock has made the most essential contribution of all in graciously giving up four evenings a week for two years while I wrote and erased and wrote again." But Marion Glastonbury is not all that impressed by this expression of gratitude on the part of the husband; she is, however, most impressed by the claims of the wife:

"*He* makes it sound as if all she did was to sacrifice the pleasure of his company now and then," whereas *her* version is very different. "She says she taught him everything he knows" (Marion Glastonbury, 1978: p. 29).

The question of whether ideas can be owned—and by whom—is one which almost always promotes controversy and while there can be no definitive answers, there can be no doubt that there is a distinct and identifiable pattern of ownership in relation to the sexes. And as with so many other resources, men *own* more than women[1] and this is not necessarily because men *produce* more.

That men may systematically take the ideas (and efforts) of women is an issue that has been raised in the academic community, particularly in relation

[1]See the United Nations statistics (1982)—that men receive 90% of the world's income and own more than 99% of the world's wealth.

to the "research wife." Among the evidence cited to support the contention of male appropriation is that of the "acknowledgement," where it seems—ironically—that in the attempt to be fair and to document in detail the contribution made by wives, some men have attributed so many skills to their spouses that all that seems to have been required of them as authors was to append their names. For while they may have graciously acknowledged that their books would not exist without the work of their wives, their "generosity" does not extend to the inclusion of wives in ownership/authorship of the text.

The historian E. P. Thompson has (paradoxically) acquired a reputation for his sensitivity to unfair practices and for his condemnation of exploitation, yet these are attributes that appear to be peculiarly lacking in his relationship to his wife. His acknowledgement—which is not atypical of male authors but which is virtually without parallel among female authors—prompts questions about the nature of his own role as researcher and writer:

"I have also to thank Mrs. Dorothy Thompson, a historian to whom I am related by the accident of marriage," writes E. P. Thompson in the preface to *The Making of the English Working Class* (1963): "Each chapter has been discussed with her and I have been well placed to borrow not only her ideas, but material from her notebooks. Her collaboration is to be found not in this or that particular but in the way the whole problem is seen" (p. 14).

On the basis of this acknowledgement, my question is—why does Mr. Thompson use the word *borrow*? He unabashedly admits to *borrowing* his wife's notes and ideas, but the term can only be euphemistic given that even if he so desired, he could not return that which he has taken.

Marion Glastonbury, however, asks different questions about Mr. Thompson's literary usages: "At first glance this seems scrupulously honest," she states as she peruses the preface, "a handsome tribute, who could say fairer than that? Then one wonders, if Dorothy played such a vital part in the project, why doesn't her name appear on the title page?" (1978: p. 29). Marion Glastonbury's question is not rhetorical: She knows why—and how—women's energy, women's intellectual, emotional, creative, and physical energy can be appropriated by men. She is one of a long line of women who has argued that society has been arranged so that women may serve as resources for the achievements of men.

Perhaps the most persuasive proponent of this thesis is the nineteenth century American feminist, Matilda Joslyn Gage (1826–1898). She developed an impressive economic theory to explain the relative poverty of women and wealth of men. It was her contention that one of the main principles of patriarchy was that men *owned* women and she drew many parallels between this arrangement and the system of slavery; the harder slaves work, the richer masters get, she argued, and asserted that the position was no different for women. United Nations statistics lend support to this broad thesis; women—who own less than 1% of the world's wealth—are working harder and getting poorer every year. "The feminisation of poverty" is the contemporary name that has been given to this particular pattern of wealth distribution (see Hilda Scott, 1984).

Even the so-called gains of the Women's Liberation Movement have been called into question by the increase in women's commitments and the decrease in women's wealth over the past twenty years. In examining the broad perspective in which the rich (men) are getting richer and the poor (women) are getting poorer, Barbara Ehrenreich (1983) has suggested that as more and more women have joined the paid labour force, they have relieved men of the sole responsibility of being breadwinners. Men don't have to pay for as much as they used to (witness too, the widespread non-payment of maintenance), so they can accumulate resources. But not only do women get paid less and have to support more (witness the dramatic rise in female-headed families) but women now have to work harder; they may have relieved men of the responsibility of breadwinning but men have rarely relieved women of the housework.

This is the context in which men feel entitled to help themselves to the fruits of women's labour. It is a context which is reinforced by numerous arrangements; by the education system which legitimates preferential treatment of males and practices wholesale theft of girls's creativity. It is a context in which men can assume that the resources of women are readily available to them—in conversations, in classrooms, in the office, in relationships, in literary activities.

Such a context is not ordinarily problematic to men; the problem arises when women attempt to withdraw their resources and when men feel they are being deprived of their traditional rights. But it is a problem which is becoming focussed for contemporary women who are much more comfortable about asserting their own worth than some of their foremothers appear to have been. Hence the introduction of such topics to women's circles as the nature of "originality" and the double standard (Berenice Carroll, 1981 and forthcoming), and the documentation of case histories where men have passed off women's contributions as their own efforts. Take Dorothy Wordsworth (1771–1855) for example.

Dorothy Wordsworth managed many of her brother William's emotional needs; she provided support, encouragement, and that inestimable attribute—faith in *his* creative ability. She also managed his household, sharing in the security she helped to establish when he was single and solicitous of the welfare of both William and his wife when he was married. She also kept a journal—for William's use.

"Her journals were begun early, spurred on by William," writes Elizabeth Hardwick (1974: p. 147) and while they were original and evocative literary documents (see Dorothy Wordsworth, 1976), they were not kept for the literary purposes of the writer. Dorothy Wordsworth's journals were used by William as a major source for his writing.

Seduced by the notion of service and sacrifice for a man, Dorothy Wordsworth worked for William. This is not to suggest that she was callously coerced into slaving for a man, but it is to suggest that when women are systematically undermined, when they are taught to believe that in the end it is men who are brighter and better and on whom they must depend, then it is a mockery to speak of women's offerings as "freely given." When the alternatives are rejection or starvation, it is understandable that women could choose to live with men—on men's terms. They could agree to give up their own aims, aspirations, and autonomy and, in the name of love, offer all that they possessed to a man. Given the options it is even conceivable that women of the past could have been grateful for the opportunity.

But had William Wordsworth recognised the wealth of the contribution that his sister put at his disposal, had he publicly acknowledged the extent to which he drew on her diaries for detail, direction, inspiration, it is still doubtful whether the reading public could have accepted his assessment of the creative worth of a woman. More likely, William would have been considered a sweet and sensitive man for providing some space for his sister within the frame of his own success; else he would have been considered misguided or mistaken to attribute some of his achievement to a woman's "housekeeping" skills. So deeply entrenched is the idea that men are the patrician artists and women the plebian servicers of their skills, that it is sometimes impossible to break the mind-set and to have the intellectual strengths of women presented as credible.

Look what happened to John Stuart Mill when he openly and fully acknowledged the intellectual contribution made by Harriet Taylor to his work! At first he was not taken seriously, but when he continued to insist that Harriet Taylor's intellectual stature was comparable to his own, he was perceived as besotted, as swayed by the wiles of an unscrupulous woman, and *his* declaration was dismissed.

Alice Rossi (1970) has offered an explanation for the absence of Harriet Taylor's name as coauthor on their joint publications; it may not necessarily have been because John didn't want to share the glory or the credit. For these two had a very unconventional relationship in that they were "just good friends" and working colleagues for many years, while Harriet was married to someone else. And this in Victorian times! For Harriet to have appeared as coauthor would have been to attract further and unwanted attention to their relationship—and to Harriet's "unwomanly" characteristics. There could have been sensible reasons for Harriet remaining the silent partner; of course another possible solution could have been for the work to have appeared solely in Harriet's name, but this option does not seem to have been contemplated.

Harriet Taylor (later Mill) was an intellectual, a clear, concise, creative thinker who, in many respects was more radical than John Stuart Mill in Alice Rossi's opinion. A study of Harriet's reclaimed writing ("Enfranchisement of Women") makes it quite clear that she was perfectly capable of participating in the intellectual partnership which John Stuart Mill claimed they shared. But when he tried to tell the world of *her* wit and wisdom—as he did in his *Autobiography* (1924)—it was his *own* wit and wisdom which was seriously questioned.

John Stuart Mill described in detail the way in which he and Harriet had worked together and where possible, he carefully separated his contribution from hers. For example, in relation to *Political Economy*, "He acknowledged that the first draft of his book had no chapter on the future condition of the working class, and that the one that was finally included was 'wholly an exposition of her thoughts, often in words taken from her own lips,'" (Alice Rossi, 1970: p. 40).

When it came to *On Liberty* he was even more specific; this was the book which was "more directly and literally our joint production than anything else which bears my name," he stated in his *Autobiography*, "for there was not a sentence of it that was not several times gone through by us together, turned over in many ways, and carefully weeded of any faults, either in thought or expression, that we detected in it" (1924: p. 176).

But his words fell on deaf ears: Worse, they prompted vicious attacks on Harriet and various assaults on his own integrity, as every attempt was made to reestablish the active artistry of men—and the passive, "clay nature" of women.

In what has become a depressingly familiar pattern of response to John Stuart Mill's praise of Harriet Taylor, Justice Holmes made a significant contribution when he said "I believe he was literally the only person who was in the least impressed by her. Mrs Grote said briefly that she was a stupid woman. Bain said she had a knack of repeating prettily what was wonderful" (quoted in Alice Rossi, 1970: p. 33).

Writing in 1961, Jack Stillinger, editor of *The Early Draft of John Stuart Mill's Autobiography* sums up the response to John Stuart Mill's claim that Harriet was his intellectual equal: "Harriet of the incomparable intellect," concludes Jack Stillinger, "was largely a product of his imagination, an idealization, according to his peculiar needs, of a clever, domineering, in some ways perverse and selfish, invalid woman" (p. 27).

Interestingly, this is one of the few areas where John Stuart Mill is charged with having got it wrong: Even more interesting is the application of the double standard which would have any "flaws" in the great man's reasoning laid at the feet of Harriet. All the evidence suggests that the only "logic" which is permitted to prevail is that—no matter what—man is to be considered creatively and intellectually superior. As Alice Rossi states, "The hypothesis that a mere woman was the collaborator of so logical and intellectual a thinker as Mill, much less that she influenced the development of his thought, can be expected to meet resistance in the minds of men right up to the 1970s" (1970: p. 36). And onwards!

But women too can come to believe in the intellectual impoverishment of their sex—particularly those very few women who have been allowed entry to male circles, whose judgement is often suspect, and who can find themselves facing constant pressure to prove that they can meet the male standards. Diana Trilling, for example, is one of the few women who in the past has enjoyed the status of a literary critic, and who has gone to great lengths to enhance the image of the male sex at the expense of her own. In taking the creative resources of women and reallocating them to men, she more than meets "the topic and terms" requirements of the discourse laid down by men:

"John Stuart Mill had characterized Harriet as his 'intellectual beacon,'" Alice Rossi informs us, "but Mrs Trilling suggests that she had in fact 'nothing more than a vest pocket flash-light of a mind . . . one of the meanest, dullest ladies in literary history, a monument of nasty self regard, as lacking in charm as in grandeur,' whose correspondence shows a 'fleshless, bloodless quality' full of 'injured vanity, petty egoism and ambition.'" (Alice Rossi, 1970: p. 35). All this from the text of course!

It seems that it was precisely because Harriet played such a major part in John's intellectual and literary life that Diana Trilling openly accuses her of being devoid of feminine grace; she had "no touch of true femininity, no taint of the decent female concerns which support our confidence in the intelligence of someone like Jane Carlyle," declares Diana Trilling, revealing her own value judgements about the place of women (Alice Rossi, 1970: p. 35).

How Diana Trilling accounts for the credible and exemplary nature of her own judgement is not explained, but what she does do is demonstrate that we cannot rely on the practices of traditional literary criticism to change, simply by the introduction of a few women into the privileged community.

A literary criticism which does not address the issue of sex-exploitation in the production of texts has left out one of the most significant areas of women's contribution. For whether one man is unable to redress the balance and reinsert women's claim to creativity—as John Stuart Mill tried to do; or whether a man takes the creativity of a woman as raw material which he proceeds to polish or refine—as William Wordsworth did; or whether a man borrows or plagiarises the work of a woman as Benjamin Spock and E. P. Thompson have done, the end result is that men are thriving. They are enriching their own resources by drawing on those of women; the arrangement is not reciprocal. And in mainstream literary history hardly a word of protest about these widespread appropriation practices has been recorded; in the literary history of women this topic is of central concern.

BY ANOTHER NAME

While the discussion of the theft of women's creative work by men has not been a prominent item on men's literary agenda, it has been a popular practice in the world of letters. My own somewhat elementary investigations have revealed a substantial number of known cases and I am convinced that further study would reveal the even more scandalous proportions of the crime. And the victims are by no means confined to the categories of the lesser known women writers; nor has it necessarily been the lesser known men who have taken what they could get. Colette and Maria Edgeworth, for example, are but two very different writers who have had their words appear under another name; and D. H. Lawrence is just one of the many well-known men writers who has taken the words of women and passed them off as his own.

Of course one reason that there has been no systematic objection to this facet of literary production is that there has not always been full recognition of the pervasive nature of the thefts. Rather, the individual examples that have been recorded are regarded as just that—as the isolated case—and not as the ordinary or routine habits of the dominant group. Such is the price that can be paid in the absence of a tradition; however when these previously "isolated" cases are drawn together and the connections among them clearly made, there can be no doubt about the general principle which operates— from women's perspective.

Take Colette for example. Born in 1873, she married young. Her husband, known professionally as "Willy," ran a "literary factory" (see Margaret Crosland, 1975: p. 59). Not long after their marriage—as early as 1894—it occurred to Willy that it might be possible to "employ" Colette as one of his ghost writers to produce novels in his name. Opposed to such work, Colette initially outwitted Willy in this scheme; she recounts what happened the first time Willy told her to write something for him:

"When I had finished I gave my husband a closely written text which respected the margins. He read it through and said:

'I was wrong, it's no good at all.'

Liberated, I went back to the divan, the cat, the books, the new friends . . . '' (quoted in Margaret Crosland, 1975: p. 68).

That she felt herself to be "liberated" when Willy dismissed her writing has been taken by some critics as evidence that Colette was indifferent to a literary career (see Janet Flanner, 1975, for example). But to me her testimony does not constitute evidence that she did not want to write—only that she did not want to write for Willy! That she would later go on to write so many books (many more than fifty) and would reveal a measure of pride and pleasure in her work, suggests that writing was a career she was content to cultivate: She could have made a living as an actress but when allowed a choice, it was a literary life that she led.

But she wanted to write in her own way and on her own terms. She wanted freedom for writing and she certainly didn't have that with Willy, which is why she thought she had escaped when initially he perceived her writing to have no value.

After her first "failure" to meet Willy's standards, Colette was for some time left alone. But the issue of working for Willy resurfaced when he "redis-covered" some of her writing that he had previously discarded. "To his surprise he found the school exercise books and the pages of tidy hand-writing," writes Colette. "He thought he had thrown them away. As he glanced at them again he remarked, 'c'est gentil,' 'it's nice'. He decided that he had been a bloody fool. He collected the notebooks together in a hurry, rushed to pick up his flat brimmed hat and dashed to a publisher's office . . . And that is how I became a writer," Colette cynically confesses (Margaret Crosland, 1975: pp. 68–69).

In 1900, under the name of "Willy," *Claudine a l'ecole*, Colette's first novel appeared. It was a sensational success, selling 50,000 copies almost immediately, a substantial number for the time. Willy was gratified by both the fame and the fortune.

Willy enjoyed the prestige and popularity and paraded round Paris culti-vating the image of a successful literary man. Sometimes he was accompa-nied by his wife, Colette: Sometimes she remained in her room writing more novels for which Willy would claim the rewards. And while it might not be an unusual occurrence in the literary relationship between the sexes for the woman to do the work and the man to take the credit, this episode of Willy and Colette ranks among the more dramatic examples of theft in literary history. This is partly because Colette is now so well known; but it is also partly because she was so explicit in her denunciation of Willy and his wily ways—once she had escaped his clutches.

That she was coerced into writing cannot be doubted. Colette herself admitted to being terrifed of Willy, and yet as someone who was completely dependent, and who had nowhere else to go, she believed she had no alternative but to do what she was told. And Willy told her to write. A lot! He was a hard taskmaster, always in a hurry, always in need of cash. And he was not averse to locking her in her room until she wrote what he required.

According to Colette's biographer, Margaret Crosland, from the moment that Willy took Colette's manuscript to the publisher (until she left him six novels later), Willy allowed Colette little or no respite: "If Colette had felt 'liberated' when her first manuscript had been relegated to a drawer in Willy's desk," writes Margaret Crosland, "that liberation was now over, for Willy was determined to exploit Claudine (Colette's fictional character) as far as he could" (1975: pp. 72–73).

Colette wrote six novels which were "signed" by "Willy," whose only (and highly magnanimous) contribution seems to have been the offer to fill in any "blanks" that she may have wanted to leave. "For at least four years," states Margaret Crosland, Colette "spent several hours a day in a room which was sometimes locked, writing books about a character that she had invented, but rarely writing in a way in which she wanted" (1975: p. 83).

Fortunately there was a limit to the exploitation. "As time went on, Willy found he had to employ even greater astuteness in 'manipulating' the activities of his wife. He realized that she would not continue year after year, to write books to his formula and submissively allow him to sign them" (Margaret Crosland, 1975: p. 87).

He was right.

When in 1904, Colette created her new character, Minne, she made every effort to be acknowledged as the author, but again, Willy refused to allow publication in Colette's name. She was angry; she was bitter; she left him. She launched her own independent literary career with her seventh novel, La Vagabonde. And she talked about, and she wrote about—openly and repeatedly—the way Willy had stolen her words, taken her rights, and pocketed her profits.

But if this is an extreme case of appropriation it is by no means an isolated one. Nor has it been but brothers and husbands who have benefited from women's talents. There have been fathers who have literally exploited their daughters. Among the minor thefts have been the exactions of secretarial services where—before and since word processors—fathers have called on daughters to provide "a clean copy." When Fanny Burney for example, was trying to write Evelina (1778) she had little time for her own work because she spent so many hours acting as an amanuensis for her father, producing clean copies of his masterpiece for him. (Needless to say, once she became a famous writer there is no evidence to suggest that he acted as scribe for her, see Joyce Hemlow, 1958.)

Then too, there have been the medium thefts, the thefts from the research daughter (or mother, sister, wife) who gathers the data, prepares the first draft—not to mention the production of meals, clean socks, and quiet space and time for the man to reflect upon her offerings—before he appends his name to the text. How much work Milton's daughters did in this respect would be interesting to quantify; and what about Eleanor Marx's contribution to her father's opus?

But this is not all. There is also the grand theft. The occasions when reams of women's writing are pilfered by men, where the work of a woman is known by another name.

Maria Edgeworth (1768–1849) is one woman who has had volumes of her writing "appropriated" by a man: her father. He was interested in educational reform and wished to be acknowledged as an expert so he chose the topics that he wanted to discuss and then he directed his daughter to do the research, and the writing. Which was then published under his name.

Of such theft, Maria Edgeworth did not complain: on the contrary it is interesting to note the construction that she put upon this practice.

Urged by her father to write *Professional Education* (a study of vocational education for boys and in which she was not greatly interested), Maria Edgeworth protested little about the hardship, though, "It cost her two or more years of hard reading and months of drudgery in the writing" (Marilyn Butler, 1972: p. 210)—however, she was much more worried about the responsibility. In a letter in 1808 to her cousin, Sophy Ruxton, Maria Edgeworth wrote of *Professional Education* that she was awaiting "its publication and fate with an anxiety and apprehension that I never felt before in the same degree—for consider my father's credit is entirely at stake! And do you not tremble for me, even when you read the heads of the chapters and consider of how much importance the subjects are and how totally foreign to my habits of thinking or writing" (quoted in Marilyn Butler, 1972: p. 210).

To Maria Edgeworth, the task of *writing as a man* was a daunting one indeed; she believed that it would be no mean feat to reach the standard set by men, and she was acutely conscious of the vulnerable position in which she was placing her father—whose reputation rested entirely upon her capabilities and competence.

Ah well: There are many means of rationalisation.

But given Maria Edgeworth's context it is not surprising that she should have experienced such anxiety about the responsibility—and such honour at being asked to "stand in" for her father. She was dependent upon him, financially and emotionally. She wanted his love and approval. And writing for him not only allowed her to find a place in his affections; it also allowed her to indulge her literary leanings. Not that she found such works as *Professional Education* a form of indulgence: but at least they constituted writing as distinct from any other form of domestic duty or drudgery. And after meeting the needs of her father she was able to use her time for her own novel writing. She didn't think that writing for her father was too high a price to pay. She would probably have been outraged at any suggestion that her father was *stealing* her resources. As far as she was concerned she and her father shared a "literary partnership" where, if there were any debts, they were owed by her.

The principle of doing it all willingly—for love—is of course not new. Nor is it confined to the world of letters as Germaine Greer has made clear; "The feminist art historian must deal with the phenomenon of willing sacrifice," she says (1979: p. 35). The feminist literary critic must also deal with the way men have been so keen to take these offerings, without any seeming sense of obligation, or qualms of conscience.

Given the extent to which men have been so prickly and protective about the ownership of ideas (about sources, footnotes, and full acknowledgements of each other, not to mention copyright and considerations of originality) their readiness to dispense with all the rules in relation to contributions from women should arouse at least some curiosity. But D. H. Lawrence, for example, is a man who seems to have seen his own appropriation of women's words as perfectly in order.

A suspicious person could well find something strange in the manner in which he incorporated the contributions of women into his publications without it being suggested that his creative method was an offence. For it is widely recognised in mainstream criticism that he did *take* the efforts of women, but this has not led to the registering of any protest. On the contrary, references that are made to this aspect of his creative practices are often tinged with admiration; this penchant of his for women's words is seen as a commendable attempt at authenticity on his part. The assumption seems to be that this is an added and valued dimension of D. H. Lawrence's art; when he wants to "get right" the psychology of women, he makes use of "the real thing"—the words of the women themselves. And for this he is customarily congratulated rather than condemned.

Of course, as Hilary Simpson (1979) has pointed out, such an assumption ignores the fact that much of the writing D. H. Lawrence "borrowed" from women has nothing to do with expressing authenticity, with evoking or analysing women's inner state. It is straight descriptive, or narrative material. The plain truth of the matter is that D. H. Lawrence took a variety of forms of writing from a variety of women, and made their words his own. And while some allusion is made to the manner in which he purportedly "polishes" the work of his diverse female sources, I can find no comment in conventional criticism which addresses the issue of whether his exploitative habits constitute plagiarism or plain theft.

Excluding the "assistance" provided by his wife, Frieda, D. H. Lawrence drew primarily on the energies of four women for his "sources": Jessie Chambers, Louie Burrows, Helen Corke, and Mollie Skinner. Catherine Carswell also contributed to his literary output and another woman, Mabel Dodge Luhan, offered herself, her services, and the substance of her life, for D. H. Lawrence's fictional purposes: It was partly because of the objections raised by Frieda that Mabel Dodge Luhan's generous offer was refused.

But it was Jessie Chambers, his first love, who was also his first "collaborator," and whom D. H. Lawrence was loath to lose. So when after a few years—when some of the "romance" had worn off and Jessie Chambers showed signs of being wearied by ill-use—their relationship was threatened, D. H. Lawrence tried to reassure her, and to reinlist her cooperation, with the compliment that she was necessary to his life. Which—as Hilary Simpson ironically observes—was in many ways an accurate statement.

"This necessity which Jessie filled in Lawrence's early life was not that of a source of inspiration, a muse," writes Hilary Simpson, "the help she gave him was practical—criticizing, discussing, supplying him with detailed notes and comments. For years her own literary ability was sunk in what she calls her 'co-operation' in Lawrence's work" (1979: p. 160).

Jessie Chambers herself has given some idea of the nature of her contribution. In her account of her relationship with D. H. Lawrence, she says that "Lawrence was constantly bringing his writing to me, and I always had to tell him what I thought of it. He would ask whether the characters had developed, and whether the conversation was natural, and if it was what people would really say" (Jessie Chambers, 1965: p. 115).

And competently, creatively, and continually, Jessie Chambers provided D. H. Lawrence with the feedback he deemed necessary, and which helped him to focus and fashion his work. While Jessie Chambers' skills—and those of many other women—were never regarded by D. H. Lawrence as the *vital* force in his literary creations, he certainly saw them as a desirable "extra": they were a means of adding what he perceived as an authentic dimension to his writing, and of easing the way to productivity in the process. This is exemplified with reference to his first novel, *The White Peacock* (1911): D. H. Lawrence wrote to Jessie Chambers describing their roles in relation to this artisitic work—"I its creator, you its nurse" he said (Jessie Chambers, 1965: p. 189).

It was, however, in the writing of *Sons and Lovers* that, for D. H. Lawrence, the cooperation of Jessie Chambers was crucial. For not only did she provide considerable "raw material" for his work, she was the critic who guided his efforts, and she was the chief source of his psychological support. It was Jessie Chambers who gave constant encouragement, who gave the counselling which helped D. H. Lawrence to deal with some of the pain that such a personal examination prompted; and it was Jessie Chambers who urged him to write from direct experience and who—according to Hilary Simpson—is therefore responsible for eliciting much of the (much lauded) spontaneity and naturalness in the novel.

D. H. Lawrence made many "requests" to Jessie Chambers to help him with this work, including requests for information on their mutual past, for comments on setting and surroundings, for details on their relationship, and her feelings. Some of the notes, passages, recommendations, and editorial suggestions supplied by Jessie have been collected as the "Miriam Papers" (housed in the Humanities Research Center, University of Texas) and they help to reveal the nature and the extent of her involvement with D. H. Lawrence and his novel. Hilary Simpson comments on the contents of the "Miriam Papers" and points to some of the implications:

"The papers consist of three manuscript sections in Jessie's hand (the recollection of incidents from their past that Lawrence requested); 23 pages of manuscript in Lawrence's hand with Jessie's interlinear and marginal comments, including material eventually omitted from *Sons and Lovers*; and four pages of extra comment in Jessie's hand." Having examined these papers, Hilary Simpson states that "It is clear that some of the most vivid scenes in the novel derive from Jessie's reminiscences. Lawrence often takes sentences directly from her manuscript; some of the descriptions of nature, especially, go into *Sons and Lovers* almost exactly as Jessie wrote them" (Hilary Simpson, 1979: pp. 161–162).

Not that many critics have seen the contribution of Jessie Chambers in this light. The consensus seems to be that her efforts constitute but another manifestation of the principle of the "raw material nature of women" and "the refinement qualities of men." This is the conclusion reached by D. H. Lawrence's biographer, Harry Moore, who resorts to the values of the sexual double-standard with his comments on the writing of Jessie Chambers and D. H. Lawrence: "Her prose is lead, his quicksilver" states Harry Moore, and proceeds to sum up the "polishing women's words" position when he goes on to pronounce that "She as a recorder gave him a sequence of remembered facts; he as an imaginative artist dramatically intensified them and made them into literature" (Harry Moore, 1974: p. 52). A bald statement of the artistic status of men and women.

If Harry Moore, however, is not aware of the significance of his stand, there is some evidence to suggest that D. H. Lawrence was aware of the price he was asking Jessie Chambers to pay by "contributing" to his work. While it neither impeded his writing nor prevented him from repeating his requests, Jessie Chambers nonetheless believed that D. H. Lawrence felt some guilt about *his* appropriation of *her* resources. Commenting on their so-called cooperation she has said that "we talked about his writing and he upbraided me for not making an effort to do something myself. He was so sure I could write if I would try. 'If you only had two books out, I shouldn't care,' he said. I knew he was reproaching himself for having occupied my time with his own work" (Jessie Chambers, 1965: p. 200).

But the guilt was not so great as to cause D. H. Lawrence to change tack and to begin to help Jessie Chambers with her work. On the contrary, he went on using her material (not always with her permission) for many years to come, and often in ways she did not like.

For Jessie Chambers' grievance was not simply that she thought her words were being taken from her: There were times when she felt that her own words were being used directly against her. This was certainly her reaction to Lawrence's representation of Miriam in *Sons and Lovers*: Purported to be an authenticated portrayal of Jessie, the character of Miriam was a distortion which caused Jessie considerable dismay. She felt betrayed by D. H. Lawrence's depiction of her and said of their relationship that "the shock of *Sons and Lovers* gave the death blow to our friendship" (Jessie Chambers, 1965: p. 203).

Among the many women who served as sources for D. H. Lawrence, Jessie Chambers was the most distressed by the use he made of her, and her response is not surprising in the circumstances. When other women have found themselves in similar situations—see Sonya Tolstoy and Zelda Fitzgerald for example, later in this chapter—with their experience and identity taken over and turned into representations that they felt were grossly unfair, they too dealt with anguish, and deep depression. But both Sonya Tolstoy and Zelda Fitzgerald were married to the men who were exploiting them, and neither thought they had the option to bring their relationships to an end. For Jessie there may have been some compensation in not having been married to Lawrence; at least there was life after Lawrence.

While she had been badly hurt by Lawrence's attitude towards her, Jessie Chambers was still free to leave their relationship and to establish a life of her own. And after reading the manuscript of *Sons and Lovers*—and registering her strong objections—she saw little of D. H. Lawrence again. But this merely minimised the extent to which he mined her work; it did not stop him.

Leading her own life—and able to work on her own writing—Jessie Chambers thought that she was taking some small revenge when in 1913 she sent to Lawrence a copy of her autobiographical novel "Eunice Temple" (later destroyed) which outlined the manner in which she believed she was exploited. For Jessie Chambers the final bitter irony was finding the evidence of this writing of hers in Lawrence's *The Rainbow* (1915).

Were Jessie Chambers the only woman to have been treated by D. H. Lawrence in this way, the practice would no doubt be perceived as peculiar, and the notion of "an isolated case" could be maintained. But given that it seems to have been Lawrence's habitual manner of relating to women (and men's habitual manner of relating to literary women, according to Gillian Hanscombe and Virginia Smyers, 1987), it is possible to discern a well-defined pattern behind the man's request, and the woman's response.

Louise (or Louie) Burrows—on whom D. H. Lawrence modelled the character of Ursula in *The Rainbow*—was also called upon to provide material along with considerable emotional support. She was asked to record details, to register reactions, to review the latest revisions of the literary man. And while she "helped" D. H. Lawrence, so too did he "help" her, though paradoxically it was probably help that she could well have done without.

Louie Burrows wanted to be a writer and D. H. Lawrence's reaction to her literary attempts was to retort that he could do better. He took her work—as he took that of other women—and proceeded to provide help in the form of rewriting, and in a manner that could do little but undermine the confidence and integrity of the woman writer.

In the counsel that he gave to Louie Burrows, D. H. Lawrence reveals his attitude to women and their writing: "I am glad you are writing stories," he informs Louie Burrows in a letter, "I can't do 'em myself. Send me them please, and I'll see if I can put a bit of surface on them and publish them for you. We'll collaborate, shall we?—I'm sure we could do well" (quoted in J. Boulton, 1968: p. 38).

Louie Burrows obliged by sending him *Goose Fair*, a story which D. H. Lawrence proceeded to "polish" and to which he initially attached a nom-de-plume when he submitted it for publication. Perhaps not fully appreciative of the significance of his words, he wrote to Louie Burrows and said, "The nom de guerre, as you will see is a happy mixture of you and me; you are the body, I am the head. Qu'en dites vous! I believe you are utterly unrecognisable under my figurehead" (quoted in J. Boulton, 1968: p. 39).

That it is D. H. Lawrence's belief that the woman can provide the "raw material" and the man, "the polish," is (inadvertently) revealed in part by his reference to Louie Burrows as "the body" and himself as "the head." And that he thinks that the woman is subsumed under the figurehead of the man is another indication of D. H. Lawrence's evaluation of the relative attributes of the sexes.

Goose Fair was at first rejected. D. H. Lawrence resubmitted it and, states J. Boulton, "when the story was finally published in *The English Review* for February 1910, it appeared under Lawrence's name alone—although he insisted to Louie that it was 'as much your child as mine' and split the fee he received for its publication with her in acknowledgement of this" (1968: p. 50). But this was a "private deal"; D. H. Lawrence retained "public ownership."

After Louie Burrows, it was Helen Corke who served as a D. H. Lawrence source. *The Trespasser*—D. H. Lawrence's second novel—was based on the diary of Helen Corke kept during the summer of 1909, when she had been on holiday with her lover—who later committed suicide. When she first "lent" D. H. Lawrence her diary, he was fascinated, and asked her whether he could use it. In her autobiography Helen Corke recounts what happened at this stage of their "collaboration":

"He returns to the subject of my Freshwater diary later—comes with the request that he may take it and expand its theme—use the poems as basis for a more comprehensive rendering of the story. He will bring me the work as it grows: nothing shall stand with which I am not in agreement. It shall be a finished study in full accordance with my suggestions" (Helen Corke, 1975: p. 178).

Hilary Simpson is in the fortunate position of having been able to compare Helen Corke's original diary with D. H. Lawrence's later novel: She suggests that "*The Trespasser* follows closely the events described in Helen's diary," and that "whole sentences of her prose are incorporated unchanged." There is, however, one distinct departure: Whereas in "real life" it appears that D. H. Lawrence made overtures to Helen Corke, and was rebuffed, there is something of a reversal in the novel. In the fiction, D. H. Lawrence "includes a self portrait, a young man called Cecil Byrne who comforts Helen and seems, at the end of the novel to have won her love." On this "revision" Hilary Simpson cannot resist a satirical comment. The presence—and preference—shown for Cecil Byrne is "not merely one feels, to provide a traditional happy ending," she remarks, "but as an act of wish fulfilment on Lawrence's part" (1979: p. 163).

Obviously "polish" can mean many things.

That D. H. Lawrence enhanced his own reputation at the expense of Helen Corke, that he owed her a debt, is an issue that has rarely been debated in literary circles, despite the fact that the Freshwater diary was not the only item of hers that D. H. Lawrence "helped himself to." According to Hilary Simpson, the origin and development of the poem, "Coldness in Love," (D. H. Lawrence, 1964: p. 98) reveals the way D. H. Lawrence worked and one of the reasons why:

"Helen Corke showed Lawrence a poem she had written called 'Fantasy,' about a trip they had made together to the coast. Lawrence promptly produced his own poem, based on the same situation, taking Helen's theme and recasting it to his own satisfaction," states Hilary Simpson. "The final printed version could be in the voice of either a man or a woman, but in fact the emotions are Helen's, as her autobiography reveals, although anyone reading the poem without a knowledge of its background would assume them to be Lawrence's" (1979: p. 156).

That the poem and the sentiments should be attributed to D. H. Lawrence, that the contribution made by Helen Corke should be so little known, is a result of the failure of D. H. Lawrence (and literary critics) to publicly proclaim the part that Helen Corke played. D. H. Lawrence did not openly advertise the assistance provided by Helen Corke, but this was in some measure because in his own actions he saw little of note—or notoriety. He thought it perfectly appropriate to draw on the resources of women as he did: It seems that he was nothing other than sincere when he wrote to Helen Corke and said, "I always feel when you give me an idea, how much better I could work it out myself" (Harry Moore, 1974: p. 102). And this, declares Hilary Simpson is "an appropriate epigraph to any discussion of Lawrence's attitude towards women's articulation of their own experience in literary form" (1979: p. 156).

In the context of polish, plagiarism, and plain theft, D. H. Lawrence can take his place as one of the worst offenders. While his behaviour may conform to the pattern that predominates among male artists—as illustrated by Germaine Greer (1979)—it must be acknowledged that in his "borrowings" D. H. Lawrence has gone further than most other members of his sex. "For Lawrence not only solicited reminiscences from Jessie, from his wife Frieda, from Mabel Dodge Luhan and others—in itself a fairly unusual procedure," states Hilary Simpson, still treating D. H. Lawrence's method as an isolated example, "he also took over women's manuscripts and rewrote them as in the cases of Helen Corke and Mollie Skinner" (1979: p. 155).

Mollie Skinner had been a nurse during World War I, and had published an account of her experiences, which D. H. Lawrence read when in 1922 he was staying in her guest house in Australia. He asked her if she had written anything else and she brought out her work in progress, the novel *Black Swans*.[2] D. H. Lawrence suggested that Mollie Skinner should write more— and send him what she wrote. He would see about getting it published.

In 1923, when he was in Mexico, Mollie Skinner took D. H. Lawrence at his word and forwarded to him her latest work—"The House of Ellis." D. H. Lawrence replied:

"I have read 'The House of Ellis' carefully—such good stuff, but without unity or harmony. I'm afraid as it stands you'll never find a publisher. Yet I hate to think of it all as wasted. I like the quality of so much of it. But you have no constructive power.—If you like I will take it and recast it, and make a book of it. In which case we should have to appear as collaborators, or assume a pseudonym.—If you give me a free hand, I'll see if I can't make a complete book out of it" (D. H. Lawrence, 1962: p. 751). No chance of anyone using *his* words under another name!

A reasonable offer on his part, however, were Mollie Skinner to get her full share of the credit, as Lawrence was to get his: Exploitation, however, when she came to be subsumed under his name. Though D. H. Lawrence has not been the only literary man to believe that it was right and proper, that the words of women should become art, in the hands of men. The practice of according the credit to the man and of eclipsing the woman is just as much the responsibility of the critics who have failed to examine this form of malpractice. It hasn't been a problem for them.

But Mollie Skinner thought it looked like a good opportunity and agreed to allow Lawrence to polish her manuscript; he "wrote the whole book over again from start to finish, putting in and leaving out, yet keeping the main substance of Miss Skinner's work." (D. H. Lawrence, 1968: p. 295). The art of polishing, it appears, is not a particularly time-consuming task, for he soon sent a letter to Mollie Skinner to say that his work was almost done, but that the ending would have to be "different, a good deal different," and that he had made "a rather daring development psychologically" (D. H. Lawrence, 1962: p. 720).

When Mollie Skinner read what he had written she was not at all pleased; she disapproved—decidedly—of the ending. It seemed to her that it was disastrous, rather than daring. It was the hero to whom she objected and the

---

[2]Published by Jonathan Cape, 1925—and a fascinating book according to Debra Adelaide, 1986.

emphasis that D. H. Lawrence placed on his emerging manhood was to her entirely unacceptable. She suggested that the ending be rewritten, and her own "character" reinstated. But no changes were made: In 1924, *The Boy in the Bush* was published, complete with D. H. Lawrence's controversial but male-affirming ending.

That Mollie Skinner was the original and substantive author, and that the changes in the story line (and the ending) were not sanctioned by her, seem to have been factors which have been "overlooked,"[3] as this novel has found its way into the literary tradition, where it is classified among D. H. Lawrence's work. The information that Mollie Skinner might have made a contribution to the book could never have been gleaned from the television production of the novel, for her name was not among the credits. And scant reference has been made to her in literary circles. While in the 1981 Penguin edition of *The Boy in the Bush* it is acknowledged that Mollie Skinner cooperated with the author, her credibility is effectively undermined by the description of her as an "amateur writer." Although how the author of more than five published works could be labelled as an amateur is not made clear! A sex-definition perhaps?

After *The Boy in the Bush*, Mollie Skinner does not appear to have collaborated with D. H. Lawrence again. He seems to have given her some "editing" assistance—particularly with a series of articles she wrote for *The Adelphi*—but there is no evidence to suggest that she provided him with further substantive sources. And as to whether she believed herself to be ill used or exploited, there is room for some debate. She was certainly grateful for the interest shown in her work by such a great literary man—but she was not completely satisfied with her relationship to D. H. Lawrence—or with its results.

How Catherine Carswell finally felt about her collaboration with D. H. Lawrence is also a matter in which there is room for debate. A novelist, critic, and friend of Lawrence, she too was wooed. He asked her to accompany him to New Mexico, to help establish a new community but she "carefully explained that she didn't feel able to leave her husband and young child," comments Hilary Simpson, and in order to "soften the blow of her refusal she began to tell him of an idea she had in mind for a new novel. Lawrence was interested in her theme and suggested that they should collaborate" (1979: p. 167).

To what extent D. H. Lawrence thought he was helping or hindering the development of the women around him is hard to determine. But that he

---

[3]There is an exception: Debra Adelaide's paper at Association for the Study of Australian Literature, Townsville, 1986.

thought it quite acceptable to take the ideas, experiences, diaries, and letters of women he liked cannot be doubted: "I like that story of yours so much," he wrote to Catherine Carswell, "that I've written out a little sketch of how I think it might go. Then if you like the idea, we might collaborate on the novel" (Catherine Carswell, 1932: p. 211).

This is not the statement of a man who is self-conscious or defensive about his actions. Even if some women were uncomfortable with the collaboration, Lawrence himself was not.

There is no evidence that Catherine Carswell was eager to enter a loving or a literary affair with D. H. Lawrence. Although he suggested that they embark on a joint novel, that she should "do the beginning and get the woman character going," and he would "go on and fill in the man" (see Catherine Carswell, 1932: p. 214), she confesses that she soon lost heart and abandoned the project. But as Hilary Simpson points out, Catherine Carswell "does not intimate whether it was Lawrence's taking over of her idea that disheartened her or whether she herself had planned a quite different treatment of the theme; but the novel remained unwritten" (1979: p. 167).

There is a fine but significant line between support and interference but there can only be speculation on how far Lawrence provided either (or neither) for the women with whom he "collaborated." And it is more than likely that there is more than one version of the cooperation. His help could well have been hindrance to some to whom he offered it: His generosity could well have been theft to some with whom he shared. But such literary partnerships of the sexes and all their dynamics should certainly be the topic of serious literary debate.

On the list of (known) women on whom D. H. Lawrence drew for literary material and support, the contributions of Mabel Dodge Luhan and his wife Frieda are among those which have yet to be evaluated. That the wealthy Mabel Dodge Luhan *volunteered* her resources to D. H. Lawrence to do with what he would cannot be in doubt: That Frieda Lawrence did not favour her husband's liaison with this lady is equally clear. But the exact nature of the assistance that Frieda Lawrence made available to her husband is not so easy to establish.

She says she helped him with his writing. In relation to *Sons and Lovers* (which was being revised in 1912), Frieda Lawrence states "I lived and suffered that book, and wrote bits of it when he would ask me: 'What do you think my mother felt like then?'" (Frieda Lawrence, 1935: p. 52). And as to Mabel Dodge Luhan, Frieda Lawrence declared that there were pages of *Sons and Lovers* which were her work. On more than one occasion Frieda Lawrence claimed to be the author of "little female bits" in her husband's writing (1961: p. 186): Given D. H. Lawrence's record for "borrowing," her claim seems not unlikely.

In summing up D. H. Lawrence's attitude to women and to writing, Hilary Simpson draws on some of the precepts more fully articulated by Sandra Gilbert and Susan Gubar (1980)—and others—when she says that "The issue of the male novelist's rendering of female experience must also take into account what Rosalind Miles has described as 'the assumption that literary creation is itself a masculine act, a process of exploring and mastering the feminine, unconscious mass of life and material'. Indeed," continues Hilary Simpson caustically, "Lawrence can frequently give the impression that he considered the evocation of feminine reality too momentous and urgent a task to be left to women," (Rosalind Miles, 1974: p. 49) and it is his belief that he, as a man, could do so much better that is responsible for his relationship to women's experience and expression. "It seems to be the pervasive concept of femininity as 'raw material' and masculinity as 'shaping force'" concludes Hilary Simpson, "which underlies (Lawrence's) use of women's writing" (1979: p. 158).

There is nothing unique—or even unusual—in D. H. Lawrence's evaluation of the sex differences in writing. What must be taken into account is that historically and currently there have been men *and* women who have accepted similar assessments of the relative strengths and weaknesses of the creative abilities of the sexes. And it can sometimes be the agreement of women that complicates the issue.

If all women possessed confidence, and were convinced of the autonomy of women's creative resources, then all women could insist that the offers of men to "refine" the raw materials of women constituted nothing other than gross interference, bolstered by false claims of superiority. If all women agreed that women's resources were *women's* entitlement, and that women's creativity should be openly acknowledged as *women's* art, then any attempt by a man to take women's work and to use it as his own could be met with accusations of exploitation and theft.

But it is not so simple.

For far from always defending the independence of women's creativity, and its products, there have been women who have welcomed the artistic interest of men, particularly prominent men. It has even been seen as the high point of their lives. And far from holding such interest to be interference or theft, they have felt gratified, even honoured, that men could have found sufficient value in their work to want to appropriate it for their own use (see Maria Edgeworth, for example). There have been women who have thought themselves privileged to be able to play such a small role in literary productions and who have claimed that they have benefited from the process. Which says a lot about women's position in society.

While I have no intention here of scapegoating women for the circumstances in which they find themselves, the fact that some women have insisted that they have been privileged to be allowed to enhance the reputation of great men,[4] does pose something of a problem. It is difficult to conduct an investigation into *theft* when there are women who state that no crime has been committed; that on the contrary, they feel flattered at being found to have something of value which they can give away to worthy men—and feel that they have gained in the giving!

Where to draw a dividing line between giving and taking—between helping and hampering—is an awkward task; and nowhere more so than in the case of Samuel Richardson.

During the eighteenth century and at a time when women were deprived of education and occupation, and definitely discouraged from "going public," Samuel Richardson acted as patron and mentor for aspiring literary women. He gathered round him a group of gifted women who enthusiastically cooperated in *his* work, while they were convinced that it was of benefit for their own. He encouraged them to write for him, and not only did some of the participants in his projects later attribute their literary success to the various forms of support that he supplied, they went so far as to suggest that without his active assistance, they might not have written at all.

And their contributions to the work that appeared exclusively under Samuel Richardson's name were substantial. It was not the occasional item that this author "borrowed": On the contrary, part of the reason for the creation of his literary circle was to provide material—particularly from the woman's perspective—for his own literary output. "He had a large circle of women friends with whom he kept up a steady correspondence about his writing, soliciting and incorporating their suggestions, and in turn encouraging them in their own literary work," writes Hilary Simpson, who evaluates the role of women in Samuel Richardson's writing. "These members of Richardson's circle played a particularly important part in the composition of Richardson's third novel . . . *Sir Charles Grandison*—they contributed whole scenes and one of them completely revised the manuscript" (1979: p. 157).

But it is a damning indictment of the options that were available to women at the time that they should have been pleased to have had the opportunity that such involvement represented. Denied systematic education, professional occupation, political influence, and literary verisimilitude, it is not surprising that these highly talented and intellectually active women should have been grateful to Samuel Richardson for holding open his door and inviting them in to support his literary reputation. Writers such as Sarah Fielding (1710–1768), Frances Sheridan (1724–1766), Charlotte Lennox (1729–

---

[4]I have often wondered about Queenie Leavis; the Australian critic, Nettie Palmer, who visited the Leavises at home, provides a fascinating account of the way F. R. Leavis unwittingly acknowledged that Queenie did much of the writing for which he took the credit (see Nettie Palmer, 1988, p. 627).

1804),[5] and Catherine Talbot (1721–1770) were among those who sang the great man's praises and who were prepared to acknowledge the boost that he gave to their own writing. They were not unaware of the nature and significance of the material they made available to him, but they were not resentful. They believed they had made a reasonable bargain, as Ellen Moers observed:

"Richardson indulged in an active collaboration with his gifted female friends," she writes, and notes that the women showed every sign of feeling delighted rather than exploited by the venture. Catherine Talbot, for example—an otherwise most serious, solemn, and sober writer—revelled in the literary game and referred to herself along with some of the other women as "the Pygmalionesses," as an indication of the way they had all fallen "head over heels in love with the ideal hero (Sir Charles Grandison) that she and the rest had helped to form" (Ellen Moers, 1977: p. 176).

And when Samuel Richardson and his literary women friends found such an *exchange* so profitable, a sequel to *Sir Charles Grandison* was planned. It "was to be an entirely collaborative effort: a collection of letters by different female hands," states Ellen Moers, who fails to raise the issue of the name under which such a novel would have been published. But such discussion is hypothetical: Despite the fact that Samuel Richardson "actively solicited in his last years among the women he called his 'daughters' and 'sisters' for the material for this new work, the project did not come to fruition" (Ellen Moers, 1977: p. 176).

In a society where, upon marriage, women have been required to give up their identity and to be known by another name, it is nothing other than consistent practice for women to be required to give up their creative resources and to have their efforts go by another, male, name. In a society where men dominate, where women are just another one of all the planet's resources which are available to them, it is predictable that women should be required to hand over their intellectual valuables and that these should go to replenish and enrich the reputations of men. How else could male supremacy be maintained?

In the interest of the autonomy of women, there has to be an end to the exploitative practices of men. Not just a shift in topic, but a complete transformation of the rules of conversation, whereby women and men enjoy an equal right to be heard, and are accorded equal authority.

But until the revolution occurs, women can continue to talk to women about the way that men have *stolen* the bodies and souls of women, Sonya Tolstoy among them.

---

[5]For further discussion of these women writers see Dale Spender, 1986.

SONYA TOLSTOY: A CASE OF REJECTION (1844–1919)

In 1862 when she was eighteen years of age, Sonya[6] Andreyevna Behrs married Nikolaevich Tolstoy and embarked on a "partnership" which was to endure for almost fifty years, and which was to be for her the source of both her greatest satisfaction and her deepest despair. Although she brought to the marriage many personal resources—she was lovely, lively, witty, and talented—Sonya Behrs' marriage could never qualify as one of equals, for Count Tolstoy was a person of powerful and prestigious dimensions: Almost twice her age, a member of the nobility, a man of liberal reputation and growing literary stature, he was elevated to the rank of virtual demi-god by his innocent and impressionable wife, who was initially flattered and affirmed by his attentions.

But a willingness on the part of his wife to accord him supremacy was not the only factor which from the outset helped to establish the nature of the couple's so-called cooperation. Along with Sonya Tolstoy's conviction that her husband was a man of much merit went his own preoccupation with lofty principles. Leo Tolstoy was concerned to lead a responsible and worthy life: That he continually fell short of his own prescriptions—and had to contend with guilt and self-contempt as a consequence—was not only characteristic of him, but created considerable problems for her.

One of the first instances where his failure to meet his own idealised standards caused immense interference in their joint life was when, on the eve of their marriage, Leo Tolstoy gave his diaries to his prospective wife and instructed her to read them. As they were the record of much more than a mildly misspent youth, the perusal of them was close to traumatising for his innocent fiancée, who, in effect, was being asked to accept the responsibility for proceeding with the marriage and who was being charged with the task of pardoning her husband for his sins. And as Andrea Dworkin has pointed out in *Intercourse*, (1987) the whole episode had overtones of intimidation and threat. Count Tolstoy could easily engage in such "vice" again, and not necessarily outside the home: Sonya could also become a "victim." In giving her his diaries and obliging her to deal with some of the sordid facts and fantasies of his life, Leo Tolstoy was setting a precedent for their partnership, and for his power.

Perhaps it was because he found it easier to communicate with her by the written personal word that upon their marriage Leo Tolstoy gave his wife "a new diary, insisting that they must each read what the other wrote; as husband and wife they must have no secrets" (Anne Edwards, 1982: p. 84). Sonya Tolstoy's reaction was ambivalent: While she was willing for her hus-

---

[6]Sometimes "Sophia," see Mary Jane Moffat and Charlotte Painter, 1975.

band to read her diary, she was reluctant to read his. She did not mind revealing to him the innocent details of her life—and was even ready to include many a reassuring word for his benefit—but she wanted no repetition of the prenuptial ordeal, no confessions of corruption from him, that would cause her fear and pain.

So she had reservations about reading his diary, and subsequent events suggest that her apprehension was not without grounds. Over the years Leo Tolstoy did come to use his diary as a weapon against his wife, first by including taunting and terrible allegations and then later—cruelly and ironically—by excluding her, by denying her access to his journals.

What began on Sonya Tolstoy's part as a readiness to hand over her diaries and a reluctance to examine his, was an attitude which was reversed over the years. For when she came to realise that her husband was taking and using the material of her diaries (and her "self"), she showed herself less willing to share with him: She felt depleted, debased, and distorted as he "lifted" her experience and restructured it for his own fiction.

And as he became firmly established as the famous and foremost Russian writer, she became more fascinated with his personal record of experience. But it is a mark of the deterioration of their relationship that the more she sought to understand him the more unavailable he became to her, so that by 1890 she could make the following entry in her diary:

> In the old days it gave me joy to copy out what he wrote. Now he keeps giving it to his daughters and carefully hides it from me. He makes me frantic with his way of systematically excluding me from his personal life, and it is unbearably painful . . . (Anne Edwards, 1982: p. 333).

To be excluded from her husband's personal life (and kept from copying his writing) stood for Sonya Tolstoy in stark contrast with the early stages of their relationship. For before they had been married but a year she was deeply involved in his literary activities and in the organisation of his life. When her husband took up his pen she took up a range of responsibilities: Apart from running the home and the estate she took on the task of making a full and fair copy of her husband's work (no mean feat given the character of his writing). She ceaselessly copied, corrected and edited, and yet for her considerable creative contribution she has received little credit; not from her husband, not from the world of letters.

While it is irrefutable that Leo Tolstoy's writings could not have been forged in the form in which they exist without the efforts of his wife, her contribution has not been taken to be integral to the artistic enterprise. Instead of being lauded, Sonya Tolstoy and her labours have frequently been distorted—and deplored (see also Andrea Dworkin, 1987: p. 5).

But there need be no puzzle as to why Sonya Tolstoy was prepared to participate so fully, even so enthusiastically, in her husband's literary activities. That she was persuaded by the premise that the greater her husband's place was in the world, the more prestigious (and profitable) would be her own, is a motive that has been attributed to her and which could well be part of the pattern of devaluation; but that she had her own good and stated reasons for providing her husband with every possible form of support is quite clear. Sonya Tolstoy wanted to be loved, she wanted to be needed, she even wanted to be indispensable, and during the first years of marriage all the signs are there that in these aims she succeeded. And one reason she was capable of becoming central to her husband's work was that she had literary aptitudes and aspirations of her own.

Not that she was ready to put her own talents to the test. She was young and, by her own admission, had much to learn. So she felt content, even honoured, to be allowed to serve someone so great and gifted, someone she judged to be a genius. And while she undertook the ostensibly tedious task of "copying" her husband's work, she was also enjoying intellectual stimulation of a kind she had not previously experienced. Like Maria Edgeworth (and some of the women around Samuel Richardson) she felt far from demeaned by such literary work. It represented an opportunity to be creative, to be useful, to learn, and to be loved: What more could a woman want?

The chance to help her husband afforded enhancement in Sonya Tolstoy's life precisely because she did more than "follow" and "enter" the narrative on clean paper: The task called for far more active intellectual involvement. Confronted with Leo Tolstoy's incomplete hieroglyphics in "his small, cramped careless hand" (Anne Edwards 1982: p. 133), his wife was required to speculate on what he might mean, and then to supply a suitable structure to convey his ideas. Sonya Tolstoy did not simply *transfer* her husband's writing to a new sheet: She *transformed* it in the process.

But the extent of her contribution has generally been denied and not always deliberately. Her biographer, Anne Edwards, who plainly wants to portray Sonya in a positive light does not, however, congratulate Sonya on her creativity. She does not praise the artistic efforts of the wife or even acknowledge that without Sonya's contribution, much of what we have accepted as "characteristic Tolstoy" would not exist. Instead, Anne Edwards also robs Sonya Tolstoy of her creativity, for she denatures the calibre of her contribution when she describes it as the "almost telepathic ability" to read her husband's thoughts. So in Anne Edward's terms it is an uncanny ability to intuit what her husband intends that Sonya Tolstoy possesses, and not an independent artistic capacity of her own.

In this context Sonya Tolstoy is perceived as but a passive medium through which her husband's thoughts and meanings can steadily flow.

And again we are confronted with the operation of the double standard. For in many respects the contribution of Sonya Tolstoy is comparable to that made by D. H. Lawrence—to the work of Mollie Skinner, for example. But whereas his efforts attracted praise for their power to transform raw material into art, Sonya Tolstoy's efforts have been minimised and passed over as those of the secretarial-spouse. Which suggests again it is not the writing, not the artistic contribution itself that is the determining factor in literary evaluations: It is the sex.

Sonya Tolstoy, as a woman, is classified simply as a scribe. And when Anne Edwards places Sonya Tolstoy in this context she robs her of her creativity almost as effectively as her husband was later to do. Not that Tolstoy ever denied that *his* contribution was anything other than a very rough draft. His cousin, Alexandra Andreyevna Tolstoy was "appalled at Sonya's workload" when the couple came to visit and she tried to alleviate Sonya's lot by undertaking some of the "editing"; she found it a demanding task. She also thought it amusing that she should be in the position of correcting the great writer's prose, but Leo Tolstoy was unabashed: "I am concerned only with the idea and pay no attention to my style," he declared (Anne Edwards, 1982: pp. 322–323).

But does such an admission detract from what is held to be Leo Tolstoy's achievement? Not at all. For the polish provided by a man is of a very different brand from that provided by a woman. When D. H. Lawrence—or F. Scott Fitzgerald—polish the raw materials of women they are praised for the glow they provide; when Sonya Tolstoy, or Alexandra Tolstoy, do the same thing for a man, they are deemed as doing no more than contributing clerical competency. So are men given gifts while women have theirs taken from them.

But Sonya Tolstoy's contribution to her husband's life and work did not end with the conversion of her husband's script into clear and comprehensible copy: Every conceivable domestic service was made available to him as well. Within a short space of time she was listening to his plans, providing him with emotional support, producing children, running the home and the estate—and working such long hours that she had little time for sleep.

Describing this period of Sonya's life and the nature of her "partnership" with her husband, Anne Edwards states that "During the day she stood between him and the household, allowing no one to disturb him when he was writing in his small study on the ground floor." If the bailiff had questions then it was the Countess who had the answers, if there were difficulties in the nursery or the kitchen it was the Countess who would find the solutions—and yet for Sonya Tolstoy this was only the beginning of her working day.

"In the evening, when the baby was asleep, the servants gone for the night, and while Tolstoy chatted with Aunt Toinette and Natalya Petrovna, she would sit down at her table in the parlour and by candlelight copy his day's work. It was a Herculean task," states Anne Edwards who suggests that Sonya brought some form of extra sensory perception born of sensitive love to this difficult chore.

The pages she was given were filled with incomplete sentences and abbreviated words. Lines were heavily scratched out and new sentences or phrases were written in balloons in the margins or scrawled between the lines, making such a maze of words that she often needed a magnifying glass to make her way. Yet somehow she managed to make sense out of pages Tolstoy himself had not been able to reread. She refused to put down her pen until every page—copied in her graceful legible script—was ready for him to read next morning. And never did she complain of fatigue or about the dreadfully marked up pages of her work which were returned to her the next evening to be copied again (Anne Edwards, 1982: pp. 144–145).

Was ever woman served so by man?

Andrea Dworkin has also commented on the tragedies of Sonya Tolstoy's life; her "labors were considerable, hard and sad," she says:

She had thirteen pregnancies, thirteen children; six died of difficult, painful illnesses—for instance, meningitis and croup. She had puerperal fever at least once, other fevers, inflamed breasts . . . She educated their children. From 1883 on she managed his estate, his money, his copyrights, fed and housed their children; she published his books, which sometimes included the necessity of pleading with the state censor for permission to publish them (she pled with the Czar for permission to publish *The Kreutzer Sonata*). It was not until July 3, 1897, that she moved out of the marital bedroom, not wanting to have intercourse any more, but Tolstoy continued to fuck her when he wanted and to ignore her the rest of the time (Andrea Dworkin, 1987: pp. 5–6).

She was used physically, emotionally, and literarily.

Perhaps in the end it would have been better if Sonya Tolstoy had not done so much, and so uncomplainingly. Perhaps it would have been better if from the beginning she had protested about the thankless nature of her task and the denial of her person. It could be said that had she placed more value on herself and her work, her husband might have had more respect for her existence and her effort. He might have felt some compunction about requiring her to rewrite his prose again and again—on occasion up to fifteen times. He might have acknowledged the integral part *she* played in *his* publications. He might have done more than roughly and rudely use her body and her mind. But this would have meant seeing Sonya as a human being, and not just as his vassal, his sex object, his wife. (And of course, there is absolutely no guarantee that he would have responded to her assertiveness with respect; he could have simply become more brutally oppressive.)

Given her circumstances however it is understandable that Sonya should have felt grateful—at least at first—for the opportunity to be needed and to participate in such a prestigious and stimulating venture. She too could "do a Dorothea" and try to find the meaning of life, and the realisation of love, by putting all her resources at her husband's disposal. And initially, she reaped rewards: As Anne Edwards comments, "the more a part of her husband's work she became, the deeper became Sonya's love for him," and this in turn prompted even further self sacrifice (1982: p. 150).

But if there were rewards there were also some reservations.

"All her own ambitions were transferred to him" observes Anne Edwards, "though not without an occasional twinge of jealousy. Although she thought from time to time about writing something of her own, she did not act on these impulses" (p. 150). This was partly because she did not have the audacity to declare any literary pretensions of her own. Of course she was intimidated by her husband's reputation—and genius—and she held her own artistic endowment to be paltry in comparison. But other factors were also influential in her decision to refrain from undertaking her own writing.

Leo Tolstoy would not have taken kindly to any independent literary foray on her part. A man of "strict principle" (in men's terms), one tenet he held to be true was the subservient and domestic nature of the wife. Besides, in his frame of reference it was beyond the bounds of comprehension that a woman should have the ability to take a place in the world of art: A woman's place was "in the bedroom," and "in the home."

That Sonya Tolstoy frequently performed some of the duties generally judged to be the province of a man (like running the estate and later publishing her husband's books) were "aberrations" Leo Tolstoy could afford to overlook while ever it suited him to do so: However, it did not suit him to have his wife—in her own right—on *his* literary stage.

If these considerations were insufficient to dissuade Sonya Tolstoy from writing, there was yet another reason behind her reluctance to take up her pen for her own purposes. It was that she felt that her husband had taken away the substance about which she could write—that he had appropriated her material, her life story.

Anne Edwards advanced this explanation in her account of Sonya Tolstoy's decision to "abdicate" from writing. Admittedly Sonya Tolstoy accepted the verdict that it was inappropriate for a married woman to lead an autonomous life, argues Anne Edwards, who also adds that this, however, did not prevent Sonya Tolstoy from adopting an independent stance in areas other than literature. And admittedly Sonya was prepared to acquiesce to the edict of male supremacy and to acknowledge that the female was not so artistically well-endowed. But according to Anne Edwards, Sonya Tolstoy would have been perfectly capable of overcoming these objections—had she believed herself to be free to write about her own life. The reason she refrained from writing was because "she felt that Tolstoy was capturing the world she would have written about, that he had absorbed all of her experiences. Scenes from her childhood and adolescence appeared in his new novel, and each day she copied brilliant pages alive with characters modelled after her mother, her father, Lisa, Tanya and herself" (1982: p. 150).

This process her husband was engaged in could not be called polishing or plagiarising but can be classified under the heading of plain theft: He appropriated her experiences—sometimes culled from her conversation, sometimes drawn from her diary—and made it his own. And this left Sonya Tolstoy feeling frequently depleted.

This was not her only reaction of course. During the first few years she had to deal with some of the many contradictions that her contribution produced, as she copied her husband's account of her and found herself distressed by the distortion and the loss of identity and independence, but flattered by the attention and the essential nature of her work. Yet as she encountered more and more of her self in her husband's work, and as she saw that self increasingly (and sometimes, it seemed to her, maliciously) misrepresented, she became more and more conscious of her loss, and more and more aware of her own exploitation.

She was confused by "the mixed emotions she experienced as she copied scenes drawn so closely from her own life," writes Anne Edwards. When she found that her husband had actually incorporated some of her own attempts at writing in his work, right down to the names of characters and all, she felt some pride in the fact that he thought her efforts worth including, but she also felt that she had nothing left which she could call her own, and "somehow it distressed her to copy the details" (1982: p. 185).

She found it difficult to come to terms with the sense that her husband was stealing from her, that he was taking her identity and reshaping it, without her consent, for his own purposes. She found it difficult to come to terms with the reality that for her there was to be no literary life in her own right. And to be engaged in the task of "polishing" the distortions of her self for her husband to obtain the artistic credit was to stretch her own emotional stability to the limit.

It was partly because she resented the way her husband was using (to her, misusing) her identity and experience in his work, and partly to resolve some of the painful contradictions of her position, that Sonya Tolstoy felt the urge to write. But she also felt frustrated in her desire for while "There were so many things Sonya would have liked to write about Tanya[7] and herself and their family" states Anne Edwards, "Tolstoy seemed to be leaving her nothing; and then, how could she dare consider writing anything serious when, first she could never meet his literary standard and second, he thought women had no place in the literary world?" (1982: pp. 185–186).

There can be no doubt that Sonya Tolstoy could write; her diaries in themselves are testimony to her literary ability[8]—and astute analysis and acerbic style. ("Sophia's view of the great man was not reverential. One day at tea he spoke of a vegetarian menu that he had read and liked: almonds and bread. In her diary Sophia wrote: 'I expect the person who wrote the menu

---

[7]Her sister.
[8]See Sophia Andreyevna Tolstoy, 1929, and Cathy Porter, 1985.

practises vegetarianism as much as the author of the *Kreutzer Sonata* practises chastity. [Thirty-seven words deleted by surviving family.]'" (Andrea
Dworkin, 1987: p. 5).

The recreations she provided for her children reveal her more than considerable creativity: "When the children were awake, she would spend every
moment she could with them. She cut out elaborate paper dolls, made up
stories, and often put the two together in staged puppet shows, designing,
drawing and painting the scenery herself . . . " (Anne Edwards, 1982: pp.
184–185). And along with the children's stories she also wrote short stories:
But again her husband was not averse to making use of her work.

Without conscious irony, without seeming to realise that it was Sonya who
was doing all the work and who demonstrated all the necessary expertise,
Anne Edwards states that in 1870, "Tolstoy was working on the ABC Book
and four reading books for children." In reality, it was Sonya who was
"translating stories from French and German, adapting them to the Russian
language and customs," although of course it seems that they all appeared in
Leo's name. For Sonya, this work on children's literature "spurred a revival of
creative activity . . . and she wrote a short story, 'Sparrows' and a children's
story. She also wrote a Russian and French grammar for use in teaching her
own children" (1982: p. 206).

I wonder whether these were published, and, if so, under whose name?

Regrettably there is no volume of the collected works of Sonya Tolstoy
which would allow study of her literary worth; to my knowledge there is not
even a study of her literary contribution to her husband's writing, though it
was undeniably central, and considerable.

By her own accounts (and those of some observers) Sonya Tolstoy had an
increasingly difficult life as she tried to maintain a harmonious relationship
with her husband and to promote and protect his literary products, generally
the absence of appreciation or approval. But the fact that his behaviour to his
wife could be inexcusably exploitative and border on the cruel and tyrannical does not seem to have detracted from the image of him as a champion
of liberty.

This complete disregard for the feelings of his wife—and the development
of her understandable trepidation—is revealed not only in Leo Tolstoy's attitude toward his wife's sexual availability, but also to breast feeding. Because
he considered it proper for a mother to nurse her own children, he insisted
that Sonya should do so, despite the open fissures in her breasts and the
agony that such feeding entailed. It was in Leo Tolstoy's terms a wife's role to
please her husband in all that he should command, and it just so happened
that he made literary demands above and beyond the prescribed domestic
duties. That the woman should find her obligations onerous or even unen-
durable caused him little consternation. Yet the appalling way Tolstoy some-

times treated his wife does not seem to count in the conventional assessments of his work as a man—or a writer.

The "partnership" into which husband and wife had entered was not one where Sonya set many—if any—of the terms. The longer it continued, the harder she worked in her husband's interest, and the less thanks she received, as Anne Edwards has observed:

> Tolstoy's handwriting went from poor to deplorable in the last sections of *War and Peace*. He still inserted "whole sentences between lines, in corners, or even right across the page." Sonya no longer sat in his room while he worked; she was, in fact, afraid to interrupt him. When written pages were truly indecipherable, she would timidly knock on his door, open it quietly and peer nervously at him, waiting for him to acknowledge her presence. Invariably he would look up from his work and ask irritably, "What is it you don't understand?" If he couldn't make out the passages, he would become even more annoyed at having to rewrite the lines. She often found grammatical errors in his work, but these she corrected silently, pointing out her recommendations to him later. Sonya spent every free moment at her desk in the sitting room struggling to decipher Tolstoy's almost illegible pages. She was working when the children went to bed and when they rose in the morning; and during these years they regarded her as the working member of the family. (1982: p. 197)

Sonya Tolstoy "copied" *War and Peace* eight times. It must have taken every ounce of her energy—and her patience—to persevere, when her clean copy was so constantly, carelessly, and callously reworked, and her efforts so little appreciated. And making a clean copy of the manuscript was by no means the end of the chore: After that came the proofs.

The "progress" of the novel *1805* was not atypical:

> "The proofs of *1805* arrived. When Tolstoy finished with them, they were black with corrections and could not be returned until Sonya disentangled the maze of nearly illegible lines, words, balloons and arrows and copied his corrections onto a fresh set. She sat up until nearly dawn for several nights and, exhausted, finally placed them on Tolstoy's desk for a last look before she mailed them back to Katkov.
> That afternoon Tolstoy returned them to her, covered once again with almost indecipherable corrections . . . '(Anne Edwards, 1982: p. 165)

The "burden" which Sonya Tolstoy bore cannot be overemphasised. There is a blasé note in much of the literary and biographical commentary which tends to gloss over some of the implications of Sonya's working life. For example, much of her plight (and pain) is concealed in sentences such as the following: "In the early hours of Dec 20 1870, having spent the night copying her husband's work, Sonya gave birth to a boy" (Anne Edwards, 1982: p. 247).

Leo Tolstoy too was disposed to disallow any frustration, suffering, or fatigue in his wife. And he was far from grateful to her for the mammoth effort she made to maintain his literary life. Instead of responding positively to her contribution he "resented his dependence upon her," and reacted accordingly (1982: p. 167).

Perhaps because he felt that women were so inherently inferior, he found it "shaming" to acknowledge his debt to his wife and registered his resistance by venting his anger upon her. But if we can only hypothesise about the reasons for Leo Tolstoy's unjustifiable exploitation of his wife, we can be sure of the consequences of his actions so far as she was concerned: "Baffled by his rejection and wounded by his sarcastic and sometimes cruel comments, Sonya was mired in self abasing speculation" states Anne Edwards (1982: p. 167).

Few are the records of "service to spouse" which could match those of Sonya Tolstoy. Even Jane Carlyle—who is often credited with holding the award for supreme self sacrifice to a literary "great"—appears to have led a relatively relaxed life in comparison.

Like Jane Carlyle, Sonya Tolstoy ran her husband's home and kept the world away so that he might write unworried and undisturbed; but unlike Jane Carlyle, Sonya Tolstoy gave birth to thirteen children whom she was also obliged to keep from her husband's study door. Sonya Tolstoy managed her husband's moods, ran his estate, acted as his publisher, polished his prose, and transformed his manuscripts. And it was partly because she worked so well for him—because she was so proficient in many of the tasks that she performed—that he accused her of being unwomanly—and immoral.

Had her husband been grateful for her "gifts" Sonya Tolstoy could well have decided that their relationship constituted a fair deal. She did genuinely seek to help him establish his literary career rather than to follow one of her own, and while this decision reflects a realistic assessment of the opportunities that were available to women at the time, it can also be taken as an indication that she could have found satisfaction in assisting her husband rise to fame: The positive features of self sacrifice, of vicarious living—of nurturing the talents of a loved one—cannot completely be overlooked. If only her husband had reciprocated, if only he had loved her in return—then she could have seen in their partnership a fair exchange.[9]

But there was no fair exchange. Sonya Tolstoy came to feel cheated and robbed of her just rewards. And it is an indication of the extent to which wives are expected to provide resources for husbands that Sonya's sense of injustice is so frequently presented as unwarranted, as the antics of a neurotic and nasty woman who was a sore trial to a great man. In the annals of mainstream literary history there is no suggestion that Sonya's grievance was genuine, only that it was a measure of the mean nature of her mind. Leo Tolstoy made his own contribution to this character study of his wife.

---

[9]In this, Sonya Tolstoy was not unlike many of the modern women included in Shere Hite's (1988) survey, *Women and Love*.

As he became more and more involved with his humanitarian experiments, as he became more and more committed to the repudiation of his wealth, he became more and more critical of what he perceived to be the mercenary demands of his wife. While Sonya was aware that it was her work which primarily provided for the welfare of the whole family she also recognised that they all found it convenient to "keep their hands clean" and to castigate her for what they called her capitalist ways. As she wrote in her diary:

> October 26, 1886
> Everyone, her Nikolaevich, as well as the children who follow him like a flock of sheep—has come to think of me as a *scourge*. After throwing on me the whole responsibility of the children and their education, household duties, money matters, and all the other material things, which they all make much greater use of than I ever do, they come along and with a cold, officious, and pious expression, tell me to give a horse to a peasant or some money, or some flour, or this, that and the next thing . . . (Sonya Tolstoy, 1975: p. 145)

It was not the work itself which distressed her: It was the way her work was used, the way it was used against her, the way her efforts were misrepresented and her motives distorted, which drove her to distraction.

Matters came to a head when Leo Tolstoy decided to give away all the rights to his writing and to place his works in the public domain. That his wife protested has been taken as a sign that she lacked vision and had a mundane mind concerned with material things. But what needs to be taken into account in this context is that apart from the fact that she was motivated to provide for her many children, Sonya Tolstoy was also resisting her husband's attempts to deprive her of further resources. For in their "partnership," while he had produced the raw material, she had polished it—and *published* it, and in giving away the rights to his writing, Leo Tolstoy was giving away her *share* in the partnership. By this stage of their relationship, Sonya didn't think that it was *his* to give.

As Anne Edwards has indicated, the message that emerges from Sonya Tolstoy's diaries is that she felt ill used, exploited, as though all that she had and wanted had been taken from her: "She had suppressed her own desire to write because Tolstoy believed that women had no place in the literary world; she had accepted his edict that woman's place was in her home with her children; she had nursed her babies as he had decreed; and although reluctantly, she had subjected herself at his whim to non-stop motherhood" (p. 256). But she would not readily give up the rights to her husband's books, willingly embrace poverty, and rear her children as peasants. She opposed her husband: He took his revenge.

As with other novels, Leo Tolstoy included many details of his family life in *The Kreutzer Sonata* but in this work, his wife decided that he had gone too far. The book contained what Sonya took to be a cruel caricature of her as the wife and she was deeply offended by this distorted and dreadful protrayal. Anne Edwards says that it was because Sonya "was certain the world now thought of her as the 'lustful evil' wife in the novel," that she protested, but Andrea Dworkin, while recognising Sonya's distress, provides a somewhat different explanation for it.

Leo Tolstoy was in Moscow in the company of an actor and a painter when—for the second time—he heard Beethoven's "Kreutzer Sonata" (the first time he had heard it, it had inspired him to "fuck his wife" states Andrea Dworkin):

> This time more restrained, he wanted each to create a work of art inspired by the sonata. Only he did. His story, *The Kreutzer Sonata*, is a powerful and distressing one. It combines an unfinished short story, "The Man Who Murdered His Wife," with a story told to Tolstoy by the painter about a stranger distraught with marital troubles met on a train; but its basic text is the Tolstoy marriage. The story is autobiographical, as is much of Tolstoy's fiction; and in *The Kreutzer Sonata* he uses the details of his sexual intercourse with Sophie, what the biographer Henri Troyat called "his periods of rut," to show his feelings of deep repugnance for the wife he continues to fuck—and for the sex act itself . . . There is a real woman Sophie, on whose body, inside whom [his "desire"] is expressed; and when he is done with her, he puts her aside with rude indifference or cold distaste. (Andrea Dworkin, 1987: p. 4)

It is this repudiation and rejection which Sonya finds intolerable, according to Andrea Dworkin. And for a lifetime of reasons, Sonya Tolstoy wanted to eliminate her husband's version of her and to present the more accurate and authentic portrayal of herself, by herself.

So, "as spring approached," Anne Edwards informs us, Sonya Tolstoy "sat down to write a story in her defence which would negate Tolstoy's conclusion by telling the story from the woman's point of view. She showed the finished story to Anna Dostoevsky, Seryozha and Lyova, and read it aloud when her friends gathered in the salon for tea and Tolstoy was safe in his study" (p. 337).

Significantly, the story was entitled "Whose Fault?" And it embodied Sonya Tolstoy's most explicit and concerted attempt to reclaim her identity and to assert her sexual and literary independence. Many of her friends were aware of her intentions and the symbolic dimension of her story which they thought to be not only excellent, but a fair and just version as well.

Although she believed that "Whose Fault?" achieved its purpose, Sonya Tolstoy elected not to publish this story, for reasons that are not made entirely clear. That she decided to let her husband's version stand, could have been because she had lost some of her spirit, that she was weary and could see no point in opposing him. Or it could have been because it would have made a mockery of her life-long service to this man she proclaimed to be a genius, if she had publicly challenged and exposed the petty nature of his fictions. Or perhaps it was because—as some have sarcastically suggested—it would have been financially foolish to proceed with her own publication which reduced the value of the publications of her husband.

But if we do not know why Sonya Tolstoy refrained from presenting her version of events to the public, we do know that the writing of "Whose Fault?" represents one of her last acts of defiance and that after this incident she became an increasingly disturbed and distressed woman. In her own terms she was never able to adequately explain what had happened to her over the years—where her store of energy, exuberance, talent, had gone. Convinced of the necessity of copying (and preserving) her husband's diaries, but driven almost to despair by the entries they contained—particularly as they related to her—Sonya Tolstoy began to believe that in the literary and life "partnership" she had embarked on with her husband most of her resources had been taken away:

> Dec 31 1890
> I am so used to living not my own life, but the life of Lyova and the children, that I feel I have wasted my day if I haven't done something for them. I have again begun to copy Lyova's diaries. It is sad that my emotional dependence on the man I love should have killed so much of my energy and ability: there was certainly once a great deal of energy in me . . . (see Mary Jane Moffat and Charlotte Painter, 1975: p. 147)

According to many commentators, Mary Jane Moffat and Charlotte Painter included, it was Sonya Tolstoy's "passion to understand" her husband which "eventually unbalanced her mind" (1975: p. 139). It was the recognition that her husband had taken so much and given so little, that he had been so calculating and so cold, that she found unbearable.

Sonya Tolstoy believed that her husband had taken all that she possessed: her love, her labour, her body, her mind. She believed that he had taken everything, and not even given her love in return. Such a realisation could have been enough to unbalance any mind and Sonya Tolstoy's was no exception; she died embittered, distrustful, discarded. But she is not alone.

Awful as her fate may seem, it stands not as an isolated example of theft in literary history; numerous are the women who have been similarly robbed of resources. Which is why at the core of women's criticism is the recognition that behind many great literary men lies a ruined woman.

ZELDA FITZGERALD (1900–1947): A PARADIGM OF PLAIN THEFT

Of all the cited examples of the appropriation of women's words by men, the case of Zelda Fitzgerald must rank as one of the most definitive and damning. And because the act was so blatant, the consequences so awful—and the issue of such significance to women writers in general—I take exception to Elizabeth Hardwick's verdict that with regard to Zelda's writing, in the end "It does not seem of much importance that the diaries and letters were appropriated, the stories wrongly attributed for an extra $500 . . . "[10] (1974: p. 95). Such an attitude has been partly responsible for the continued treatment of the systematic theft of women's resources as "the isolated example." And for the failure to recognise the high price that is paid by women who are the victims of looting literary men.

In many respects the life story of Zelda Fitzgerald is one which, like that of Sonya Tolstoy, documents her ever decreasing resources, and which ends in destruction and despair. For, in his efforts to take over her resources, her husband, F. Scott Fitzgerald, allowed her no respite. He was a firm believer in the principle that whatever was hers—belonged to him. He made it perfectly plain that it was out of the question that Zelda should ever use her resources for her own ends—and that he would never let her set herself up to challenge him as a writer of fiction.

Much has been made of the melodrama of the Fitzgerald marriage, partly because so many of the miseries it entailed have surfaced in F. Scott Fitzgerald's highly acclaimed work. And as with the Tolstoy "partnership," the perspective which has usually been presented is that of the literary man—and one in which his own status is enhanced. In critical circles little attention has been given to women whose life, work, and sanity have been plundered.

Of course there are some who would suggest that Zelda Fitzgerald should have known from the outset what she was letting herself in for and that she should have been a little more circumspect when it came to "husbanding" her own resources. For the signs were all there from the start, but in the beginning it suited Zelda to go along with her prospective husband's fancies.

It wasn't F. Scott Fitzgerald who gave Zelda his diary to read before they were married: It was she who gave him hers. And he wasn't shocked, he was most impressed, sufficiently so to offer praise and to commandeer the diary for future use in his fiction.[11] Far from being offended by this confiscation of her writing, Zelda Fitzgerald—like Sonya Tolstoy when she too had been in love—was flattered, and felt that the fact that it was of value to F. Scott Fitzgerald was an affirmation of her own worth. At this stage, Zelda's experience was a positive one: She felt good about her own writing, she felt good about being seen to be good. She even began to contemplate a whole range of possibilities.

---

[10]While I disagree with this particular assessment of Elizabeth Hardwick's I find myself in overall sympathy with her work; after all she has pointed out what happened to Dorothy Wordsworth, Jane Carlyle, and Zelda Fitzgerald even if she has not attached quite the same importance to their exploitation. Her criticism is well within women's tradition.

[11]Before their marriage "Zelda showed him a diary she kept which Scott found so extraordinary that he was to use portions of it in his fiction in *This Side of Paradise, The Beautiful and Damned,* and 'The Jelly Bean'" (Nancy Milford, 1975: 38).

If she was as good with words as Scott pronounced her to be, why should she not be a writer too?

For F. Scott Fitzgerald, this might not have been the required response from the woman in his life, but Zelda was doing nothing unreasonable or even unusual, when she used his words of praise to boost her confidence in her own artistic aspirations. After all, if women are informed that they have talent, then surely some of them might prefer to write in their own right, instead of working to produce more and better offerings for a man. Not surprisingly, Zelda Fitzgerald could have found this early appropriation of her work complimentary, and a spur to greater things. If her husband had permitted it.

But he did not. Unfortunately these jottings of Zelda's, which were appraised and appreciated by Scott, were not to be used for her benefit, but for his own. For her they did not represent the start of an independent artistic life, but the beginning of availability for her husband's literary achievements. The more he saw the potential of her writing, the more he wanted it for his own use. This is one reason that the story of Zelda Fitzgerald is such a sad tale of harassment and abuse (see Nancy Milford, 1975).

It was some time however, before Zelda came to recognise that her own creative resources were being depleted, and when she did, there was a painful struggle as she tried to assert her right to her own work. Initially though—particularly in those heady days of first love—she found it not only affirming, but amusing, when her husband took her words and presented them as his own. For example, as part of the promotion that accompanied the publication of *The Beautiful and the Damned*, Zelda was asked to write a review of her husband's efforts. Her response was flippant, and has since become famous:

> It also seems to me that on one page I recognized a portion of an old diary of mine which mysteriously disappeared shortly after my marriage, and also scraps of letters, which, though considerably edited, sound to me vaguely familiar. In fact, Mr Fitzgerald—I believe that is how he spells his name—seems to believe that *plagiarism begins at home*. (Nancy Milford, 1975: p. 99, my italics)

Her husband's habits were perceived as *playful* plagiarism at this stage and represented no problem. While ever Scott Fitzgerald could call for literary materials and his wife would duly, dutifully, and docilely provide, the issue of unfair practices—of theft—simply didn't arise.

But the seed of contention was sown when Zelda Fitzgerald was asked to do more than write the occasional promotional review in support of her husband's work. The issue of who owned what began to emerge when literary men—other than her husband—showed signs of appreciating the significance of Zelda's writing, and commissioned her to work for them in her own right.

She "cooperated." She wrote the required material—to which her husband then appended his name. And to this action, Elizabeth Hardwick attaches no great significance. F. Scott Fitzgerald of course saw nothing problematic in his response. That the piece would be better paid if it appeared under his name was the rationalisation that he gave for his appropriation.

But if his manner seemed reasonable, his explanation was spurious. The publishers were not paying for *his* name, or *his* work. They knew that his contribution to Zelda's output was minimal—even non-existent on occasion. It was *Zelda's* creative efforts they admired and wanted—and were prepared to pay for—regardless of whether it carried her name. So any attempt to justify F. Scott Fitzgerald's theft on financial grounds simply will not suffice.

Why Zelda should have complied with his requisitioning is however, a more complex matter.

Commenting on Zelda's apparent early diffidence to the appropriation of her work, Nancy Milford refers to one occasion when George Nathan approached Zelda for some material for publication. The editor of *The Smart Set*—which first published F. Scott Fitzgerald—George Nathan was staying with the couple when he came across Zelda's diaries: "They interested me so greatly," he said, "that in my capacity as a magazine editor I later made her an offer for them. When I informed her husband, he said he could not permit me to publish them since he had gained a lot of inspiration from them and wanted to use part of them in his own novels and short stories . . . "

And, continues Nancy Milford without any great emphasis, or explanation, "Zelda apparently offered no resistance to this rather high handed refusal of Nathan's offer, and the diaries remained Scott's literary properties rather than hers" (1975: pp. 79–80).

Nancy Milford outlines what happened to Zelda's writing but at this stage she does not draw attention to the act, or dwell upon the significance of such appropriation. Like so many other commentators and critics she seems to have assumed the "normalcy" of this state of affairs whereby the labours of the wife are held to belong to the husband. Only when Zelda herself starts to protest does Nancy Milford start to point to the many injustices.

But if she remained acquiescent in public, and caused no scenes when George Nathan was not permitted to publish her material, there is evidence that Zelda Fitzgerald was not quite so passive in private. For when both her esteemed husband and his editor declared that she could write, Zelda Fitzgerald was spurred to even greater authorial efforts. And as she sought to establish her own identity, as she tried to find a creative area in which she could excel, she turned more and more to writing as a form of serious work, and as a means of self-realisation. Not that she risked her husband's displeasure by declaring her commitment to her own literary independence, or even by openly opposing his claim to ownership of her writing. But unobtrusively she began to study and to develop her own skills, and she was as defiant, determined, and dedicated as she could be, under the circumstances.

"Zelda worked harder at her writing than she admitted," states Nancy Milford, "During 1922–3 she sold two short stories, a review, and at least two articles, earning $1,300 for her efforts." But although she was published, and paid, it would be erroneous to presume that Zelda was permitted to own her own work, as the fate of one of her stories, "Our Own Movie Queen," reveals.

Her husband "helped" her with this story and we learn of the nature of his assistance from his entry in his literary ledger (in which he kept the—now incriminating—details of his work and their "collaboration"): In relation to "Our Own Movie Queen" he records "two thirds written by Zelda. Only my climax and revision." And Nancy Milford continues with the next chapter in this particular tale:

> The story was not published until 1925, when it won two stars in O'Brien's short story collection for that year. Zelda however was not given credit for it and the story was published under Scott's name alone. He was paid $1,000 for it, which they split. (1975: pp. 113–114)

That the image of Zelda as foolish and frivolous has been fostered is hardly surprising, given that so much of her serious literary work appeared under her husband's name. And of course it was not only her literary resources that he took from her. In her study of Zelda Fitzgerald, Nancy Milford portrays a young woman of considerable creative potential, who is frustrated whenever she tries to use any of it for her own ends. When she recognised the threat that her fiction-writing posed for Scott, Zelda decided to find an outlet for her talents that would not challenge his literary career; this was when she turned to ballet. But even this resource and form of self-realisation Scott would not allow her to have for herself. Not only did he mock her commitment and her performance, he went to great lengths to "persuade" her teacher to inform Zelda that dancing was not her forte. This was far from the teacher's professional assessment of Zelda's ability, but it was enough to make Zelda abandon her efforts at artistic achievement and autonomy in dance. Once more she found herself without any resources of her own to command.

The picture of Zelda that has persisted, however, is predominantly the distorted one which Scott helped to create, where her desire to be a writer or a dancer is derided as a disposition to dabble in the arts. And while it is sometimes acknowledged that *both* members of the Fitzgerald household aspired to be artists it is almost always assumed that only *one* of them was being realistic. In literary and biographical studies F. Scott Fitzgerald is perceived to be the *proper* writer and this is partly because his own attitude and actions have helped to ensure that Zelda is not often given due credit for her own creative achievements.

But we should not take F. Scott Fitzgerald at his "public" word and presume that Zelda Fitzgerald could not write. For despite his contribution to the portrayal of Zelda as an amateur, it is perfectly plain that in private Scott believed Zelda was a talented writer. Why else would he have wanted to exercise proprietary rights to her work?

What F. Scott Fitzgerald most certainly did not want was a wife who was a competitor on the literary scene, and he seems to have had few inhibitions about insisting that Zelda play a supportive role. Not that this prevented Zelda from writing: What it did do was to prevent her from publicly proclaiming she was a writer—with such a serious commitment to her art.

And as a result of these early writing efforts there are some good articles written by Zelda, a few of which were published under her own name. But sadly, the fact that she does have some substantial pieces in print has not helped to enhance her reputation as a writer. Again, her achievement can be denied, this time by the simple shift in explanation—which would account for anything of value in her writing as emanating from her husband's pen. Because it is known that there was some "collaboration" in the writing, the existence of good and disciplined writing in Zelda's name does not necessarily dispel the image of her as a dilettante: Instead the positive features of the writing can be seen to be the product—of a man.

Once more sex and status are intertwined. In the history of collaborative couples, high status writing has been attributed to the high status sex; this has happened with the Mills, the Lawrences, the Tolstoys, and the Fitzgeralds (to quote but a few possible examples). Yet such conclusions are often contrary to the evidence; sometimes they stand in direct contradiction to the claims of the couples themselves. Not that the testimonies of Jessie Chambers, Sonya Tolstoy, or Zelda Fitzgerald, for example are likely to challenge these findings. When a respected and rational man of the stature of John Stuart Mill cannot manage to convey the message that a woman may make a positive intellectual contribution, it is unlikely that lesser mortals, particularly mere women, could help to establish the claim for female creativity and integrity.

With Zelda, however, there was no champion to proclaim her worth. Her situation was quite the reverse. Initially it was her husband who took her resources, but because this injustice has not been remedied and her literary reputation restored to her, she has "lost" even more over the years.

In contrast to the received wisdom, what is revealed in an investigation and analysis of the Fitzgerald "partnership" is that Zelda wrote much, and she wrote well. That she is not portrayed in this particular light is primarily because her husband took over so much of her literary output. He appropriated her work directly—by attaching his name—and indirectly, by incorporating her efforts in his work; by depriving her of her own literary resources, he contributed to the image of her as a pretentious and capricious woman, who could boast of neither talent nor accomplishment in her own name.

But this is not all he did. F. Scott Fitzgerald went to considerable lengths to prevent his wife from writing in her own right and to ensure that instead of gaining a literary reputation of her own, she contributed to his. If and when he did feel obliged to justify his actions he did so on the grounds that he was the *true* writer in the partnership, on the grounds that he was the *man*. And there was no doubt in his mind that a man was entitled to the labours of his wife.

Perhaps because it is so widely and readily taken for granted that behind every great man there is a woman—and perhaps because it is so widely and readily assumed that this is how it should be—the contribution that Zelda Fitzgerald made to her husband's writing has attracted so little attention. Yet Zelda Fitzgerald's efforts were crucial to her husband's writing—and in more ways than one.

Undeniably Zelda Fitzgerald helped her husband substantially with his work. And not just by making available "raw material" although this she did, if not always knowingly or willingly. But she also served as a trusted reader who provided valuable feedback and who could be relied upon for sound commentary and advice. F. Scott Fitzgerald's ledgers make his dependence on his wife's work and judgement patently clear, and there are many entries which record Zelda's reports and his responses. Yet this aspect of their collaboration—where Zelda makes a positive contribution and where her husband is to some extent in her debt, has been disregarded. Instead we have the pervasive portrayal of a partnership where it was always F. Scott Fitzgerald who paid.

So the double standard allows F. Scott Fitzgerald to take the credit—and the sympathy as well. It all went his way; there was nothing reciprocal in their so-called partnership. Not that this is how he or his actions are perceived in the world of letters where he remains the literary *asset* and Zelda is labelled the *liability*.

The reality of their lives was very different: their routine—as registered in her diary and his ledger—reveals that for much of the time when they were not revelling they were both persevering with their writing. And when not "helping" her husband, Zelda often enjoyed the greater success, much to his chagrin. For above and beyond the material and the support she provided for him (Scott once stated in his ledger that he must stop referring everything to Zelda—see Nancy Milford 1975: p. 114), Zelda found the space to produce, and polish, her own work.

During 1927, "Zelda worked energetically on four articles, three of which were published the following year. The first, 'The Changing Beauty of Park Avenue' was signed by both Fitzgeralds, but in his ledger Scott gave Zelda credit for the article. The style was obviously hers," states Nancy Milford, who has compared the published version with the original, and who cannot resist the somewhat satirical comment: "There were minor corrections on the manuscript which are in Scott's hand (he wrote in both the title and the authors' names, putting his own name first)," but interestingly some of the changes he made do not appear in the published piece (1975: p. 146).

Was it Zelda—or some other editor—who disregarded his advice and eliminated his revisions?

There can only be speculation as to whether Zelda asserted her artistic independence and integrity on this occasion and ignored her husband's intrusions. Perhaps she did not possess the confidence to countermand her husband's advice: Certainly she confessed to feeling constantly undermined and not just by the way he commandeered her writing but by the way he commandeered her life. And she was not alone in thinking that her experience was being exploited.

As Nancy Milford has indicated, in so many social settings, "Scott was splendidly at ease with women, charming them with his graciousness and his interest in them. If that charm soured, it was always because of his having drunk too much. Then it became apparent that what he wanted from the woman he was talking to was her story, and one sensed a certain coolness, a detachment in him, which could be chilling" (p. 148).

To have one's existence reduced to raw material for a literary man to mine is sufficient to drive one to distraction—as Sonya Tolstoy claimed. When, in her endless copying of Tolstoy's manuscripts she found—again and again— that her husband was drawing on her "most private and tormented experiences to create his fictional world" (Anne Edwards, 1981: p. 228) she saw the result of such appropriation leading to her sense of desolation and despair. And while few, apart from Nancy Milford, have traced a direct link between F. Scott Fitzgerald's appropriation of Zelda's experience and Zelda's breakdown, the evidence suggests that the connection was by no means tenuous.

There can be no doubt that Zelda Fitzgerald felt the need to establish her own identity and that for her this necessitated the attainment of independence and an artistic achievement of which she could be proud. But her husband would not allow her this in the literary world—which, as has been indicated, is one reason that she took up ballet.

A mature woman, and aware of the limitations under which she worked, Zelda Fitzgerald nonetheless threw herself into her ballet lessons in her desperate determination to excel. Yet even while she worked so hard on her new art she did not abandon the old: Throughout the winter of 1928–29, in energetic bursts, she wrote a series of short stories on young women for the magazine College Humor.

F. Scott Fitzgerald organised the deal with his agent, Harold Ober: While Zelda did the writing, the stories were to be published in both names.

Five of Zelda's stories were published in College Humor but F. Scott Fitzgerald was not particularly pleased. He felt that some of his resources had been siphoned off by Zelda, in her work. He complained to Harold Ober that these stories had "been pretty strong draughts on Zelda's and my common store of material" and that in the use of two of her female characters he found cause for discontent for he had both of them "in my notebook to use" (Nancy Milford, 1975: p. 166).

The fate of the sixth story in this set of Zelda's typifies the treatment that she and her writing received at her husband's hands. "'A Millionaire's Girl' was published by the *Saturday Evening Post* and although it was Zelda's story, Scott's name alone was signed to it," Nancy Milford comments wryly. "Scott later wrote that the story 'appeared under my name but actually I had nothing to do with it except for suggesting a theme and working on the proof of the completed manuscript. This same cooperation extends to other material gathered . . . under our joint names, though often when published in that fashion *I had nothing to do with the thing from the start to finish except supplying my name*'" (1975: p. 166, my emphasis).

As with Sonya Tolstoy there is no collection of Zelda Fitzgerald's short stories: Indeed, it is not even widely acknowledged that she wrote sufficiently—in quantity or quality—in her own right to warrant such a collection. Yet without such an anthology it is difficult to establish Zelda Fitzgerald's reputation as a writer. But Nancy Milford, who has made a study of Zelda's writing has said of these stories which appeared in *College Humor* and the *Saturday Evening Post* that "they remain a remarkable expression of Zelda's considerable talent as an essentially descriptive writer"[12] (p. 167).

Covertly, if not overtly, F. Scott Fitzgerald recognised Zelda's talent, which is why he tried to harness it for his own use, and why he was so concerned that she should not compete with him, for she constituted a formidable challenge. But the fact that she could write well was not all that he resented: as his own literary attempts became increasingly onerous he also held it against Zelda that she wrote so readily. When she embarked on her short stories in 1928–29, he was "astonished by her productivity and even resented it in comparison to his own vexing inability to move forward on his novel" (Nancy Milford, 1975: p. 168).

Even Elizabeth Hardwick counteracts the image of Zelda Fitzgerald as an amateur whose flirtation with the arts was part of her pattern of mental instability. It is as a serious artist who undertakes serious work, that Elizabeth Hardwick sees Zelda when she says, she had "the precious gift of fantastic energy—not energy of a frantic chaotic sick sort, but that of a steady application, formed and sustained by a belief in the worth of the work and the value of each solitary self" (1974: p. 95).

But in the end the strain proved too much for Zelda Fitzgerald: The strain of her ballet training, the strain of her writing, the strain of dealing with her

---

[12]Is this too a put-down? Zelda is a "descriptive" writer, while Scott, presumably was "analytical": the split between emotion and reason again?

unsteady husband. In 1930 she had a breakdown and entered a clinic in Switzerland from where she wrote intensely moving letters to her spouse, about her inner state. Some of these letters were later incorporated (virtually unchanged) in F. Scott Fitzgerald's novel, *Tender is the Night*.

This was the first but by no means the last time that Zelda entered a mental institution, and tried to shape her world though the process of writing. In 1932, back in the United States, she again collapsed and was admitted to the Phipps Clinic where, as part of her own prescription for her improved mental health, she wrote her novel, *Save Me the Waltz*.

And this was the work which became the battleground in the struggle to establish whether it was the husband or the wife who *owned* Zelda's life experience, and writing.

As a writer might be expected to do, Zelda Fitzgerald sent her completed novel off to a publisher—in this case, Scribner's, where she had contacts. She did not show the manuscript to Scott first: Why should she? And if there was no good reason to show him her work, there were numerous reasons why she should not. It was not as if they were living together, and that she had taken to hiding her work: As a resident of an institution it would have been a more significant act to forward her writing to her husband than it was to undertake it "in private." And besides, she was wary about distracting Scott from his own work: He was always complaining that his writing was not going well because he was not left in peace. But in sending off her novel without first giving it to Scott to read, Zelda Fitzgerald's main concern was to escape his criticisms and condemnations.

She was quite right to think that there could be an "explosion" and that she might not be psychologically strong enough to withstand it—as she later tried to explain to her enraged husband when he heard about her novel. Lacking in confidence, Zelda wanted him to realise that she was not sure of the quality of her work and that she feared it might "be a dubious production due to my own instability," but she didn't want Scott to tell her so, not in the harsh terms he had so often used. While she had no intention of hiding her novel from him she was determined to protect herself, for (as she wrote to him) "I did not want a scathing criticism such as you have mercilessly—if for my own good—given my last stories poor things. I have had enough discouragement generally . . . " (Nancy Milford, 1975: p. 242).

As Zelda had anticipated, F. Scott Fitzgerald was furious when he found out about the manuscript. He was furious that she had written at all (when he was suffering from a "block"), and furious that she had acted independently. But most of all he was furious that she should have written a novel. Sustained fiction was *his* territory, and he accused Zelda of *trespassing*.

When the manuscript came into his hands his worst fears were confirmed. He wrote to Zelda's doctor at the clinic and complained bitterly. And F. Scott Fitzgerald did not mince words: The substance of his protest was that in writing about her life Zelda had *stolen his* sources and some of his work. For four years, he insisted, he had been prevented from working methodically on his own novel because of the pressure of keeping Zelda in sanitariums. And what little of his novel he had been able to write, Zelda had now taken from him. He was adamant that there were whole sections of his wife's novel— which belonged to him.

"Zelda had for the first time directly invaded what Scott considered his own domain," comments Nancy Milford, "and the violence of his reaction was telling. Her novel was intensely, even naïvely autobiographical and as she drew on her own life, so she drew on her life with Scott, for it was her material as well as his." But with this belief that she had a right to her own life, "Scott strenuously disagreed" (1975: p. 239).

Although she tried to appease him, Zelda would not abandon her attempts at publication, with the result that Scott's anger did not abate. And when he realised that he was not going to be able to stop Zelda from going ahead with her novel, he took steps to ensure that he had little to lose and something to gain from the publication of the work.

First, he took over arrangements for the publishing deal with Scribner's and had a clause inserted in the agreement which "stipulated that one half the royalties earned would be retained by Scribner's to be credited against 'the indebtedness of F. Scott Fitzgerald' until a total of $5,000 had been repaid" (Nancy Milford, 1975: p. 250). And then he demanded that Zelda remove any material from her novel that he deemed to be *his*.

Zelda was conciliatory, and with most of his requests she readily complied. But she would not give up everything. Like Sonya Tolstoy, who had found it crucially important to rectify the false images created by her husband, and to put forward her own view of events (as she had done in the short story, "Whose Fault?"), Zelda Fitzgerald also recognised the necessity of retaining her own versions of her experience and her own identity.

"The Pershing incident which you accuse me of stealing occupies just one line and will not be missed. I willingly relinquish it," Zelda wrote to Scott, but then she added her word of warning, "However, I would like you to thoroughly understand that my revision will be made on an aesthetic basis: that the material which I will elect is nevertheless legitimate stuff which has cost me a pretty emotional penny to amass, and which I intend to use when I can get the tranquillity of spirit necessary to write the story of myself versus myself. That is the book I really want to write . . . " (Nancy Milford, 1975: p. 144).

Zelda's assertion of autonomy and integrity were just too much for her husband, who reacted with rage. His use of the double standard to justify his response is insufferable. For he never questioned his right to appropriate Zelda's experience and writing, he only protested that she had no right to make use of his. He ignored any effect that his theft of her work may have had on her mental health, but complained loud and long about the effects that her writing was having on his mental state. Without compunction, and without compassion, he maintained that Zelda's "story" was his property, and that it was she who was behaving abominably when she would not "hand over" her records to him.

"Zelda had used him, he insisted—his writing, his life, his material—to her own advantage," and he wrote to her doctor, without conscious irony, and decried her determination to "build this dubitable career of hers with morsels of living matter chipped out of my mind, my belly, my nervous system and my loins" (Nancy Milford, 1975: p. 245).

But he did more than complain. After this outburst F. Scott Fitzgerald resorted to even more deplorable tactics in his attempts to prevent Zelda from utilising her own resources, and competing with him in the literary world. Just as he had "persuaded" Zelda's ballet teacher to tell her that she was no good as a dancer and that dancing was no good for her, Scott now tried to persuade the doctors to tell Zelda that she would only do herself damage if she persisted with her determination to write.

Of course F. Scott Fitzgerald did not state that it was in his interest that he wanted his wife to withdraw from the literary world: On the contrary, he declared that it was entirely in her own interest that he recommended retirement. He was simply trying to protect her from the pressure. . . .

With this justification he asked the doctors to dissuade Zelda from writing. He tried to discourage her by warning her against anticipating any success with her work. And just to make sure of his scheme, he requested the publishers to keep any praise they might have "on the staid side" and excused his strange intervention by way of explaining that "it was important to the doctors . . . that Zelda not be made to feel too jubilant about the fame and money that might come to her through publication" (Nancy Milford, 1975: p. 248). A dreadful theft: a damnable "cover-up."

Giving a clear indication of what he believed to be his literary status, and hers, F. Scott Fitzgerald informed Zelda's editor that his wife "must not try to follow the pattern of my trail which is of course blazed distinctly on her mind" (Nancy Milford, 1975: p. 249).

That F. Scott Fitzgerald should have gone to such lengths to keep Zelda away from fiction writing borders on the incredible: But that his manouvres have attracted so little attention in the literary world, and have been accorded so little space in any discussion of his literary life and style would be—in a just world—incomprehensible.

But despite her husband's rage and machinations, the courageous Zelda would not abandon her writing, which she believed was helping to restructure herself and to rebuild her life. And while she persevered with her work, her husband persisted with his protest, which he backed up by threats. In and out of the clinic, in and out of the papers,[13] in and out of letters, he carped and he quarrelled. A long list of incidents reveals how resistant Zelda had become and how uncompromising F. Scott Fitzgerald could be in his belief that whatever Zelda had belonged to him. And while he maintained this stance there could be no resolution of their problem. However, so frequently did he threaten Zelda, and her writing, that she finally and understandably reached the stage where she became secretive, where she refused to tell him what she was writing or to let him see it. And Scott finally and unforgivably reached the stage where he was ready to explode.

When he was unable to get his own way it was F. Scott Fitzgerald who became irrational. During 1933 his behaviour to Zelda was increasingly harassing and the life and literary "partnership" of the Fitzgeralds underwent further deterioration: "Throughout the fall Zelda worked on her new novel, the one that dealt with psychiatric material and her own hospitalisation," writes Nancy Milford, and "Scott was beside himself with anger and in a long and forceful letter to Dr Rennie (Zelda's doctor) said he thought they had all agreed that he was to finish his novel before Zelda took up any extended piece of fiction, and she was violating that promise" (pp. 293–294).

With this lament from F. Scott Fitzgerald we are confronted with the situation where Zelda is in the mental institution but it is Scott who claims to be enduring the mental anguish. And it was partly because *he* had worked himself into such an anxiety state over Zelda's writing that her doctors proposed that the couple should meet, and with the assistance of a "moderator" attempt to find a solution to what had become a most pressing problem. Zelda and Scott agreed: On May 28, 1933, they sat down "with a stenographer and Dr Rennie . . . to discuss their troubles or at least to air them. The 114 page transcript of their talk provides . . . " the most vividly illustrated and damning evidence of the extent to which a man believes he is entitled to seize the resources of a woman—with impunity (Nancy Milford, 1975: p. 301).

Because of F. Scott Fitzgerald's blatancy, the substance of this transcript borders on the bizarre: It is most definitely a case of having to be read to be believed. And one factor which soon emerges is that for Scott the fact that Zelda was female was sufficient reason for seeing her efforts as those of an amateur—while he of course reserved the status of *professional* for his own. Reticent when it came to defining his categories—"the difference between the professional and the amateur is awfully hard to analyze, it is awfully intangible. It just simply means the keen equipment: it means a scent, a smell

---

[13]For example, "Scott gave an interview to the Baltimore *Sun* in which he mentioned Zelda's forthcoming novel. The headline for the article ran, 'He tells of Her Novel' with subtitle, 'Work Sent to Publisher is Autobiographical at Suggestion of Her Husband'. That must have been hard for Zelda to swallow" (Nancy Milford, 1975: pp. 283–284).

of the future in one line" (p. 302)—Scott was nonetheless sure that he had what it takes, while Zelda did not. He conceded that she might be able to write some "nice little sketches," and that she could cultivate a satirical standpoint towards her friends, but he remained convinced that her writing did not count because in the end, "she has nothing essentially to say." This was in stark contrast to his own ability of course; he steadfastly claimed for himself more substance, more skill—and more suffering! "To have something to say," he remonstrated, "is a question of sleepless nights, and worry, and endless motivation of a subject, and endless trying to dig out the essential truth, the essential justice" (Nancy Milford, 1975: p. 302). His art hurt more in the making.

Again and again—and quite in line with patriarchal values—F. Scott Fitzgerald argued that *his* writing was worth more than his wife's. And the sole basis of his case was that it was the sex and not the writing that was responsible for the value. Again and again, without reference to the writing, he insisted that as a man his work was concerned with the fundamentals while Zelda's interests were simply superficial. Again and again he decreed that he was for truth and justice, as a man, while Zelda was only for amusement as a woman. And he offered not a shred of evidence for his views. Only the blind conviction that a man and his writing by definition are superior to the efforts of any woman—and that the husband has an absolute right to the resources of the wife, to ensure that it stays that way.

That Zelda wanted to write, and was even judged by others to write well, were not the only perceived instances of injustice with which Scott had to contend: His sense of order was outraged by the fact that Zelda appeared to write with such ease. And he seized on this supposed effortlessness and turned it against her, again managing to invoke the double standard however, again managing to have his cake and to eat it too.

In the first place, on the premise that a writer must suffer in order to produce worthwhile work, Scott accused Zelda of writing so readily and painlessly that there could be no possibility that her work could be any good. This, while she was still in a mental institution. But at the same time, he was so incensed by Zelda's capacity to "discipline" herself and to produce (in contrast to his own poor performance) that he turned Zelda's "success" and his comparative "failure" into Zelda's fault.

From the transcript of the couple's conversation Nancy Milford concludes that "as they talked one aspect of the problem became clear: Scott had not published a novel for eight years (in the transcript he said 'seven years—six years') and he blamed it on Zelda" (1975: p. 302).

He blamed her and he bludgeoned her: That she should have become mentally distressed under such an onslaught is not at all surprising. As they ostensibly tried to clarify who, what, and where they had gone wrong, Scott lost control and delivered a diatribe against Zelda: He "turned to Zelda and told her outright what he thought of her talents: 'It is a perfectly lonely struggle I am making against other writers who are freely gifted and talented. You are a third rate writer and a third rate ballet dancer.'

'You have told me that before,''' replies Zelda (Nancy Milford, 1975: p. 302).

Perhaps if she had been a third-rate writer (were there such a thing) or even a third-rate ballet dancer, then maybe Scott would have had nothing to fear. But it was the fact that he knew her to be good, capable of achievement in her own right, that he found intolerable. She threatened his superior status as a man as well as his existence as a writer. Scott had few objections to Zelda being talented while her resources were employed behind the throne and used to augment his. What he could not endure was Zelda's attempt to establish her own credentials. What if she were to exist "apart" from him, what if she were to achieve more than he could claim?

But it was not just insecurity that motivated him; there was malice in his manner as well. It is clear that he decided that if he could not have access to Zelda's strengths, no one else would either. Not even Zelda.

Scott thought that a wife should be a "complementary intelligence" (Nancy Milford, 1975: p. 304)—what nice names for such pernicious ploys— and that there was no room in a well-ordered world for a married woman to "do her own thing." And when Zelda would not conform to this view of the world, and a woman's place within it, his only way of dealing with her "defiance" was to turn to blustering and bullying, to violence. But by this stage, Zelda felt that she had little or nothing to lose: to her, writing seemed to offer the only hope of salvation and she wasn't going to give it up. The transcript of the contest between the couple reveals Scott trying to establish his right, and exercise his authority—while Zelda is refusing to be intimidated: "I am a professional writer with a huge following," he declares, "I am the highest paid short story writer in the world. I have at various times dominated . . ."

And Zelda replies: "It seems to me you are making a rather violent attack on a third rate talent then" (Nancy Milford, 1975: p. 303).

The arguments advanced by F. Scott Fitzgerald (as recorded in the transcript) are the classic ones which have been used to bolster the claim for male supremacy. They are the arguments which have helped to justify the availability of women's resources to men, and which directly and indirectly have helped to establish the reality that it is men who are the "proper" writers and whose work comprises the legitimate literary heritage. Nancy Milford has summarised F. Scott Fitzgerald's case as it was stated in the exchange with his wife:

"Repeatedly throughout the afternoon they came back to the point," comments Nancy Milford, "Scott was the professional writer and he was supporting Zelda: therefore the entire fabric of their life was his material, none of it was Zelda's. He spelled it out: 'Everything we have done is my . . . I am the professional novelist and I am supporting you. That is all my material.'"

Zelda would not be convinced: She fought back in an attempt to protect her own resources. She "told him he was 'absolutely neurotic on the subject of your own work anyway. You are so full of self-reproach about not having written anything for that long period of time you stoop to the device of accusing me . . . '" (Nancy Milford, 1975: p. 303).

There is no mystery as to why F. Scott Fitzgerald should have been so rigidly insistent (and irrational) about the role of his wife. His behaviour was based on the unquestioned (and socially sanctioned) belief in the sexual division of labour and on the premise that his wife—and all that she possessed—was rightfully his. He did not see his attitude as unusual or unreasonable. He did not see his actions as reprehensible or as constituting any form of robbery. He did not acknowledge the extent of the suffering he was inflicting on Zelda. He felt that his rights were the important ones, and that they were being violated: Hence his blind and stubborn refusal to allow the implications of his stance for his wife.

"Scott had very fixed ideas on what a woman's place should be in a marriage," writes Nancy Milford, and he was not averse to making them known to Zelda: "'I would like you to think of my interests. That is your primary concern, because I am the one to steer the course, the pilot'" he pompously announced. And to which she replied:

"'I tell you my life has been so miserable that I would rather be in an asylum. Does that mean a thing to you?'

'It does not mean a blessed thing,'" her husband brutally retorted (Nancy Milford, 1975: p. 303).

Reluctant though she was to relinquish her writing (or to turn her experience and expression over to him), Zelda was wearied and weakened by Scott's unrelenting assault and in the end, more from desperation than desire, she asked Scott what would satisfy him, what it was that he wanted her to do.

The answer was as simple as it was revealing: "*I want you to stop writing fiction*" he told Zelda (Nancy Milford, 1975: p. 303, my emphasis).

Because Scott's demand was so absolute, Zelda saw her choice as one of either pleasing him or of pursuing the path of her own survival. It was beyond her to do what he wanted: She simply could not stop writing fiction. Not because she was perverse, not because she wanted to harm or hurt her husband—but because *his* demand was so unreasonable. It was a demand that she deny the development of her own artistic and psychological potential, that she sacrifice her sense of self and her search for sanity.

And while her husband could have accepted all these reasons as sensible and satisfactory in his own case, as quite in order for a man, he would not cope with them in a woman, in his wife. While Zelda—the amateur writer of third-rate talent—dabbled in fiction, and drew on the details of her life, her husband held her to be stealing his resources, and mocking his mastery. He was incensed at her insubordination.

During this period Zelda was working on her novel on psychiatry, on "the story of myself versus myself" as she had put it, and she was of course making use of her own suffering in her work. Scott was consumed with bitterness and anger as he saw her once more "stealing" material he insisted was his: It was Zelda's experience of mental instability that he wanted to exploit in *Tender is the Night*, and he was beside himself as he contemplated the prospect of Zelda *taking* this aspect of her life for her own fictional (and psychological) purposes.

It was in this context that Scott threatened to ruin Zelda and her writing: He openly declared that if ever he got hold of her work he would destroy it. So to protect herself and her novel, Zelda installed a double lock on the door of the room in which she wrote on her visits "home" (Nancy Milford, 1975: p. 303).

If she would not give up her writing, however, Zelda was still prepared to make a deal: It is clear that she would have liked to have found a way to both continue her writing, and to retain her "companionship" with Scott. But for her husband there could be no compromise: His wife's life experience would be available to him as a writer and would not be put to any other use.

"The argument kept returning to the question of Zelda's writing," says Nancy Milford after studying the transcript of their session, and "Finally Scott gave her an ultimatum: she had to stop writing fiction. She asked, 'Of any kind?'

" 'If you write a play, it cannot be a play about psychiatry, and it cannot be a play laid on the Riviera, and it cannot be a play laid in Switzerland, and whatever the idea is, it will have to be submitted to me' " (1975: p. 304).

That Zelda's resistance should have been worn away by such treatment is not surprising—but how far her husband is responsible for the non-appearance of her psychiatric novel is not, and cannot be fully known. What is known is that she wrote no "psychiatric fiction" which would compete with his. So Zelda's story of herself versus herself is presented by her husband in his novel, *Tender is the Night*. It is not—of course—a direct account of Zelda's experience of mental illness, but a "blending of sources" which drew "deeply upon Zelda's and his life together" and in which F. Scott Fitzgerald's unchallenged version of his wife's existence prevails.

Nancy Milford delivers her verdict on the author's actions—and achievements. F. Scott Fitzgerald "mercilessly exposed Zelda in his characterisation of Nicole Diver," she says. "He drew upon Zelda's most terrible and private letters to him, written in the anguish of the early months of her illness in Switzerland, snipped and pieced them together in Book II with very little regard for Zelda's reaction or for the precarious balance of her sanity." Nancy

Milford points out—by way of comparison between the originals and the novel—that Nicole Diver's letters in *Tender is the Night* "were not simply echoes from Zelda's letters to Scott: there were whole phrases used exactly as he had received them" (1975: p. 314).

By no stretch of the imagination can such a practice be perceived as a "polishing" one. And credibility is strained to the limit if such systematic and substantial "lifting" of someone else's material is called simply plagiarism. There is only one way that this behaviour of F. Scott Fitzgerald can be classified: It is plain theft.

And it could be argued that he stole more than his wife's experience and writing; it would not be too much to claim that he robbed her of her sanity as well.

Not that his practices have been perceived this way in the world of letters where the sexual double standard persists and where the topic of men's theft of women's creativity is virtually never raised. Yet in women's criticism there should be a resounding condemnation of these sexually harassing and heinous practices of great literary men.

Encoded in the paradigm of literary criticism that we have inherited is the basic belief, as expressed by F. Scott Fitzgerald, that men are entitled to the resources of women, and that such an arrangement is not problematic. But within the paradigm of literary criticism which women are currently constructing, and which assumes the autonomy and integrity of women's artistic achievement, there must be the fundamental recognition that when men rob women of their creativity, they are committing a crime. Enshrined in women's literary criticism must be the condemnation of unfair practices, of harassment, of exploitation. And in this framework the contributions of Zelda Fitzgerald (and Sonya Tolstoy, and many more) along with the thefts of the men who exploited them, will be assessed very differently—and will produce a very different profile of great writers.

POSTCRIPT

At the core of Gillian Hanscombe's and Virginia Smyers' innovative and excellent analysis of writing women (1987; *Writing for Their Lives; The Modernist Women, 1910–1940*) is a crucial understanding about the relationship between the sexes in a male-dominated society. It is that women who live with men are customarily called upon to support them—domestically, emotionally, and artistically (see also Sally Cline and Dale Spender, 1987; *Reflecting Men*). Because of this arrangement, and because it is non-reciprocal, it is the opinion of Gillian Hanscombe and Virginia Smyers that *women* who want such support—who want to be "nourished," in Virginia Woolf's terms—must live with *women*. And the authors offer this interpretation as one explanation for the frequency with which the women writers in their study—as well as women writers in general—have chosen to live with members of their own sex.

"Some made commitments to permanent partnerships," they comment, "Amy Lowell, Gertrude Stein and Sylvia Beach, for example. Others lived more covertly, leaving us to speculate about the obscurities pertaining to relationships such as Margaret Anderson's with Jane Heap, or Harriet Weaver's with Dora Marsden." (p. 244). There's no shortage of examples to support their thesis that women have turned to women for nurturance in the literary world: Djuna Barnes, Thelma Wood, "Bryher," "H.D." They acknowledge that a very few women writers have enjoyed the services of men, but they regard this (as I and many others do) as the exception and not the rule. And not of the same order, either, as women's services to men:

> . . . on the whole, women writers are few in number who can—or ever could—depend on a man for the constant support that writers need. Male writers have almost automatically derived such support from the women close to them, whether it is intense and stormy like the Lawrences, or conventionally wifely, like the Joyces. . . . (Gillian Hanscombe and Virginia Smyers, 1987: p. 244)

Whether any human being should take on the responsibility of someone else's "shitwork"—be it providing them with meals, clean clothes, interruption-free space, or facilitating their conversation/image/art (often at the expense of their own)—is a matter for debate. But what can be claimed with certainty is that no person should be obliged to fulfil this role for another simply on the basis of class, creed, colour, or sex. The arrangement whereby women are expected to provide such services for men because men are men and women are women simply cannot be defended. Not in terms of human rights; not in terms of literary excellence.

But this principle should not be confined to "personal relationships," to the so-called private realm where the exploitation of women like Jane Carlyle, Emma Hardy, Sonya Tolstoy, and Zelda Fitzgerald can to some extent be shielded from the public eye. For when throughout the entire society one sex is dominant and the other subordinate, it's not just in personal relationships that the subordinates are "ripped off," denied the fruits of their own labour. In the workplace in general, and in the academic community in particular, women's resources are still being stolen on a grand scale. As Annette Kolodny pointed out in her address to the MLA (1987), now that women, through a process of painfully hard, often penalised, and almost always disparaged work, have produced a body of knowledge known as *feminist literary criticism*, they are in danger of having it stolen from them. Now that it is perceived as valuable it is at risk of being taken over by academic men.

Just as men in mixed-sex conversations try to take over women's ideas and recast them in their own terms with the common utterance—"What you mean is . . . "—so are literary men trying to take control of the topics and terms in feminist literary criticism. "What you mean is . . . " is not an un-common response from a male to a female feminist literary critic.

Says Annette Kolodny, these manouvres suggest the condescending "judgement that feminists still haven't got it right and that our enterprise would be much better off in male hands . . . one hears . . . one male critic after another either chide . . . the feminist for not doing things *his* way or for not meeting *his* expectations of what she should be about" (in press).

Worse, women are supposed to acknowledge the error of their ways, to apologise, and to thank men for the benefit of their greater wisdom.

But in the end, this is back where this book begins; with the links between the spoken and written discourse, and the institutions of society. The dangers that Annette Kolodny alerts us to are of the same kind that women face in mixed-sex discussions, where the contribution of women is ignored, only to be taken over by a man, and applauded. "That's a good idea Ms. Jones, we'll wait until a man puts it forward."

The reality with which women's literary criticism must currently contend is that the literary reputations of so many men have been built upon the exploitation of women; which is why it is difficult, if not impossible to keep "social issues" out of literary evaluation. Until we address, and remedy, some of these injustices we cannot speak of women *willingly* giving their creative efforts to men. We cannot expect women to be free to enjoy the fruits of their own literary labour. We cannot assume that women's writing will suffer no penalties on the grounds of sex.

This is why I am perplexed when some people ask me why I have aban-doned the political arena for the safe place/sideline of women's literary history and criticism. I know that despite the "information revolution" and the glorification of technology (as if it can ever be a human solution!!), there's nothing more dangerous than "the word." Women's words. And a fair hearing. This is why women's writing and reading is an area of continual expansion, why women's literary criticism is one of the most dynamic (and dangerous?) areas within the academy. Why too men want to take it over.

As Annette Kolodny has said, "The practice of feminist literary criticism is the most demanding practice I know . . . it is and always has been a moral and ethical stance that seeks to change the structures of knowledge and with that, the institutional structures in which knowledge gets made and codified" (in press).

As with all feminist practices, the object of literary study is to forge in-sights, to generate liberating ideas which can help to promote a more just and equitable society. And one of the reasons that women have been discour-aged from writing—and that their writing has been dismissed—is that the *woman* writer has presented an alternative world. Which is why it could be said—that you don't have to read women's writing to know that it is (patriar-chally) subversive.

Appendix

In the daily practice of literary criticism, many men make comments which expose their attitude toward women, and toward women's writing. Yet such expressions of blatant prejudice rarely appear in print, and in an academic community where the spoken word does not carry the same weight or authority as the written word, women's criticism can be disadvantaged while it cannot *quote* these outrageous judgements of literary men: For such comments call into question their right and their ability to practice their profession.

There is no reason to suspect that the eminent men who make these revelations would be able to put aside their prejudices when they approached the seemingly serious, scholarly, and scientific task of evaluating the literary contributions of women; no reason to suspect that they would dispense with their discriminatory standards when they engaged in the task of objectively assessing the aptitude of women candidates for professional appointments. So in the interest of accounting for the judgements of literary men as they have impinged on the achievements of women, the following quotations are provided.

I am sorry that legal considerations preclude the naming of the men; I am grateful to the women critics who have so generously allowed their own research findings in the area to be included here.

DALE SPENDER

1. *Male academic:* None of the women writers of the eighteenth century were of any significance.
   Dale Spender: How many have you read?
   MA: Enough to know they have no place in a course concerned with the

study of innovation and excellence in the novel.
(England, 1986).

2. *Male academic:* Even if there were more women novelists in the nine-teenth century, and I have no reason to believe that to be the case, they wrote about domestic matters, not about the human condition.
Dale Spender: How many have you read?
MA: I think it's a case of if you've read one, you've read them all.
(USA, 1986).

3. *Male academic:* There are no women writers on the contemporary course because we want to study the *best* writers. It's got nothing to do with sex.
Dale Spender: How many twentieth-century women writers have you read?
MA: Woolf, Lessing, they're interesting enough I suppose, but we'd have to put two of the men out to put them on, and that wouldn't be justified.
(Australia, 1987).

4. *Male academic:* Look, if you could find the time to go back to the begin-ning, and read all the women's books, sure, you'd find a couple of gems that slipped through the net. But you'd find a few men that way, too. And there just isn't the time to do it. We have to accept the judgements of the past, take it as a guide, see what has stood the test of time. It's a good method, even if it isn't perfect. If the women had been any good, they would have been there. But there's been the consensus that only the occasional woman has had what it takes.
Dale Spender: But it's been a consensus among men and about men; what about the new consensus among women about women? Women who think women's books are good?
MA: Well, they would, wouldn't they? Compensation. But it doesn't change the fact that the great works have been written by men. It mightn't stay that way of course, but that's how it is at present.
DS: How many women's books have you read?
MA: A few. Not as many as I'd like to, but there isn't the time to go into anything that isn't absolutely first rate.
(Scotland, 1987).

5. *Male academic:* These women's books, they're an interesting specialty. I believe there's a woman in Melbourne who studies them. I don't go in for them much myself.
(Australia, 1987).

6. *Male academic:* Writing is one area where women haven't been dis-criminated against, where they have had the same opportunities as men. They could even use male names if they wanted to. But they never made it in the same numbers as men, and it's not because anyone has stopped them.
Dale Spender: How many eighteenth- and nineteenth-century women writers have you read?

MA: Well, I would have liked to have read more, but they're not available, are they?

DS: What about the Virago and Pandora reprints?

MA: Oh those! Are you joking? They're just scraping the bottom of the barrel, yesterday's *Harlequins*, past pulp-romance. I mean something of the calibre of an Eliot or a Burney.

(Canada, 1987).

[Note: Virago has reprinted an Eliot; Pandora a Burney; and of course there are many women writers of comparable calibre who have not achieved favour.]

7. *Male academic:* O come off it . . . There's too many women writers on the course now. They dominate everything . . . .

Dale Spender: You come off it. Look at this Drama Anthology[1] "An Introduction to Fifty British Plays from 1660–1900," it says. Not a woman in it. Doesn't say "Fifty Plays by Men" you know.

MA: Well that's alright. That's the one area where women haven't done so well, in the Drama.

DS: Are you crazy? Is this the sort of professional expertise you are being paid for. What about the Restoration Period? Where women were the most successful . . . Aphra Behn, Delarivière Manley, Susannah Centlivre, Catherine Trotter—all those women in *The Female Wits*?[2] What about Elizabeth Inchbald, the first drama critic? . . .

MA: Well, I don't know about any of them. They hardly qualify as mainstream.

DS: What do you have to do to get to be mainstream? Just be a man? 'Cause they won't qualify as mainstream while you keep doing the Catch 22 bit. They're not there so they can't be any good, and they're not good so they're not there . . . But you said women *dominate* the courses here. That's what I want to get at. What about poetry. Look at the courses this institution teaches . . . not a woman poet on them.

MA: You can't take an isolated example. We have had women in the past. Elizabeth Barrett Browning. It's just a coincidence this year. Besides it was really fiction I was talking about . . . that's where the women are over represented.

DS: Are you serious? How can you keep saying that when a four-year-old could go and check your courses and find out that's a lie.

MA: If you're going to get nasty about this, there's no point in me continuing to talk to you. But you know as well as I do that women have dominated fiction.

---

[1] John Cargill Thompson, 1979, Pan Literature Guides, London and Sydney.
[2] Fidelis Morgan (ed) 1981, *The Female Wits: Women Playwrights of the Restoration*, Virago, London.

DS: Name them.

MA: Be serious. What do you mean, name them? You know them. Austen, Eliot, the Brontës, Woolf. They're the main ones.

DS: Any more? Only five. The Famous Five as Elaine Showalter calls them.[3]

MA: Hundreds. You know them. Lessing. Just start . . .

DS: Five. That's all you can come up with? Five. A cast of thousands of men and five women. And you're supposed to be a man of intellectual stature . . . (at this stage male academic stalks off) . . . and you say that five women dominate the men. I find such behaviour totally unprofessional. (Australia, 1987).

CATHY DAVIDSON

Anti-feminist critic: I just don't understand the point of feminist literary criticism. I mean, literature is the *one* area where women have excelled. All feminist criticism does is make it seem that good women writers are really second class, need some kind of affirmative action.

Cathy N. Davidson: Wait—I never even had a woman professor in graduate school. I read only two books by women in my entire graduate career.

AFC: I keep hearing feminists say that but it's just anecdotal. In my graduate school at least half the books were by women.

CND: Who?

AFC: Oh, I don't really remember now—you know all those women local color writers. I can't remember their names off hand.

(USA, 1987).

AFC: Women's writing just isn't universal the way men's writing is.
(USA, 1985).

AFC: Feminist criticism is an insult to women. Is there anything more ridiculous than this whole French debate about what body part women write with?

CND: Personally, I don't find the question very interesting. But you're a Freudian critic, and it was Freud who started it all by saying men write with the phallus.

AFC: There's a logic to Freud. But vaginas? Labias? Nipples? At least you can *hold* a phallus.

CND: Have you ever tried to write with one?

(USA, 1987).

---

[3]See Elaine Showalter, 1977, *A Literature of Their Own: British Women Writers from Brontë to Lessing*, Princeton University Press, Princeton.

AFC: There never has been and never will be a female Shakespeare. (USA, 1985).

Observation: My husband, literary critic Arnold E. Davidson, has published many articles on women writers. Even when he has articles rejected, he has never *once* been advised to send his work to a feminist journal, nor even had his work identified as feminist. In contrast, until recently I have had articles returned with the suggestion that *Signs* or *Women's Studies* would be a more appropriate forum (the buzz word) for my work. This has happened enough times for us to be convinced that the different response is not subject or ideology, but that his name is "Arnold" and mine is "Cathy." Whether we like it or not writing by women (including women critics) is peripheralized. (Cathy N. Davidson, March 1988).

MARILYN FRENCH

Observations: An article I submitted to a learned journal was returned with the comments of the critic (unnamed) . . . The article was either Shakespeare or Spenser . . . and the critic scrawled, "Tell her to try one of them 'feminist' journals".

I remember at the age of nearly forty going to visit an eminent male novelist-in-residence at Harvard for a year. I told him I had been writing for a long time and needed an agent. He looked at me for a while appraisingly, rubbed his chin, said 'Ummm. Well, what d'ya write, love stories?' (Marilyn French, April 1988).

ANNETTE KOLODNY

(Overheard in a corridor in the University of New Hampshire when Annette Kolodny had been denied promotion for the second time; two tenured male colleagues talking to each other).

Male A: What the hell is this "women-in-the-west" stuff that Kolodny's working on now? I don't see what it has to do with *literature*.

Male B: Yes, she's overrated.

Male A: Really belongs in women's studies where they do that sort of thing.

Male B: Just another fad. Won't last. As I said, she's overrated.

(Annette Kolodny, March 1988).

SUSAN KOPPELMAN

Along with others in the room I waited with trembling eagerness for the famous man who was our teacher in my first creative writing class at Barnard to return our first assignments. He passed out our papers, gave us a moment to read his comments, sighed, and said "What a shame so many of you are so talented!"

You can bet he got our attention with *that* remark.

After a dramatic mini-pause, he continued; "It's a pity when literary talent is wasted on girls who can never have the kinds of experiences that catalyze talent into genius."

The experiences he was bemoaning our absence of access to were: war, whoring, the good fellowship of men reeling drunk down dark mean city streets, and the hunt.

That was 1958 or 1959. Fifteen or so years later, at an MLA forum, I listened to Erica Jong tell the same story, almost word for word. She had been at Barnard when I was, a member of the class a year younger. I assumed her teacher had been my teacher but to check it out I asked her in private, after her talk. "No." she told me, "It wasn't Professor X; it was Professor Y".

I began to wonder then if it *wasn't* a genuine conspiracy . . .

(Susan Koppelman, March 1988).

JOANNA RUSS

. . . Some years ago I served as the one woman on a committee of three professors of writing; our job was to screen candidates for an MA program in creative writing. As we proceeded in our tedious and unpleasant chore of reading perhaps two hundred manuscripts, some interesting facts emerged:

- Our rankings of the top 50% of the manuscripts were almost identical.
- My ranking of the top twenty samples of the prose and verse written by men was almost identical with my colleagues.
- My ranking of the top twenty samples of the prose and verse written by women was almost exactly the inverse of theirs.

I remember in particular a short story, funny and classically feminist, which ended with the female protagonist lying in bed next to her sleeping husband, wishing she had the courage to hit him over the head with a frying pan. The last detail is distinctive; I suspect the story appeared later in a feminist literary magazine. My colleagues, who did not like the story, could not understand why the protagonist was so angry; my explanations (which connected the story with feminist consciousness) brought from one only the polite but baffled response that the story was about "a failure in human communications" in that particular marriage.

The other manuscript I remember very well was a poem I found impressive and will try to reconstruct from memory. A fifteen-year-old girl, after a date with a boy she didn't like, "so I had to work at it," returns (alone) to "my mother's kitchen," opens the gleaming, white refrigerator and finds that something startling has happened—the interior of the refrigerator has miraculously (and spontaneously) become entirely covered with red cabbage roses. As I tried to explain to my two colleagues the extraordinary elements compressed into that last image, I realized that I was speaking to ignorance. What did they know of the elaborate rating-dating scheme fifteen-year-old girls went through, of the wrench that occurs in puberty when one moves out of the female world (mothers and friends) into the one with a totally different set of standards, a world one must "work at" even if one doesn't like it, so that coming back to the familiar women's world ("my mother's kitchen," not "*the* kitchen") can be a great relief? Or of the gleaming white refrigerator which is only a "sanitary" or "efficient" fake—no laboratory appliance but the fountain of plenty, *my mother* in reality, with its immaculate bloom that is at once emotional, uterine, and the center both of the house and one's life? The bond between mother and daughter blooms inside technology, in the middle of a world in which relations with men are, alas, not a pleasure, but work. The poem is a kind of transubstantiation.

So much for my memories of kitchens, dates and my mother! But my experience was clearly not theirs. How could it be? And female experience of that sort was sufficiently invisible in literature at that time (it may still be so) to make it impossible that they should recognize it from literary sources. None of the women admitted into the program was my choice. None of my female choices were accepted into the program.

Joanna Russ, from *How to Suppress Women's Writing*, 1983, The Women's Press, London, pp. 45–46.

ELAINE SHOWALTER

Male academic: Feminist Critic "X" is by far the worst scholar in this field. She just doesn't know very much or go very deep, and she can't even write well.

Elaine Showalter: Have you read her book?

MA: Of course not, it would take a miracle to make me change my mind . . .

(Elaine Showalter, March 1988).

References and
Further Reading

Abbot, C. C. (ed) (1935). *The Correspondence of Gerard Manley Hopkins and Richard Watson Dixon*, Oxford and London: Oxford University Press.

Adelaide, Debra (1986). 'Mollie Skinner' paper given at Association for the Study of Australian Literature, Townsville, July.

Adelaide, Debra (ed) (1988). *A Bright and Fiery Troupe*, Melbourne, Australia: Penguin.

Altick, Richard (1957). *The English Common Reader*, Chicago: University of Chicago Press.

Altick, Richard (1962). "The Sociology of Authorship." In *Bulletin of New York Public Library LXVI*, pp 389–404.

Angelou, Maya (1985). "Maya Angelou." In Claudia Tate (ed), *Black Women Writers at Work*, (pp 1–11) Harpenden: Oldcastle Books.

Atwood, Margaret (1985). "Sexual Bias in Reviewing." In Ann Dybikowski *et al* (eds), *In the Feminine: Women and Words: Conference Proceedings 1983* (pp 151–152) Toronto: Longspoon Press.

Atwood, Margaret (1986). "Paradoxes and Dilemmas: The Woman as Writer." In Mary Eagleton (ed), *Feminist Literary Theory* (pp 74–76) Oxford: Basil Blackwell.

Bambara, Toni Cade (1980). "What It Is I Think I'm Doing Anyhow." In Janet Sternburg (ed), *The Writer on Her Work* (pp 153–179) New York: W. W. Norton.

Barthes, Roland (1977). *Image—Music—Text*, (transl. Stephen Heath) London: Fontana.

Bartlett, Nora (1983). "An Excerpt from My Unpublished Writing." In Michelene Wandor (ed), *On Gender and Writing* (pp 10–16) London: Pandora Press.

Batsleer, Janet, Tony Davies, Rebecca O'Rourke, and Chris Weedon (1985). *Rewriting English: Cultural Politics of Gender and Class*, London: Methuen.

de Beauvoir, Simone (1972). *The Second Sex*, Harmondsworth: Penguin. (originally published France, 1949).

Beer, Gillian (1986). *George Eliot*, Brighton: Harvester Press.

Bernard, Jessie (1974). "My Four Revolutions: An Autobiographical History of the A.S.A." In Joan Huber (ed), *Changing Women in a Changing Society* (pp 11–29). Chicago: University of Chicago Press.

Bernard, M. E., L. W. Keefauver, G. Elsworth, and F. D. Naylor (1981). "Sex role behavior and gender in teacher-student evaluations" In *Journal of Educational Psychology, 73*, pp 681–696.

Bernikow, Louise (1980). *Among Women* New York: Harmony Books.

Boulton, J. (1968). *Lawrence in Love—Letters to Louie Burrows* Nottingham: University of Nottingham Press.

Brittain, Vera ([1957] 1981). *Testament of Experience* London: Fontana.

Brody, Miriam (1983). "Mary Wollstonecraft: Sexuality and Women's Rights." In Dale Spender (ed), *Feminist Theorists* (pp 40–59) London: The Women's Press.

Brydges, Egerton (1835). *The Life of John Milton* London: John Macrone.

Butler, Marilyn (1972). *Maria Edgeworth: A Literary Biography* Oxford: Clarendon Press.

Cann, A., W. D. Siegfried, and L. Pearce (1981). "Forced attention to specific applicant qualifications: Impact of physical attractiveness and sex of applicant biases." In *Personal Psychology, 34*, 67–76.

Carroll, Berenice A. (forthcoming). "The politics of originality." In Cheris Kramarae and Dale Spender (eds), *The Knowledge Explosion; Disciplines and Debates*, Athene Series, Elmsford, New York: Pergamon Press.

Carswell, Catherine (1932). *The Savage Pilgrimage: A Narrative of D. H. Lawrence* London: Martin Secker.

Cawelti, John (1976). *Adventure, Mystery and Romance* Chicago: University of Chicago Press.

Chambers, Jessie (1965). *D. H. Lawrence: A Personal Record* London: Frank Cass.

Chapple, J. A. V. and A. Pollard (eds) (1966). *The Letters of Mrs. Gaskell* Manchester: Manchester University Press.

Chesler, Phyllis (1971). "Marriage and Psychotherapy." In Radical Therapist Collective (eds) *The Radical Therapist* (pp 175–180) New York: Ballantyne.

Chesler, Phyllis (1972). *Women and Madness* London: Allen Lane.

Chesler, Phyllis (1985). "Account Rendered: Writers Response to Writing." In Dale Spender, *For the Record* (pp 213–215) London: The Women's Press.

Christian, Barbara (ed) (1985). *Black Feminist Criticism: Perspectives on Black Women's Writing*, Elmsford, New York: Pergamon Press.

Cholmeley, Jane (1985). "Silver Moon: Setting up a Feminist Business in a Capitalist World." Unpublished MA Thesis, Kent: *University of Canterbury*.

Clarricoates, Katherine (1978). " 'Dinosaurs in the Classroom': A re-examination of some aspects of the hidden curriculum in primary schools." In *Women's Studies International Quarterly, Vol I, No. 4*, pp 353–64.

Cline, Sally and Dale Spender (1987). *Reflecting Men: The Management of the Male Ego* London: Andre Deutsch.

Coles, Robert (1976). See cover, Tillie Olsen, *Tell Me a Riddle* New York: Laurel, Dell Publishing.

Cooke, Helen (1975). *In Our Infancy—An Autobiography, Part I, 1882–1912*, Cambridge and London: Cambridge University Press.

Crosland, Margaret (1975). *Colette: the Difficulty of Loving*, New York: Laurel, Dell Publishing.

Cross, John Jacob (ed) (1924). *Autobiography of John Stuart Mill*, New York: Columbia University Press.

D'Alpuget, Blanche (1986). "Blanche D'Alpuget." In Jennifer Ellison, *Rooms of Their Own*, (pp 10–27) Australia: Penguin.

Davies, Kath, Julienne Dickey, and Teresa Stratford (eds) (1987). *Out of Focus: Writings on Women and the Media*, London: The Women's Press.

Delavenay, E. (1969). *D. H. Lawrence: L'Homme et la Genese de Son Oeuvre—Les Annes de Formation, 1885–1919*. Paris: Librarie C. Klincksieck.

Denmark, F. L. (1979). "The outspoken woman: can she win?" Paper presented at the New York Academy of Sciences, New York City.

Dipboye, R. L., R. D. Arvey and J. E. Terpstra (1977). "Sex and physical attractiveness of raters and applicants as determinants of resume evaluations." In *Journal of Applied Psychology, 66*, pp 288–294.

Drabble, Margaret (1983). "A Woman Writer." In Michelene Wandor (ed), *On Gender and Writing*, (pp 156–159) London: Pandora Press.

Duelli Klein, Renate (1986). The Dynamics of Women's Studies. An Exploratory Study of Its International Ideas and Practices in Higher Education. Ph.D. Dissertation, University of London (unpubl.).

Dworkin, Andrea (1988). *Letters from a War Zone*, London: Secker and Warburg.

Dworkin, Andrea (1987a). "The Authors: Andrea Dworkin." In Women in Publishing (eds) *Reviewing the Reviews: A Woman's Place on the Book Page* (pp 81–84) London: Journeyman.

Dworkin, Andrea (1987b). *Intercourse*, London: Secker and Warburg.

Eagleton, Mary (ed) (1986). *Feminist Literary Theory: A Reader*, Oxford: Basil Blackwell.

Edwards, Anne (1982). *Sonya: The Life of Countess Tolstoy*, London: Coronet/Hodder & Stoughton.

Ehrenreich, Barbara (1983). *The Hearts of Men: American Dream and the Flight from Commitment*, London: Pluto Press.

Elbert, Sarah (1977). "Introduction." In Louisa May Alcott, *Work: A Story of Experience*, (pp ix–xliv) New York: Schocken Books.

Elbert, Sarah (1978). "Work: A Study of Experience." In Sarah Elbert and Marion Glastonbury, *Inspiration and Drudgery: Notes on Literature and Domestic Labour in the Nineteenth Century*, (pp 11–26) London: WRRC Publication.

Ellison, Jennifer (1986). *Rooms of Their Own*, Australia: Penguin.

Epstein, Cynthia Fuchs (1976). "Sex role stereotyping; occupations and social exchange." In *Women's Studies*, (3), 190, pp 193–194.

Etaugh, C. and H. C. Kasley (1981). "Evaluating Competence: effects of sex, marital status and parental status." *Psychology of Women Quarterly*, 6, pp 196–203.

Evans, Mari (ed) (1984). *Black Women Writers. (1950–1980). A critical evaluation* New York: Anchor Books, Doubleday.

Evans, Nancy Burr (1972). "The Value and Peril for Women of Reading Women Writers." In Susan Kopplemann Cornillon (ed) *Images of Women in Fiction*, (pp 308–314) Bowling Green, Ohio: Bowling Green University Popular Press.

Fairbairns, Zoe (1987). "The Authors: Zoe Fairbairns." In Women in Publishing (eds) *Reviewing the Reviews*, (pp 84–87) London: Journeyman.

Fennema, Elizabeth (1987). Findings presented on lecture tour of Australia. Unpublished.

Finch, Anne (1974). "The Introduction." In Joan Goulianos (ed) *By A Woman Writt*, (pp 71–73) Penguin: Harmondsworth.

Fishman, Pamela (1977). "Interactional Shitwork" In *Heresies: A Feminist Publication on Arts and Politics, No. 2, May*, pp 99–101.

Flanner, Janet (1975). "Introduction" in Margaret Crosland, *Colette: the Difficulty of Loving*, (pp 14–21) New York: Laurel, Dell Publishing.

Flynn, Carol Houlihan and Lee Davidoff (1978). "Introduction." In Sarah Elbert and Marion Glastonbury, *Inspiration and Drudgery*, (pp 1–10) London: WRRC Publication.

Fowles, John (1981). *The Aristos*, London: Triad, Granada.

Fraser, Antonia (1986). Private communication.

French, Marilyn (1984/1985). "Survey New York Times Book Review" Unpublished.

Friedan, Betty (1963). *The Feminine Mystique*, New York: W. W. Norton.

Frye, Northrop (1957). *Anatomy of Criticism*, Princeton: Princeton University Press.

Gage, Matilda Joslyn ([1983] 1980). *Woman, Church and State: The Original Expose of Male Collaboration Against the Female Sex*, (intro. by Sally Roesch Wagner; foreword by Mary Daly), Watertown, Massachusetts: Persephone Press.

Gaskell, Elizabeth (1966). *The Letters of Mrs. Gaskell*, J. A. V. Chapple and A. Pollard (eds) Manchester: Manchester University Press.

Gilbert, Sandra M. (1986). "What Do Feminist Critics Want? A Postcard from the Volcano." In Elaine Showalter (ed) *The New Feminist Criticism*, (pp 29–45) London: Virago.

Gilbert, Sandra M. and Susan Gubar (1979). *The Madwoman in the Attic: The Woman Writer and the Nineteenth Century*, New Haven, Connecticut: Yale University Press.

Gilman, Charlotte Perkins ([1892] 1981). "The Yellow Wall-paper" (reprinted) Ann J. Lane (ed) *The Charlotte Perkins Gilman Reader*, London: The Women's Press.

Gittings, Robert (1975). *Young Thomas Hardy*, London: Heineman.

Gittings, Robert (1978). *The Older Hardy*, London: Heineman.

Glastonbury, Marion (1978). "Holding the Pens." In Sarah Elbert and Marion Glastonbury, *Inspiration and Drudgery: Notes on Literature and Domestic Labour in the Nineteenth Century*, (pp 27–47) London: WRRC Publication.

Glastonbury, Marion (1979). "The best kept secret—how working class women live and what they know" In *Women's Studies International Quarterly*, Vol. 2, No. 2, pp 171–182.

Godwin, Gail (1980). "Becoming a Writer." In Janet Sternburg (ed) *The Writer on Her Work*, (pp 231–255) New York: W. W. Norton.

Goldberg, Philip (1974). "Are Women Prejudiced Against Women?" In J. Stacey, S. Bereaud and J. Daniels (eds) *And Jill Came Tumbling After: Sexism in American Education*, (pp 37–42) New York: Dell Publishing.

Gordon, Mary (1980). "The Parable of the Cave or: In Praise of Watercolours." In Janet Sternburg (ed) *The Writer on Her Work*, (pp 27–32) New York: W. W. Norton.

Goreau, Angeline (1980). *Reconstructing Aphra: A Social Biography of Aphra Behn*, New York: The Dial Press.

Goulianos, Joan (ed) (1974). *By a Woman Writt: Literature from Six Centuries by and about Women*, Harmondsworth: Penguin.

Greer, Germaine ([1970] 1987). *The Female Eunuch*, London: Paladin.

Greer, Germaine (1979). *The Obstacle Race: The Fortunes of Women Painters and their Work*, London: Secker and Warburg.

Griffin, Susan (1980). "Thoughts on Writing: A Diary." In Janet Sternburg, (ed) *The Writer on Her Work*, (pp 107–120) New York: W. W. Norton.

Gutek, B. A. and D. A. Stevens (1979). "Effects of sex of subject, sex of stimulus use, and androgyny level on evaluations in work situations which evoke sex-role stereotypes" In *Journal of Vocational Behavior, 14*, pp 23–32.

Hamilton, Cicely ([1909] 1981). *Marriage as a Trade*, London: The Women's Press.

Hanscombe, Gillian and Virginia L. Smyers (1987). *Writing for Their Lives: The Modernist Women 1910–1940*, London: The Women's Press.

Hardwick, Elizabeth (1974). *Seduction and Betrayal: Women and Literature*, London: Weidenfeld & Nicolson.

Hardwick, Elizabeth (1974). "Victims and Victors: Zelda." In *Seduction and Betrayal*, (pp 87–103) London: Weidenfeld & Nicolson.

Heilbrun, Carolyn G. (1986). "Bringing the Spirit Back to English Studies." In Elaine Showalter (ed) *The New Feminist Criticism*, (pp 21–28) London: Virago.

Heilbrun, Carolyn (1973). *Towards Androgyny–Aspects of Male and Female in Literature*, London: Victor Gollancz.

Hemlow, Joyce (1958). *The History of Fanny Burney*, Oxford: Clarendon Press.

Heneman, H. G. (1977). "Impact of test information and applicant sex on applicant evaluations in a selection simulation" In *Journal of Applied Psychology, 62*, pp 524–526.

Hennegan, Alison (1984). "Report on Review of Reviews" from First Feminist International Book Fair, 1984. Unpublished.

Howe, Florence (1972). "Feminism and Literature." In Susan Koppelman Cornillon (ed) *Images of Women in Fiction* (pp 253–277), Bowling Green, Ohio: Bowling Green University Popular Press.

Huff, Cynthia, A. (1987). "Chronicles of Confinement: Reactions to Childbirth in British Women's Diaries" In *Women's Studies International Forum, Vol. 10, No. 1*, pp 63–68.

Humm, Maggie (1986). *Feminist Criticism: Women as Contemporary Critics*, Brighton: The Harvester Press.

Jacobus, Mary (1979). "A Difference of View." In Mary Jacobus, (ed) *Women Writing and Writing About Women*, (pp 10–21) London: Croom Helm.

Jelinek, Estelle C. (ed) (1980). *Women's Autobiography: Essays in Criticism*, Bloomington and London: Indiana University Press.

Jensen, Margaret (1984). *Love's Sweet Return: The Harlequin Story*, Toronto: The Women's Press.

Jerrold, Walter and Clare, Jerrold (1929). *Five Queer Women*, London: Brentanos.

Jespersen, Otto (1922). *Language: It's Nature, Development and Origin*, London: Allen & Unwin.

Jones, Carol (1985). "Sexual Tyranny: Male Violence in a Mixed-Sex Secondary School." In Gaby Weiner (ed) *Just a Bunch of Girls*, (pp 26–39) Open University Press, Milton Keynes.

Jong, Erica (1980). "Blood and Guts: The Tricky Problem of Being a Woman Writer in the Late Twentieth Century." In Janet Sternburg (ed), *The Writer on Her Work*, (pp 169–179) New York/ London: W. W. Norton.

Kaschak, E. (1981). "Another look at sex-bias in students' evaluations of professions: Do winners get the recognition they have been given?" In *Psychology of Women Quarterly, 5*, pp 767–772.

Kaplan, Cora (1976). "Language and Gender" In *Papers on Patriarchy*, (pp 21–37) Brighton: Women's Publishing Collective.

Kaplan, Cora (1978). "Introduction" Elizabeth Barrett Browning, *Aurora Leigh and Other Poems* (pp 5–36) London: The Women's Press.

Kaplan, Cora (1983). "Speaking/Writing/Feminism." In Michelene Wandor (ed) *Gender and Writing*, (pp 51–61) London: Pandora Press.

Kavanagh, Julia (1863). *English Women of Letters: Biographical Sketches*, Vol. I and II, London: Hurst & Blackett.

Kolodny, Annette (1981). "Dancing Through the Minefield: Some Observations on the Theory, Practice and Politics of Feminist Literary Criticism." In Dale Spender (ed) *Men's Studies Modified*, (pp 23–42). Oxford: Pergamon Press.

Kolodny, Annette (1986). "A Map for Rereading: Gender and the Interpretation of Literary Texts" In Elaine Showalter (ed), *The New Feminist Criticism*, (pp 46–62) London: Virago.

Kolodny, Annette (in press). "Dancing Between Left and Right: Feminism and the Academic Minefield in the 1980's" (M.L.A. address, 1987). In Betty Jean Craige (ed) *Literature, Language and Politics in the 1980's*, Athens, Georgia: University of Georgia Press.

Koppelman Cornillon, Susan (ed) (1972). *Images of Women in Fiction: Feminist Perspectives*, Bowling Green, Ohio: Bowling Green University Popular Press.

Koppelman, Susan, private communication, 1988.

Kramarae, Cheris (1981). *Women and Men Speaking*, Rowley, Mass: Newbury House.

Kramarae, Cheris (ed) (1980). *The Voices and Words of Women and Men*, Oxford: Pergamon Press.

Kramarae, Cheris and Paula Treichler (1985). *A Feminist Dictionary*, London: Pandora Press.

Kramer, Cheris (1975). "Women's Speech: Separate but Unequal." In Barrie Thorne and Nancy Henley (eds) *Language and Sex: Difference and Dominance*, (pp 43–56) Rowley, Mass: Newbury House.

Kramer, Cheris (1977 April/June). "Perceptions of Female and Male Speech" In *Language and Speech, 20, No. 2*, pp 151–161.

Kuhn, Thomas (1972). *The Structure of Scientific Revolutions*, (2nd ed) Chicago: University of Chicago Press.

Lawrence, D. H. (1962). *Collected Letters*, (Harry T. Moore, ed) London: Heinemann.

Lawrence, D. H. (1964). *Complete Poems*, (V. deSola Pinto and W. Roberts, eds.) London: Heinemann.

Lawrence, D. H. (1968). *Phoenix II—Uncollected, Unpublished and Other Prose Works*, (W. Roberts and Harry T. Moore, eds.) London: Heinemann.

Lawrence, Frieda (1935). *Not I, But the Wind*, London: Heinemann.

Lawrence, Frieda (1961). *Memoirs and Correspondence* (E. W. Tedlock, ed) London: Heinemann.

Leavis, F. R. (1962). *The Great Tradition*, Harmondsworth: Penguin.

Lee, Anne (1980). "'Together We Learn to Read and Write': Sexism and Literacy." In Dale Spender and Elizabeth Sarah (eds), *Learning to Lose: Sexism and Education*, (pp 121–127) London: The Women's Press.

Leighton, Angela (1986). *Elizabeth Barrett Browning*, Brighton: Harvester Press.

Levy, Bronwen (1985). "Women's Writing: It's Critical Reception. (1) Women and the Literary Pages: Some recent Examples" In *Hecate, Vol. XI, No. 1*, pp 5–11.

Levy, Bronwen (1987/1988). "Qualitative methods? Reading recent Australian women's fiction" In *Hecate, Vol. 13, No. 2*, pp 149–157.

Lewes, G. H. (1850). "Currer Bell's *Shirley*" In *Edinburgh Review, 91*, p 165.

Lifshin, Lyn (1982). *Ariadne's Thread: A Collection of Contemporary Women's Journals*, New York: Harper & Row.

Lloyd, Susan M. (ed) (1982). *Roget's Thesaurus of English Words and Phrases*, London: Longman.

Lombardo, J. P. and M. E. Tocci (1979). "Attribution of positive and negative characteristics of instructors as a function of attractiveness and sex of instructor and sex of subject" In *Perceptual and Motor Skills, 48*, pp 491–494.

Lorde, Audre (1985). "Audre Lorde." In Claudia Tate (ed), *Black Women Writers at Work*, (pp 100–116) Harpenden: Oldcastle Books.

Lott, Bernice (1985). "The devaluation of women's competence" In *Journal of Social Issues, Vol. 41, No. 4*, pp 43–60.

Lovell, Terry (1986). "Writing Like a Woman: A Question of Politics." In Mary Eagleton (ed) *Feminist Literary Theory: A Reader*, (pp 83–85) Oxford: Blackwell.

Mailer, Norman (1984 Dec. 16). "Advertisements for Myself" quoted in Elaine Showalter, "Women Who Write Are Women" in *The New York Times Book Review*, 31.

Mahony, Pat (1983). "Boys will be boys: teaching women's studies in mixed-sex groups" In *Women's Studies International Forum, Vol. 6, No. 3*, pp 331–334.

Mann, Peter (1969). *The Romantic Novel: A Survey of Reading Habits*, London: Mills & Boon.

Mann, Peter (1974). *A New Survey: The Facts About Romantic Fiction*, London: Mills & Boon.

Mansfield, Katherine (1981). *The Letters and Journals of Katherine Mansfield: A Selection*, (C. K. Stead [ed]) Harmondsworth: Penguin.

McClusky, Margaret (1988 May 7). "What's this about a feminist Mafia?" *The Sydney Morning Herald*, p 72.

McWilliams-Tullberg, Rita (1975). *Women at Cambridge: A Men's University—Though of a Mixed Type*, London: Victor Gollancz.

Mead, Margaret (1971). *Male and Female*, Harmondsworth: Penguin.

Meek, Margaret, Aidan Warlow, and Griselda Barton (eds) (1977). *The Cool Web: The Pattern of Children's Reading*, London: The Bodley Head.

Miles, Rosalind (1974). *The Fiction of Sex: Themes and Functions of Sex Difference in the Modern Novel*, London: Vision.

Milford, Nancy (1975). *Zelda Fitzgerald*, Harmondsworth: Penguin.

Milford, Nancy (1980). "De Memoria." In Janet Sternburg (ed) *The Writer on Her Work*, (pp 33–43) New York: W. W. Norton.

Mill, John Stuart (1924). *Autobiography* (John Jacob Cross, ed) New York: Columbia University Press.

Miller, Casey and Kate Swift (1981). *The Handbook of Non-Sexist Writing for Writers, Editors and Speakers*, London: The Women's Press.

Millett, Kate (1972). *Sexual Politics*, London: Abacus/Sphere.

Mitchison, Naomi (1986). Private communication.

Moers, Ellen (1977). *Literary Women: The Great Writers*, New York: Anchor Press, Doubleday.

Moffat, Mary Jane and Charlotte Painter (eds) (1975). *Revelations: Diaries of Women*, New York: Vintage/Random House.

Moore, H. T. (1974). *The Priest of Love: A Life of D. H. Lawrence* (revised edition), London: Heinemann.

Moore, Honor (1980). "My Grandmother Who Painted." In Janet Sternburg (ed) *The Writer on Her Work*, (pp 45–71) New York: W. W. Norton.

Morgan, Fidelis (ed) (1981). *The Female Wits: Women Playwrights of the Restoration*, London: Virago.

Moorman, Mary (ed) (1976). *Journals of Dorothy Wordsworth, The Alfoxden Journal 1798: The Grasmere Journals 1800–1803* (2nd edition) (Helen Darbishire, intro.), Oxford: Oxford Paperbacks.

Mullen, Jean S. (1972 October). "Freshman Textbooks" In *College English, Vol. 34, No. 1*, pp 79–80.

Murray, Michele (1980). "Creating Oneself from Scratch." In Janet Sternburg (ed) *The Writer on Her Work*, (pp 71–93) New York: W. W. Norton.

Oakley, Ann (1974). *The Sociology of Housework*, London: Martin Robertson.

Ohmann, Carol (1986). "Emily Brontë in the Hands of Male Critics." In Mary Eagleton, (ed) *Feminist Literary Theory: A Reader*, (pp 71–74) Oxford: Basil Blackwell.

Olsen, Tillie (1976). *Tell Me A Riddle*, New York: Laurel, Dell Publishing.

Olsen, Tillie (1977). *Yonnondio, from the Thirties*, New York: Laurel, Dell Publishing.

Olsen, Tillie (1980). *Silences*, London: Virago.

Palmer, Nettie (1988). "Fourteen Years: Extracts from a Private Journal." In Dale Spender (ed) *The Penguin Anthology of Australian Women's Writing*, Melbourne, Australia: Penguin.

Pattison, Mark (1923). *Milton*, London: MacMillan.

Peters, Margot (1977). *Unquiet Soul: A Biography of Charlotte Brontë*, London: Futura.

Plath, Sylvia (1976). *Letters Home*, Aurelia Schober Plath (ed) Toronto, New York, London: Bantam Books.

Porter, Cathy (transl.) (1985). *The Diaries of Sonya Tolstoy*, London: Jonathan Cape.

Prichard, Katharine Susannah (1982). *Wild Weeds and Windflowers: The Life and Letters of Katharine Susannah Prichard* (Ric Throssell, ed) Syndey: Angus & Robertson.

Raban, Jonathan (1988, February 13). "Money that Talks in a Literary Accent." In *The Age* (Melbourne).

Reeve, Clara (1785). *The Progress of Romance*, reprinted 1970. New York: Garland Publishing.

Rich, Adrienne (1979/1980). *On Lies, Secrets and Silence: Selected Prose 1966–1978*, New York: W. W. Norton and London: Virago.

Rogers, Barbara (1988). *Men Only: An investigation into Men's organisations*, London: Pandora.

Rose, Phyllis (1978). *Woman of Letters: A Life of Virginia Woolf*, London: Routledge and Kegan Paul.

Rose, Phyllis (1985). *Parallel Lives: Nine Victorian Marriages*, Harmondsworth, Middlesex: Penguin.

Rosen, B., and T. H. Jerdee (1974). "Effects of applicants' sex and difficulty of job on evaluation of candidates for managerial positions" In *Journal of Applied Psychology, 59*, pp 511–512.

Rossi, Alice S. (ed) (1970). *John Stuart Mill and Harriet Taylor Mill: Essays on Sex Equality*, Chicago: University of Chicago Press.

Ruddick, Sara and Pamela Daniels (eds) (1977). *Working It Out: 23 Women Writers, Artists, Scientists and Scholars Talk About Their Lives and Work*, New York: Pantheon.

The Writing or the Sex

Russ, Joanna (1972). "Why Women Can't Write." In Susan Koppelman Cornillon (ed) *Images of Women in Fiction*, (pp 3–20) Bowling Green, Ohio: Bowling Green University Popular Press.

Russ, Joanna (1972). "The Image of Women in Science Fiction." In Susan Koppelman Cornillon (ed) *Images of Women in Fiction*, (pp 79–94) Bowling Green, Ohio: Bowling Green University Popular Press.

Russ, Joanna (1984). *How to Suppress Women's Writing*, London: The Women's Press.

Said, Edward (1975). *Beginnings: Intention and Method*, New York: Basic Books.

Sale, William M. Jr. (ed) (1963). "Biographical Notice of Ellis and Acton Bell" in *Wuthering Heights: An Authoritative Text with Essays in Criticism*, New York: W. W. Norton.

Schneir, Miriam (1986, April). "The Prisoner of Sexism: Mailer Meets His Match" In *MS*, pp 82–83.

Schofield, Mary Anne and Cecilia Macheski (eds) (1986). *Fetter'd or Free? British Women Novelists 1670–1815*, Athens, Ohio: Ohio University Press.

Schultz, Muriel (1975). "The Semantic Derogation of Women." In Barrie Thorne and Nancy Henley (eds) *Language and Sex: Difference and Dominance*, (pp 64–75). Rowley, Mass: Newbury House.

Scott, Hilda (1984). *Working Your Way to the Bottom: The Feminization of Poverty*, London: Pandora.

Showalter, Elaine (1974). "Women in the Literary Curriculum" (1970). In Judith Stacey, Susan Bereaud and Joan Daniels, (eds) *And Jill Came Tumbling After*, (pp 317–325) New York: Dell.

Showalter, Elaine (1977). *A Literature of Their Own: British Women Novelists from Brontë to Lessing*, Princeton, New Jersey: Princeton University Press.

Showalter, Elaine (1979). "Towards a Feminist Poetics." In Mary Jacobus (ed) *Women Writing and Writing About Women*, (pp 22–41) London: Croom Helm.

Showalter, Elaine (1984, December 16). "Women Who Write are Women." In *The New York Times Book Review*, pp 1, 31 and 33.

Showalter, Elaine (1986). "Introduction: The Feminist Critical Revolution." In Elaine Showalter (ed), *The New Feminist Criticism*, (pp 3–17) London: Virago.

Showalter, Elaine (ed) (1986). *The New Feminist Criticism: Essays on Women, Literature and Theory*, London: Virago.

Showalter, Elaine (1987). *The Female Malady: Women, Madness and English Culture 1830–1980*, New York: Pantheon Books.

Simpson, Hilary Croxford (1979). "A literary trespasser: D. H. Lawrence's use of women's writing" In *Women's Studies International Quarterly, Vol. II, No. 2*, pp 155–169.

Smith, Barbara (ed) (1983). *Home Girls: A Black Feminist Anthology*, New York: Kitchen Table: Women of Color Press.

Smith, Dorothy (1978). "A peculiar eclipsing: Women's exclusion from man's culture" In *Women's Studies International Quarterly, Vol. I, No. 4*, pp 281–296.

Spencer, Jane (1986). *The Rise of the Woman Novelist: from Aphra Behn to Jane Austen*, Oxford: Basil Blackwell.

Spender, Dale (1980, 1985). *Man Made Language*, London: Routledge & Kegan Paul.

Spender, Dale (1981). "The Gatekeepers: A Feminist Critique of Academic Publishing." In Helen Roberts (ed), *Doing Feminist Research*, (pp 186–202) London: Routledge & Kegan Paul.

Spender, Dale (1982a). *Women of Ideas—And What Men Have Done To Them*, London: Routledge & Kegan Paul.

Spender, Dale (1982b). *Invisible Women: The Schooling Scandal*, London: Writers' and Readers' Publishing Co-operative, (2nd ed. forthcoming, The Women's Press, London).

Spender, Dale (1984a). "Sexism in Teacher Education." In Sandra Acker and David Warren Piper (eds), *Is Higher Education Fair to Women?*, (pp 132–142) Surrey: SRHE & NFER Nelson.

Spender, Dale (1984b). "A Difference of View." Paper presented at St. John's College, Cambridge, 26th April. Later used as basis for discussion, First International Feminist Book Fair, London, June, 1984.

Spender, Dale (1985). *For the Record: The Making and Meaning of Feminist Knowledge*, London: The Women's Press.

Spender, Dale (1986). *Mothers of the Novel: 100 Good Women Novelists Before Jane Austen*, London: Pandora Press.

Spender, Dale (1988). *Writing a New World: Two Centuries of Australian Women Writers*, London: Pandora.

Spender, Dale (ed) (1988). *The Penguin Anthology of Australian Women's Writing*, Melbourne, Australia: Penguin.

Spender, Dale (1988, July). "Women's Book Buying and Reading Habits: A Survey in Silver Moon" (unpublished) London.

Spender, Dale (forthcoming). *Novel Knowledge: A Guide to the Woman's Novel of the Nineteenth Century*, London: Pandora Press.

Spender, Dale and Elizabeth Sarah (1981). "An Investigation of the Implications of Courses on Sex Discrimination in Teacher Education" Unpublished *Equal Opportunities Commission Report*, Manchester.

Spender, Dale and Janet Todd (eds) (1989). *The Anthology of British Women Writers*, London: Pandora.

Spender, Dale and Lynne Spender (1984, 1986). *Scribbling Sisters*, Sydney: Hale and Iremonger, and London: Camden Press.

Spender, Dale and Lynne Spender (eds) (1983). "Gatekeeping: The denial, dismissal and distortion of women" In *Women's Studies International Forum, Vol. VI, No. 5*.

Spender, Dale and Margaret Littlewood (1986). "Sex and Reviews: British Periodicals and Newspapers March 1986" Unpublished research report.

Spender, Lynne (1983). *Intruders on the Rights of Men: Women's Unpublished Heritage*, London: Pandora Press.

Spender, Lynne (1986). Sex and Reviews: Australia, Unpublished research report.

Stanley, Julia (1975). "Sexist Grammar" Paper presented to Southeastern Conference of Linguistics, Atlanta, Georgia, November 7.

Stanley, Liz (1985). "Feminism and friendship: Two essays on Olive Schreiner" In *Studies in Sexual Politics*, No. 8, University of Manchester.

Stanton, Elizabeth Cady, Susan B. Anthony and Matilda Joslyn Gage (eds) (1881). *History of Woman Suffrage, Vol. I, 1848–1861*, New York: Fowler and Wells.

Stanworth, Michelle (1981). *Gender and Schooling: A Study of Sexual Divisions in the Classroom*, London: WRRC.

Stead, C. K. (ed) (1981). *The Letters and Journals of Katherine Mansfield: A Selection*, Harmondsworth, Middlesex: Penguin.

Sternburg, Janet (ed) (1980). *The Writer on Her Work: Contemporary Women Writers Reflect on Their Art and Their Situation*, New York, London: W. W. Norton.

Stillinger, Jack (ed) (1961). *The Early Draft of John Stuart Mill's Autobiography*, Urbana: University of Illinois Press.

Tate, Claudia (ed) (1985). *Black Women Writers at Work*, Harpenden: Oldcastle Books.

Tennant, Kylie (1986). *The Missing Heir*, Sydney: Macmillan.

Theroux, Paul (1987, Oct. 3–4), "The Male Myth" In *The Weekend Australian*, 6.

Thompson, E. P. (1963). *The Making of the English Working Class*, London: Victor Gollancz.

Todd, Janet (ed) (1984). *A Dictionary of British and American Women Writers 1660–1800*, London: Methuen.

Tolstoy, Sophie (1975). "Diary." In Mary Jane Moffat and Charlotte Painter (eds) *Revelations: Diaries of Women*, New York: Vintage Books, Random House.

Trahey, Jane (1974). "The Female Facade: Fierce, Fragile and Fading" In Maggie Tripp (ed) *Woman in the Year 2000*, (pp 54–67) New York: Dell Publishing.

Trudgill, Peter (1975). "Sex Covert Prestige and Linguistic Change in the Urban British English of Norwich" In Barrie Thorne and Nancy Henley (eds) *Language and Sex: Difference and Dominance*, (pp 88–104) Rowley, Mass: Newbury House.

Tweedie, Jill (1983). "Strange Places" In Michelene Wandor (ed) *On Gender and Writing*, (pp 112–118), London: Pandora Press.

Tweedie, Jill (1986a, July 22). "Away from it all" In *The Guardian*, p 12.

Tweedie, Jill (1986b). *Internal Affairs*, London: Heinemann.

Tyler, Anne (1980). "Still Just Writing." In Janet Sternburg (ed), *The Writer on Her Work* (pp 3–16), New York: W. W. Norton.

Van Snellenberg, Richelle (1986). "Sex and Reviews: Canadian Globe and Mail, March 1986." Unpublished research report.

Walker, Alice (1980). "*One* Child of One's Own: A Meaningful Digression Within the Work(s)." In Janet Sternburg (ed), *The Writer on Her Work* (pp 121–139), New York: W. W. Norton.

Walker, Margaret (1980). "On Being Female, Black and Free." In Janet Sternburg (ed), *The Writer on Her Work*, (pp 95–106) New York: W. W. Norton.

Walters, Anna (1977). "The Value of the Work of Elizabeth Gaskell for Study at Advanced Level" Unpublished M.A. thesis, *University of London Institute of Education*.

Walters, Anna (1983). "Introduction." In *Elizabeth Gaskell: Four Short Stories*, (pp 1–22) London: Pandora Press.

Wandor, Michelene (ed) (1983). *On Gender and Writing*, London: Pandora Press.

Wandor, Michelene (1986). "The Impact of Feminism on the Theatre" In *Feminist Review* quoted in Mary Eagleton (ed), *Feminist Literary Theory: A Reader* (pp 104–106), Oxford: Basil Blackwell.

Watt, Ian (1957). *The Rise of the Novel: Studies in Defoe, Richardson and Fielding*, London: Chatto and Windus.

Weldon, Fay (1983). "Me and My Shadows." In Michelene Wandor (ed) *On Gender and Writing*, (pp 160–165) London: Pandora Press.

West, Rebecca (1916). *Henry James*, London: Nisbet, New York: Henry Holt.

West, Rebecca (1983). "Rebecca West." In Dale Spender, *There's Always Been a Women's Movement this Century*, (pp 45–84) London: Pandora Press.

White, Janet (1986). "The writing on the wall: Beginning or end of a girl's career?" In *Women's Studies International Forum, Vol. 9, No. 5/6*, pp 561–574.

Whitmore, Clara H. (1910). *Woman's Work in English Fiction: From the Restoration to the Mid-Victorian Period*, New York and London: G. P. Putnam's Sons, Knickerbocker Press.

Wilhelm, Kate (1975, April 3). "Women Writers: A letter from Kate Wilhelm." In *The Witch and the Chameleon*, pp 21–22.

Williams, Raymond (1975). *The Long Revolution*, Harmondsworth: Penguin.

Wimsatt, W. K. (1970). *The Verbal Icon: Studies in the Meaning of Poetry*, London: Methuen.

Wollstonecraft, Mary (1792). *A Vindication of the Rights of Woman*, London: Joseph Johnson.

Wollstonecraft, Mary (1984). *Mary and the Wrongs of Women*, Oxford: Oxford University Press.

Women in Publishing (eds) (1987). *Reviewing the Reviews: A Woman's Place on the Book Page*, London: Journeyman.

Wood, Ellen, Mrs. (n.d.). *Roland Yorke*, London: Ward Lock.

Woolf, Virginia (1972). *Collected Essays II*, (Leonard Woolf, ed) London: Chatto and Windus.

Woolf, Virginia (1972). "How Should One Read a Book?" In Leonard Woolf (ed) *Collected Essays: Virginia Woolf, Volume II*, (pp 1–11) London: Chatto and Windus.

Woolf, Virginia, ([1929] 1972). "Women and Fiction." In Leonard Woolf (ed) *Collected Essays of Virginia Woolf, Vol. II*, (pp 141–148) London: Chatto and Windus.

Woolf, Virginia (1972). "Professions for Women." In Leonard Woolf (ed) *Collected Essays of Virginia Woolf, Vol. II*, (pp 284–289) London: Chatto and Windus.

Woolf, Virginia (1984). *A Room of One's Own/Three Guineas*, London: Chatto and Windus.

Wordsworth, Dorothy (1976). *Journals*, (2nd edition) (Mary Moorman, ed) Oxford: Oxford Paperbacks.

Index

THE ATHENE SERIES
An International Collection of Feminist Books
General Editors: Gloria Bowles, Renate D. Klein, and Janice Raymond
Consulting Editor: Dale Spender

EDUCATION